Kristy and her friends love babysitting and when her mum can't find a babysitter for Kristy's little brother one day, Kristy has a great idea. Why doesn't she set up a babysitting club? That way parents can make a single phone call and reach a team of babysitting experts. And if one babysitter is already busy another one can take the job. So together with her friends, Claudia, Mary Anne and Stacey, Kristy starts THE BABYSITTERS CLUB. And although things don't *always* go according to plan, they have a lot of fun on the way!

Catch up with the very latest adventures of the Babysitters Club in these great new stories:

89 Kristy and the Nasty Nappies

90 Welcome to the BSC, Abby

91 Claudia and the First Thanksgiving

92 Mallory's Christmas Wish

93 Mary Anne and the Memory Garden

94 Stacey McGill, Super Sitter

95 Kristy + Bart = ?

96 Abby's Lucky Thirteen

And coming soon...

97 Claudia and the World's Cutest Baby

98 Dawn and Too Many Sitters

The Babysitters Club

COLLECTION 12

Book 34
MARY ANNE AND TOO MANY BOYS

Book 35
STACEY AND THE
MYSTERY OF STONEYBROOK

Book 36
JESSI'S BABYSITTER

Ann M. Martin

Scholastic Children's Books,
Commonwealth House, 1–19 New Oxford Street,
London, WC1A 1NU, UK
A division of Scholastic Ltd
London ~ New York ~ Toronto ~ Sydney ~ Auckland ~
Mexico City ~ New Delhi ~ Hong Kong

Mary Anne and Too Many Boys
First published in the US by Scholastic Inc., 1990
First published in the UK by Scholastic Ltd, 1992
Stacey and the Mystery of Stoneybrook
Jessi's Babysitter
First published in the US by Scholastic Inc., 1990
First published in the UK by Scholastic Ltd, 1993

First published in this edition by Scholastic Ltd, 1999

Text copyright © Ann M. Martin, 1989
THE BABY-SITTERS CLUB is a registered trademark of Scholastic Inc.

ISBN 0 439 01112 4

All rights reserved

Typeset by M Rules
Printed by Cox & Wyman Ltd, Reading, Berks.

1 2 3 4 5 6 7 8 9 10

The right of Ann M. Martin to be identified as the author of this work has been asserted by her in accordance with the Copyright, Designs and Patents Act, 1988.

This book is sold subject to the condition that it shall not, by way of trade or otherwise, be lent, resold, hired out, or otherwise circulated without the publisher's prior consent in any form of binding or cover other than that in which it is published and without a similar condition, including this condition, being imposed upon the subsequent purchaser.

CONTENTS

Mary Anne and Too Many Boys   1

Stacey and the Mystery of
   Stoneybrook   135

Jessi's Babysitter   263

MARY ANNE AND TOO MANY BOYS

The author gratefully acknowledges
Mary Lou Kelly
for her help in
preparing this manuscript.

1st CHAPTER

I was so excited I felt like doing cartwheels across Claudia Kishi's bedroom floor. It was summer (at last!) and my friends and I had gathered for a special meeting of the Babysitters Club.

I looked round the room, and it was pretty obvious that my friends were as excited as I was. Of course, everyone was trying *very hard* to be calm, because that's the way our club chairman, Kristy Thomas, expects us to be.

Even though we were starting our summer holidays, she insisted on business as usual. Kristy was perched in a director's chair, wearing a red T-shirt, faded jeans, and a visor. She glanced at her watch just as our two junior officers, Mallory Pike and Jessi Ramsey, scooted into the room and flopped down on the floor.

"You're late," Kristy said sternly.

5

Jessi and Mal are younger than the rest of us (and happen to be best friends) but Kristy believes that rules are rules. She takes her role as chairman very seriously and believes that nothing – short of an earthquake – is an excuse for being late. But I can understand why she feels that way. The Babysitters Club was her idea, and I can still remember the day she told Claudia and me about it. All of us had grown up together in Bradford Court and loved babysitting, but it took someone like Kristy to set the wheels in motion for an actual sitting business.

But back to Mal and Jessi. "Sorry," they murmured in unison. They looked like they were trying hard not to giggle. Mal and Jessi always stick together, and besides, how could anyone take things seriously on the first day of summer?

"I can't believe you're going to California tonight," I whispered to Dawn Schafer. Dawn is my stepsister (her mother married my father), and she was going to the West Coast to visit her father and brother for two weeks.

"I can't believe it, either. It will be so much fun to go home. I mean, to my second home," she added quickly.

Her second home? I think I should explain that. Even though she lives in Stoneybrook, Connecticut, now, Dawn is a California girl at heart. She loves the sun and the ocean, and is into health food in a big way. She even looks like someone out of a Californian beach film. If you've already guessed that she's blonde, blue-eyed, and has the kind of dazzling smile you see in toothpaste adverts – you're right! Besides being my stepsister, Dawn is my "other" best friend. (Kristy Thomas is also my best friend.) There was definitely some jealousy involved when Dawn and I became stepsisters. Kristy seemed hurt that Dawn and I were spending so much time together, and I had to reassure her that it wouldn't affect our friendship.

I've just realized that I haven't told you who I am, so here's a summary, as my English teacher would say. My name is Mary Anne Spier. I am thirteen years old and an eighth-grader at Stoneybrook Middle School. I don't have a mass of corn-coloured hair like Dawn. Instead, I have brown hair, brown eyes, and think of myself as quite ordinary. Oh, yes, one more thing. I have a fantastic grey kitten called Tigger.

"Have you said goodbye to Logan?" Dawn asked in a low voice.

"I phoned him last night."

I knew it would be hard to say goodbye to Logan, so I'd decided to get it over with quickly. Logan Bruno is my boyfriend, but I still have a bit of trouble getting used to the idea. Logan is gorgeous. He looks just like Cam Geary, my favourite TV star, and he comes from Louisville, Kentucky. He has a smooth southern accent and a voice that makes me think of warm syrup. Logan is an associate member of the BSC, which means he doesn't come to meetings, but he fills in occasionally when all the regular members are busy. (Our other associate member is Shannon Kilbourne, a friend of Kristy's.)

"He's really going to miss you," Dawn said softly. "But I suppose the feeling is mutual."

I nodded. Even though I had a wonderful two weeks at Sea City, and a fantastic beach in New Jersey, to look forward to, I knew I would miss Logan. A lot.

"Can we please settle down?" Kristy said abruptly. I glanced round the room as the meeting began. It's amazing how many good things have happened for me because of the Babysitters Club. Dawn feels the same way. When we became friends, which was straight after she moved here from California, I talked the BSC members into letting her join the club. About a year later we became stepsisters. But you're probably wondering how the club got started, and this would be a good time to tell you a little bit about it.

One day Kristy noticed that her mum was having a terrible time trying to find a sitter for David Michael, Kristy's little brother. Kristy couldn't sit for him, and neither could her two older brothers. So Mrs Thomas was phoning all over town and getting nowhere. Then Kristy had a great idea. Why not form a babysitters club to solve that kind of problem?

This is how it works. A group of us meet on Mondays, Wednesdays, and Fridays from 5:30 to 6:00 in Claudia Kishi's bedroom. Why did we pick Claudia's room? Because she has her own phone and her own private number. Anyone who wants a babysitter can phone us at that time, and immediately reach seven sitters at once. The idea is perfect – and so simple, we wondered why we hadn't thought of it before.

Kristy is the chairman, because the club was her idea, and Claudia is the vice-chairman, since her room is our headquarters. Stacey McGill likes numbers, so she's our treasurer. My stepsister, Dawn, is our official alternate officer. Dawn has to be familiar with the job of every club officer and be able to substitute for anyone who can't make a meeting. She really likes being an alternate officer because she gets to take on lots of different roles in the club.

Mal and Jessi are the junior officers as I've mentioned. Since they're eleven years old, they can only babysit after school and at weekends, but they're *very* responsible. (They don't have actual club duties, though.) Mal and Jessi have a lot in common. They're both the oldest children in their families, and both of them complain that their parents treat them like babies.

I have the best job of all. (In my opinion.) I am the club secretary, and I keep our record book. The record book lists all our babysitting appointments, along with the rates our clients pay, and how much each of us earns at each job. I also have to keep track of each member's schedule – I could tell you when Jessi has a ballet lesson or Kristy has softball practice – and I have never yet made a scheduling mistake.

I was flipping through the record book when Kristy called on Stacey McGill to give the treasurer's report. Stacey looked very "New York" as usual, in a pair of khaki safari pants, topped with a jungle-print blouse and a leather belt that must have cost two months' pocket money. Stacey is a real city girl. She grew up in New York, and when her family moved to Stoneybrook, Claudia became friendly with her and invited her to join the club. Stacey is really sophisticated, but she does have her problems. Her parents recently got divorced and her father lives in New York. And she has a disease called diabetes, which means she has to stick to a strict no-sweets diet and give herself daily injections of something called insulin.

"Well, that's about it," Stacey said, finishing her report. She looked at me and grinned. "Do you realize where we'll be at this time tomorrow?"

"I do!" I blurted out. "Sea City!"

Kristy frowned. "I know everyone's excited about their holiday plans, but could we *please* keep this meeting going?"

"Sorry about that." I tried to look serious, but it was difficult because I knew I was still grinning from ear to ear. Stacey McGill and I were going to spend two fantastic weeks at a real beach town, and I couldn't wait to get started! It wasn't exactly a holiday (we were going to be mother's helpers for a family – the Pikes – just as we'd done the last time they went on holiday to the beach), but it would be wonderful. I was sure of it! I tried to restrain myself, though, because I remembered that Kristy's family hadn't made any holiday plans. Kristy would be in Stoneybrook for the next couple of weeks. Of course some people would say that Kristy is *always* on holiday, because she lives in a house that is straight out of a film. Kristy used to live next door to me, but when her mother (who was divorced) married a millionaire called Watson Brewer, the whole family immediately increased in size. Watson has two small kids who spend every other weekend with him, and recently Kristy's mum and Watson adopted an adorable little Vietnamese girl. She's two years old and her name is Emily.

Kristy nudged me impatiently. "How does the record book look, Mary Anne?" Kristy likes to plan everything days in advance and doesn't like surprises.

"You're going to be busy," I told her, flipping through the calendar pages. "Of course, you'll have Jessi to help you." (Jessi didn't have any holiday plans, either.)

Jessi is a really great black girl who moved to Stoneybrook from Oakley, New Jersey. She's in the sixth grade (like Mallory), and is a very talented ballet dancer. She has an eight-year-old sister named Becca, and a baby brother nicknamed Squirt. Jessi can handle almost any situation, and proved it once by petsitting for a houseful of animals for a week.

"It looks like you both have interesting jobs lined up," I went on.

Jessi beamed. "I'm sitting for Charlotte Johanssen one afternoon." Charlotte is one of our favourite kids.

"I'm sitting for Jenny Prezzioso," Kristy said glumly.

Jenny Prezzioso. Everybody was silent for a moment while the name sank in. Jenny is the kind of kid who gives babysitting a bad name, although I suppose it isn't really her fault. She's only four years old, but she's heading for the "World's Most Spoilt Brat" award.

"You'll be able to handle her," Claudia said cheerfully. "Just don't let her eat pizza if she's wearing one of her Little Bo-Peep dresses."

"Pizza!" Mal exclaimed. "I wish you hadn't said that. I'm starving!" As soon as the words were out of her mouth, her stomach gave a loud growl, just like a sound effect in a film. "Oh, how awful." She clutched her stomach in embarrassment and giggled.

Claudia reached under the bed and pulled out a shoe box. "Help yourself." The box tipped open and I could see it was filled with crisps, Mars Bars, and M&M's.

Nobody thought it was odd that Claudia kept snacks under the bed. Claudia is a junk-food addict, and she has crisps and biscuits stashed all over her room. Her parents aren't thrilled about it, so she keeps her "treats" safely tucked away. Claudia, by the way, is definitely the most dramatic looking person in the club. She's Japanese-American, and has long black hair and almond-shaped eyes. She's a great artist and has an incredibly brainy sister, Janine. (Claudia is *not* the world's best pupil, so it's just as well that she's talented in other areas.)

"Mary Anne," Stacey said dreamily, "remember the pizza at Sea City?"

"How could I forget?" I sighed happily. "Even pepperoni tastes better in Sea City." When Stacey and I had been to Sea City with the Pikes before, we'd had a brilliant time. If you like to eat, you would go crazy at Sea City, because you can find everything from banana fudge to foot-long hot dogs there.

"And Burger Garden," Stacey went on. "Remember those Crazy Burgers?"

"Of course I do," I said. "Burgers topped with bacon, Swiss cheese, pickles, and orange sauce."

"Orange sauce? Yuck!" Jessi looked slightly sick.

"It's not what you think," I told her. "They just mix the ketchup and mustard together. The Pike kids love it, don't you, Mal?"

"We certainly do." Mal nodded enthusiastically. Mallory is the oldest of *eight* kids, so naturally she's a terrific babysitter. The last time she went to Sea City she was a little too young to babysit, so Stacey and I had all the responsibility for her brothers and sisters. Now that Mal is older, her parents have decided to pay her to help us out. But just from time to time. For the most part, they want her to have fun and enjoy her holiday.

Every year Mal's family rents a big house overlooking the beach, and the kids love it. Stoneybrook is on the water, but it isn't the same thing. It isn't a "beach town" the way Sea City is. There must be a million things to do in Sea City, and I don't mean just the ocean and the boardwalk.

"Remember how much fun we had at Trampoline Land?" Stacey said.

"And Fred's Putt-Putt Course!" Mal exclaimed. "I love miniature golf. And the Big Wheel, and oh, Candy Kitchen and Ice-cream Palace!"

Kristy looked a little put out by this trip down memory lane, so I decided to change the subject.

"How about you, Claudia? Are you all ready for Vermont?"

"I think so," she said softly. She looked a bit wistful and I knew she was thinking of Mimi, her grandmother. Mimi died recently, and this year's holiday in the mountains just wouldn't be the same without her. The Kishis were even going to a different spot, because it would be too painful to go back to the old place.

"I suppose we can finish the meeting now," Kristy said reluctantly. I know she was disappointed that most of us were taking off for exciting places, while she and Jessi would be stuck at home in Stoneybrook.

"Gosh, I'm going to miss everybody," I said suddenly. It had just dawned on me that I wouldn't see my friends for two whole weeks!

Before I had a chance to get misty-eyed (I cry *very* easily), Kristy thumped me on the shoulder. "Hey, don't turn on the waterworks. We're all going to write to each other!"

"That's true," I said, trying to cheer up, "but it won't be the same." I could feel a lump rising in my throat and swallowed hard. "I'll send everybody tons of postcards. And make sure you all write back," I pleaded. (We'd already exchanged addresses.)

"Of course we will," Jessi promised. "Kristy and I will tell you about our babysitting jobs."

"And we'll write everything in the club notebook," Kristy said. (The club notebook is like a diary. We write up about what happens on every job we go to. Trust Kristy to be businesslike at a time like this.)

I hate goodbyes, so I didn't object when Stacey pulled me towards the hallway. "Have a great time, everybody!" she yelled over her shoulder. Dawn and Mallory were already ahead of us, thundering down the stairs, eager to start their holidays. Kristy and Jessi looked a little sad standing in Claudia's bedroom, and I could feel myself getting weepy again.

"Come on, Mary Anne!" Stacey exclaimed. "Sea City is waiting for us."

She was right. I wiped away a tear that was threatening to trickle down my cheek. Who could cry when it was holiday time!

2nd CHAPTER

"Which do you like better? The pink or the blue?"

Dawn snatched up two identical bikinis from her drawer and waved them at me.

"Um . . . I like them both," I said.

"Honestly, Mary Anne! You must like one a teeny bit more than the other." She collapsed on the bed next to her open suitcase. It was late on Friday afternoon, and her bedroom looked like a tornado had just ripped through it. Dawn was packing for California, and every single surface was littered with clothes. She could have held a jumble sale. When our parents got married, we started out as roommates, but it was a disaster, and we decided on separate rooms. I glanced at the piles of clothes scattered everywhere and remembered why.

"You look great in pink *and* blue," I said defensively. "I wasn't just being polite.

Anyway, why don't you bring both of them? You can always do with an extra costume at the beach."

Dawn started to laugh. "An extra costume!" she said, sitting up and drawing her knees to her chin. "I'm bringing *six* with me – three bikinis and three swimming costumes."

"Oh," I said, feeling a bit silly. Dawn really dresses like an "individual", and to her, swimwear is more than something to swim in. It's a fashion statement.

"Hey, I've just thought of something," she said. "I've got a string bikini that would look great on you. It's one of those green metallic ones. You know, the kind that always looks wet?"

"No thanks," I said quickly. "I'm all prepared." I could just picture what my father would do if he thought I was packing a string bikini for Sea City! Even though Dad has mellowed a lot in the last few months, he's still pretty conservative. It's hard to believe, but in the old days, I had hundreds of rules. I had to be home by nine, I had to wear my hair in plaits, and worst of all, my father chose *all* my clothes for me. I think part of the reason is that my mother died when I was little, and Dad had to be a mother *and* a father to me. Luckily, he's calmed down a lot, even though he'll never be as casual about things as Sharon (Dawn's mum) is.

I was Dawn's first friend when she moved to Stoneybrook after her parents got divorced. We got along really well from day one. You can imagine how surprised we were when we discovered that her mum and my dad went to high school together, and that they'd even gone *steady*. Their story is very romantic (and a bit sad) because although they'd loved each other, they'd broken up. Why? Because Dawn's grandparents didn't approve of my father! Anyway, years later, when Sharon and my dad met each other again, they realized that they were still in love and finally decided to get married. All of us moved into Dawn's house, and although things were a bit rocky at first, everyone is happy now.

"Mary Anne, I've got some suntan lotion for you." Dad tapped on the open bedroom door and then came in, followed by Sharon.

"Thanks, Dad, but I've got tons of sunblock." I'd learned my lesson the last time I went to Sea City and ended up looking like a lobster. For some reason, I'm one of those people who *never* tan. I just go directly from dead white to flaming red, followed by some painful peeling.

"How about toothpaste, shampoo, and stationery?" Dawn's mum asked. She fumbled in the pocket of her pink jumpsuit, looking a little distracted. "And I bought each of you a roll of stamps, but what in the world did I do with them?"

It's really funny when Sharon tries to be organized and in control, because she's the most disorganized person I've ever met. If you don't believe me, you should see our kitchen. Last week, I found the grocery list (with a pencil still attached) in the fridge, and a very ripe tomato in the cutlery drawer. I couldn't tell you how they got there, and I bet Sharon couldn't, either.

"Oh, dear," she said, searching in her pocket again. "Would you believe I actually made a list of what you would both need for two weeks?" I'd believe it. Sharon is a great list-maker. The trouble is she always loses a list five minutes after she writes it.

"Don't worry, Mum," Dawn said reassuringly. "I'm ready to go. I just have to throw in a beach cover-up and a hair dryer, and then I'll be all packed."

"It's true," I said, catching Dad's worried glance. "The room just *looks* like a disaster. She's really got everything organized."

"You could have fooled me," Dad said, shaking his head.

One of the reason's Dawn's room looked so cluttered is that it is very small. All the rooms in Dawn's house are small, because that was the style back then. I should explain that when Dawn's mother moved to Stoneybrook from California after her divorce last year, she bought a house for herself, Dawn, and Jeff. (Jeff is Dawn's younger brother.) But not just any house –

a farmhouse that is so old it's practically an historic landmark. It was built in 1795, and has an outhouse, a barn, and an old smoke-house. It looks like a large, creepy doll's house, the kind of place that a ghost would love to call home. (And probably does!) Dawn and her mum love it. Jeff, her brother, wasn't crazy about it. Jeff wasn't crazy about *anything* in Stoneybrook, though, so he eventually moved back to California to be with his dad.

But back to Dawn, who was sitting on her suitcase to close it. "I think that about does it," she said, looking a little flushed with the effort. Dawn was dressed for travelling, which meant she was wearing a beautiful Laura Ashley dress and had swept her long blonde hair back in a pearly hairslide.

"Then let's have a quick dinner and be off to the airport," Sharon said. "I've made something special for your last meal here, Dawn," she added, heading for the door.

Dad and I exchanged a look. Neither one of us likes health food as much as Sharon and Dawn do.

"Something special?" I ventured. I was *starving* and hoped she hadn't made one of her famous tofu casseroles.

"Something you *both* like," Sharon said, stopping to put an arm around me. "Spinach lasagna, tossed salad, and Italian bread."

"That sounds great!" I breathed a sigh of relief.

"And for dessert," she went on, "Tofu Delight!"

It was nearly seven o'clock when we got to the airport, and I could tell Dawn was feeling a little bit nervous about her flight to California. She checked her bag three times to make sure she had her ticket, while the four of us strolled up and down the long concourse.

"Did you bring some snacks for the trip?" I asked her.

"Of course," Dawn grinned and patted her duffel bag. "An apple, some dates, and two muesli bars. And they give you something to eat on the plane."

"Something cardboard," Sharon said crisply.

"No," Dawn laughed. "Something edible. I checked." She paused and looked at me. "I've left that new mystery book on your chest of drawers for you to read. And if you want to take any of my tapes to Sea City, they're in the shoe box in my wardrobe."

I smiled. Dawn and I don't usually have the same taste in music, but it was a nice thought. "Thanks," I said slowly. I was surprised to find that my voice was a bit quavery. It was silly, but I was already starting to miss Dawn.

Maybe she felt the same way, because she looked at me seriously. "I wish you were coming with me, Mary Anne. You'd love California."

I shrugged. "I'll have my hands full with all those Pike kids in Sea City."

She smiled. "I know, but remember not to work all the time. Take some time to have fun."

Dawn's flight was announced then, and Sharon enveloped Dawn in a big hug. "Are you *sure* you've got everything?" she asked for the dozenth time. "Tickets, money. . ."

"Everything, Mum," Dawn told her. They looked amazingly alike. Blonde, blue-eyed, and pretty.

Dad hugged Dawn then, even though I think he felt shy about doing it. Dad always feels a little uncomfortable with kids, probably because I'm his only child and the two of us have lived alone for so many years.

Dawn turned to me with her arms outstretched, and the tears welled up in my eyes. "Oh, Dawn, I'm really going to miss you!" I blurted out.

"Me, too," she said awkwardly, patting my back. "I hate goodbyes." She pulled away to look at me and I saw that her eyes were misty. "Don't make me cry, okay? I can't get on that plane with mascara dribbling down my cheeks!"

"Okay," I said, sniffling a little. I was trying hard to be brave, but deep down, I felt like bawling. I couldn't believe I was losing my stepsister for two whole weeks.

"Send lots of postcards!" Dawn called as she headed towards the gate. "And tell me *everything*!"

"I will," I promised. I dabbed at my eyes with a tissue.

"She'll be back before you know it," Dad said consolingly.

I nodded, afraid I would start crying again. Suddenly two weeks seemed like two years.

It was impossible to sleep that night. I tossed and turned, thumped the pillow, and tried to imagine what Dawn would do when she reached California. I pictured her having lemonade with Jeff and her father. Maybe they were relaxing outside on the balcony. Dawn told me that her father has a really cool house with terracotta floors and skylights in almost all the rooms. Also they have a housekeeper, so she doesn't have to worry about kitchen duty.

Then I started thinking about my trip to Sea City in the morning. I went through a checklist of everything I needed to take. And *then* I started thinking of all the things the Pikes would need to take for eight kids. Try to imagine it. Buckets and spades, beach blankets, and swimming costumes, plus tons of rainy-day toys for kids of all different ages. Just thinking about it must have made me tired, because the next thing

I knew, I had buried my face in my pillow and fallen sound asleep.

"Mary Anne, we're going to be late!"

"I'm coming, Dad. Just one more hug." I crouched down so that Tigger and I were on eye level (he was stretched out on the sofa) and kissed the top of his head. I couldn't stand to say goodbye to him.

"We'll take good care of him," Sharon promised.

"I know you will." Sharon isn't exactly a cat fan, but I think Tigger is growing on her.

After I'd hugged Sharon goodbye, Dad dropped me off at the Pikes'. *Another* goodbye, I thought as he got all my things out of the car.

"Take care of yourself, darling," Dad said. I wasn't sure, but I thought he hugged me extra tightly, since I was going to be gone for a long time. I got through this last goodbye pretty easily, though, because Claire, Margo, and Nicky Pike all came charging out of the garage, carrying suitcases.

"Come on, Mary Anne-silly-billy-goo-goo," Claire said. "It's time to go!" Claire is the youngest Pike and is going through an incredibly silly stage.

I helped load both cars (the Pikes always take two estate cars to Sea City) and at the very last minute, Stacey arrived with her mother. Stacey's mother looked a bit sad and I knew she was going to miss her. Stacey is her only child, just as I'm Dad's only child. But Mrs McGill would be alone for the next two weeks, while my dad would have Sharon and Tigger.

We finally decided who was going in which car. (I was going with Mrs Pike, Vanessa, and the triplets, and Stacey was going with Mr Pike, Mallory, Claire, Margo, and Nicky.)

We were just pulling out of the drive when Vanessa yelled, "Wait a minute. We've forgotten Frodo!"

Mrs Pike turned round to smile at her. Frodo is the Pikes' pet hamster. "Vanessa, Jessi's taking care of him at her house, remember?" Jessi's got a hamster of her own called Misty, so she'd know how to look after Frodo.

"Oh, yeah." Vanessa settled back, sighing with relief.

"Now if there are no more problems, it's—"

Right on cue, the triplets sprang to life. "Sea City, here we come!"

3rd CHAPTER

Saturday

Hi, Kristy!

We made it to Sea City, but I feel like I've been through some sort of natural disaster — maybe an earthquake or a hurricane. I suppose that's what a car trip with a bunch of kids does to you. Vanessa recited poetry nonstop, the triplets staged a running battle with Nicky, who rode in Stacey's car, and Claire gave us all the scare of our lives. I have no idea what will happen next!

More later, Mary Anne

Do you know *exactly* how many words rhyme with cat? I do. Vanessa used every single one of them during our trip to the beach. Vanessa is nine years old and wants to be a poet. I should say, she is a poet, because she is always making up poems. And you know what? It must be contagious, because now I find myself doing the same thing when I'm with her!

We were only a few miles out of Stoneybrook when it started. Vanessa and I were sitting in the front with Mrs Pike, and the triplets were bouncing around in the back. The triplets, in case you don't know, are called Adam, Jordan, and Byron, and they're ten years old.

"Can we stop for doughnuts?" Adam yelled.

"Certainly not," Mrs Pike said. "We'll stop at the Little Chef at the halfway point as always."

"Oh, Mum . . ." Adam whined. "We're starving."

"Adam, don't be a pest. It's all for the best." Vanessa looked very pleased with herself.

Oh, no. Here we go, I thought. "Come on. Adam. You can hold on for another hour or so," I said encouragingly.

"That's right," Vanessa went on. "It's a very short ride, and you'll soon see the tide." Jordan stuck his fingers in his ears, but she ignored him. "A day at the beach is like a fresh peach. A trip to the shore leaves you begging for more. A drive to the ocean is like a . . ." she paused, temporarily stumped.

"Mum!" Byron screeched. "Make her stop. She's driving me mad!"

Mrs Pike just smiled and shook her head. I should tell you that the Pikes have very liberal ideas about bringing up kids. (Totally opposite from my father's ideas.) The Pike kids are allowed to do pretty much what they want, within reason. They don't have to eat foods they don't like, and they can stay up as late as they want, as long as they're in bed. Mrs Pike would *never* tell Vanessa to stop making up poems because she thinks that kids should be allowed to express themselves.

"Vanessa," I said gently, "you've picked a bad *time* to make up a—" I nearly said "*rhyme*," but luckily I stopped myself.

"Make up a what?" she asked with a knowing smile.

"A . . . a poem."

She shrugged. "But there's nothing to do." I braced myself for what was coming. "And you know that it's true."

"Vanessa," Jordan said warningly from the backseat.

I thought fast. "I know. We'll all play a game—"

"But it won't be the same." Vanessa grinned.

I sighed. I could see it was a losing battle.

"Hey, I've got one," Adam shouted. "How's this? We're stuck in the car, and the ocean is far."

Vanessa turned round and stuck out her tongue at him. I don't think she liked being upstaged by her brother.

"Hah! You're a poet, and you didn't know it!" Jordan chimed in.

I was about to suggest a game of I Spy when Mr Pike suddenly pulled up next to us on the three-lane motorway.

"There's Daddy!" Vanessa shrieked. Mr Pike tooted the horn, and Nicky, who's eight, pulled out his cheeks and made a really disgusting face against the window.

"Yuck!" Jordan yelled as Mr Pike sped away. "Let's get him back!"

"Drat. It's too late now, but if we hurry up we can get him next time." Adam reached for a pad of paper I'd tucked into a bag. "Quick! Anybody got a Magic Marker?"

Byron grinned. "Write something really gross!" he said, fumbling in a box of toys and art materials for rainy days.

"Um, I'm not sure this is a good idea," I began. I felt I *had* to say something, since Mrs Pike was humming along with a song on the radio and watching the road. She didn't seem the least bit worried that the triplets were planning a major battle!

Adam frowned, waiting for inspiration to

strike. Then he smiled, just like Road Runner plotting some awful revenge, and wrote: Batman has a Bird Brain.

Batman has a Bird Brain? I turned round to stare at Adam. "I don't get it," I said. I noticed that Mrs Pike was catching up with Mr Pike, and the two cars would be side by side at any minute.

Adam hooted. "Nicky is *so* proud of his new Batman T-shirt, he's been wearing it day and night."

"Yeah, he bought it with his own money, and he thinks he's really cool," Byron piped up.

"He won't think he's so cool when he sees your sign," Jordan said happily.

Jordan was right. Nicky was furious. He stared at the sign, glanced down at his shirt, and turned beetroot. He shook his fist at us, just as our car suddenly changed lanes and charged ahead of them.

The triplets were practically rolling off the seats with laughter as I racked my brain, trying to think of something to do to distract them. For the next few minutes, they turned down every single car game I could think of. I suppose "Get Your Brother" was more fun.

They held up the Batman sign about five more times during the next hour – every time the two cars came side by side. Nicky was so annoyed, I expected to see smoke coming out of his ears!

At last we reached the halfway point. "This is it," Mrs Pike said cheerfully.

I have never been so glad to see a Little Chef in my life. Everyone piled out of the car, and after a quick trip to the toilets, we all met at the take-away counter. Mallory and Stacey were ordering ice-cream cones for Claire and Margo, while Nicky was struggling to make up his mind.

"Get Cherries Jubilee," Mal suggested. "Or Rocky Road."

"Don't get Rum and Raisin," Margo said. "It looks like vanilla ice cream with flies."

Stacey and I led the kids to a small picnic area while Mr and Mrs Pike sat at the counter and ordered coffee. Stacey was the only one of us without an ice-cream cone – because of her diabetes – so she was munching on an apple.

"Tough trip," she said, and sighed. "It's a good thing Nicky was in a separate car from the triplets or it would have been World War Three."

I nodded. For some reason Nicky and the triplets manage to fight over *everything*, and I noticed that Nicky was sitting as far away from them as possible.

"How's your Pistachio Crunch?" Stacey asked me.

"Fantastic." I used to feel guilty about eating ice cream and chocolate in front of Stacey, but she handles her diabetes so well, I hardly think about it any more.

Mr and Mrs Pike wandered out with the remains of their coffee then, and joined Mal and the triplets at one of the long wooden picnic tables.

Stacey sat on the grass and turned her face up to the sun. A few people glanced over at us curiously, probably wondering if we were part of the huge Pike family. I scanned the two picnic tables then, and something seemed out of place. What was wrong?

I did a quick head count. And came up with eleven. *Eleven?* There should be twelve of us. The eight Pike kids, Mr and Mrs Pike, Stacey and me.

"Ohmigosh," I muttered under my breath.

"What's up?" Stacey asked lazily. She was stretched out like a cat, enjoying the warm sun.

"Stacey," I said, not taking my eyes off the kids, "we're missing somebody."

She sat up fast. "Are you sure?" She did her own head count, without waiting for my answer.

"I'm sure." I gulped. "There are the triplets and Mal and Vanessa and Nicky and Margo." And no Claire, I added silently.

"Where's Claire?" Mrs Pike said loudly.

"I was just wondering the same thing," I said, as Stacey scrambled to her feet. "Have any of you kids seen her?" The triplets solemnly shook their heads, and Mrs Pike glanced nervously at the car park.

"Maybe she went back to the car," she said a little breathlessly. I know she was really worried, even though she was trying not to show it.

Mr Pike stood up. "I'll go and check the car. Stacey, why don't you look round the play area." (There were some swings at the far side of the car park.)

"I'll go back inside," I said suddenly. "Maybe she had to go to the toilet."

Mr Pike nodded and hurried off, his expression tense. Claire's only five years old, and at that age, kids shouldn't be out of your sight even for a minute.

I quickly checked the toilets, the water fountain, and the phone booth. No sign of her. I was about to dash outside when I spotted her at the counter, happily spinning on a stool.

"Claire!" I said, rushing up to her. "We thought you were missing." I hugged her, my heart still doing flip-flops in my chest.

"I'm not missing," she said seriously. "I'm right here. All my ice cream leaked out, so I came back to get another cone." She held up an empty cone. The bottom was jagged as if she had bitten it off.

"We can fix that," a boy behind the counter said. "What kind of ice cream did you have?"

"Vanilla. I always get vanilla."

He handed her a new cone and winked. "Make sure you eat this one from the top down, not the bottom up."

We hurried outside, just as Mr and Mrs Pike were coming through the glass double doors. They swept Claire into their arms and hugged her, just like I'd done.

We piled back into the cars, and after endless rhyming, Vanessa shrieked with joy.

"There's the cow sign!" she said, jabbing me in the ribs and forgetting to make up a poem. The cow sign is one of the Pike kids' favourite landmarks. It's a billboard with a three-dimensional purple cow, and they look for it every year.

"And there's Crabs for Grabs!" Jordan yelled a few minutes later. Crabs for Grabs is a seafood restaurant on the outskirts of Sea City.

"And the suntan girl!" Adam and Byron shouted together. The suntan girl is *another* billboard that they always watch for. "And *there*'s Sea City!"

We're finally here, I thought. I started to relax and then caught myself. Who knew what would happen next!

4th CHAPTER

Saturday

Dear Dawn,
 I'd have to write a book to tell you all about the trip down here, so I'll just say it was an adventure. The Pike kids are really excited to be back in Sea City, and so am I. Even though I miss all of you (and a certain person with the initials L.B.) I think I'm in for a very interesting two weeks, and I want to swap stories the minute you get back. I bet you're tanned already!
 Bye for now,
 Mary Anne

"The wind chimes are still here!" Jordan shouted.

"And they've left the swing up!" Adam said, throwing himself into a white wicker swing on the front porch.

"The honeysuckle bush is blooming, just like before," Vanessa said dreamily. She buried her face in the soft blossoms for a moment.

"Okay, gang," Mr Pike said firmly. "I know you want to run around and look at everything, but what do we have to do first?"

"Unpack?" Nicky suggested.

Mr Pike nodded, and there was a chorus of groans.

I took a deep breath of salty air while Mrs Pike unlocked the front door of the house. The Pikes rent the same place every year, and it looks like something out of Hansel and Gretel. It's a giant gingerbread house, which Mrs Pike says is Victorian style. It's painted yellow with a white trim, and has carved railings and posts and eaves and edges. Best of all, it has a big front porch, so you can sit for hours and look at the ocean (if you're not busy running after eight kids). The Pikes love it because they have the beach right in their own front garden.

After we'd helped unload the car, Stacey and I ran upstairs to the yellow bedroom we'd shared the last time. It's very old-fashioned (maybe a little too much for

Stacey) and has two high, dark wood beds, a bare wood floor, and yellow flowered wallpaper. It also has a great view of the ocean, and I stood and watched the sun glittering on the water for a moment before I tackled my suitcase. I saw a lifeguard talking to some little kids splashing in the sea, and I thought of a lifeguard we'd met here the last time. His name was Scott, and Stacey'd had an *incredible* crush on him. Unfortunately he was much too old for her (I tried to tell her so at the time), and besides that, he was interested in another girl.

She must have read my mind because she joined me at the window, eyeing the little group on the shore. She watched them for a minute and then said softly, "Thank goodness I'm more grown up this time."

I knew exactly what she meant. "You've got to admit it was an interesting holiday."

"Interesting!" Stacey hooted. She curled up on the bed, her knees tucked under her chin. "I can't *believe* I made such an idiot of myself over Scott." She paused, inspecting a frosted-pink fingernail. "Of course, it wasn't a total loss. You met Alex and I met Toby."

"That's right." I sat down next to her. "Do you think they ever think about us?"

Stacey twisted a lock of blonde hair around her finger and frowned. "Probably just once in a while. Toby was really *nice*, wasn't he?"

I nodded. Toby was one of those totally cool boys (really Stacey's type), but I preferred Alex. Alex was the first mother's helper I'd ever met who was male! Alex was great with kids, and we hit it off right from the start.

"Whatever happened to that ring he gave you?" Alex and I exchanged rings on our last night in Sea City, but it didn't mean there was anything really serious between us. (Also, I didn't know Logan then.) We found this place where you can buy rings and have things engraved on them for five dollars each. Alex has a ring with my initials on it and I have one with his.

"Um, I'm not sure. It's either in the bottom of my dressing table drawer, or in a shoe box in my wardrobe."

Stacey pretended to be shocked. "I thought you slept with it under your pillow every night."

I knew she was only teasing. I don't even think of Alex in a romantic way, especially since I've met Logan. I suppose Alex played an important part in my life, though, because he was the first boy I was ever interested in.

"Wouldn't it be funny if Alex and Toby showed up again?"

I didn't get a chance to answer because Claire bolted into the room just then and wrapped herself around my knees.

"Can we go to the beach, please, please, please, Mary Anne-silly-billy-goo-goo?"

"We've got to finish unpacking," I told her, and Claire's mouth turned down, just like one of those Greek masks that are supposed to stand for "tragedy".

Then she brightened up. "What if I help?" she asked. She picked up one of my T-shirts and held it up to her chest. It hung all the way down to her knees.

"The best way you can help is to go back to your own room and get Mal to help you find your bathing suit and beach towel. Then when you're all dressed – and your suitcase is unpacked – we'll go to the beach," I said.

"Promise?"

"Promise." That seemed to satisfy her because she gave a wild whoop of joy and dashed down the hall.

I probably should explain about the sleeping arrangements. Claire and Margo bunk together, Vanessa and Mallory share a pink bedroom, and Stacey and I have the yellow bedroom. The boys have a big bedroom at the end of the hall. There are plenty of rooms to go around, and there's even a spare room with a window seat up on the third floor. It's one of my favourite places to curl up (Mal's too), and once she and I went up there to watch a lightning storm. Very exciting!

It took at least half an hour to unpack, because Stacey and I kept reminding each other of funny things that had happened with Alex, Toby, and Scott, the lifeguard. Actually, the incident with Scott wasn't exactly *funny* (Stacey saw him kissing another girl and dissolved into tears), but I was pretty sure that she was over him now.

"How will you feel if you bump into Scott on the beach?" I asked her.

"I don't know, but I certainly won't rush out and buy any more chocolates." She laughed, and I knew everything would be okay. She had actually bought Scott a ten-dollar box of chocolates as a going-away present, just before we saw him kissing his girlfriend. Talk about bad timing!

Mal stuck her head round the door just as I was putting the finishing touches to my beach outfit.

She stared at me, and her jaw dropped open. "Gosh, Mary Anne," she said, "you look like you're going to the desert."

As I've said, I burn very easily, so I have to cover every square inch of myself with sunblock – even on cloudy days.

"This is my beach cover-up, if you remember," I said, feeling a bit defensive. I was wearing my white caftan that flows around me like a tent. And just to make sure that no rays would sneak in, I put on giant black sunglasses, a straw hat, and covered my nose with sunblock.

Stacey and Mal exchanged a look, and I know they were trying not to burst out laughing. "Are you sure you need all that?"

Stacey said, trying to be tactful. "It's a bit late in the day to get burnt."

I glanced at myself in the mirror. I *did* look a bit strange, but I didn't dare take any chances.

"I'm ready, Mary Anne-silly-billy-goo-goo!" Claire shrieked. She was dressed in a bright red swimming costume and was wriggling with joy like a puppy.

"Okay, let's go," I said, scooping her up. We met the triplets and Margo in the hall, and I automatically counted heads as we went down the stairs. "Where's Vanessa?" I asked. (After the scare with Claire, I wasn't taking *any* chances.)

"I'm out here," she called from the front porch. Vanessa was curled up in a wicker chair, balancing a notebook on her knees. She had a dreamy expression on her face, as if she was lost in thought.

"Beach time!" I said, ruffling her hair as we went by.

She gave a little smile. "I'll be there in a few minutes," she said. "I've got something I want to finish."

Stacey raised her eyebrows. Vanessa's usually the first one to plunge into the waves and never complains even when the water is freezing.

"I'll catch up with you later, okay?" She obviously wanted to be by herself.

"Okay," I said doubtfully, "but don't wait too long or the sun will go down."

"Where does it go?" Claire asked, grabbing my hand and dragging me towards the beach.

I was still watching Vanessa, wondering if something was wrong. "Where does what go?"

"The sun!" She rolled her eyes. "Where does it go when it goes down?"

"Oh." I was stumped.

"Behind a cloud?" Stacey suggested.

"Good answer," I said, just like they say on TV game shows.

Stacey grinned at the compliment. "Any time," she told me.

5th CHAPTER

Sunday

Dear Logan,
 Sea City is fantastic! The beach is great (even though I am wrapped up like a mummy to avoid the sun). The weather is perfect and all the kids are getting along with each other. I think this is going to be the best holiday ever. You would really love it here! How are things in Stoneybrook? If you see Tigger sitting

in the front window, be sure to wave to him. I miss you!
            Lots of ooo's and xx's,
                  Mary Anne

You wouldn't believe how many times I rewrote my postcard to Logan. You'd think I was doing an essay for an Advanced Composition lesson. Of course, it was a lot harder to write than an essay, because I had to find the perfect "tone", as my English teacher would say. I had to be funny (I thought the part about the mummy was pretty good), and I had to sound as if I was having a wonderful time. Of course, I wanted Logan to know that I would be having an even *better* time if he were there with me. You see what a problem I had. I didn't want Logan to think I was pining away for him, but I also didn't want him to think I was having such a good time that I didn't even miss him. What a dilemma! (Another expression my English teacher uses a lot.)

I tucked the postcard in the bottom of my underwear drawer before I went to bed on Saturday night. When I woke up on Sunday morning, I discovered that everything I'd said about the weather had been totally wrong. There was *no* sunshine, and the sea looked grim and choppy. The sky was a flat grey colour, as if someone had gone over it with a gallon of semigloss paint and a roller. I thought it looked very depressing, although I know that some people don't mind cool, windy days at the beach.

Breakfast was hectic as usual. Mr Pike was flipping pancakes in what looked like the world's largest frying pan, while Mal was busily making gallons of orange juice. Vanessa buttered a mountain of raisin-bread toast while I microwaved the bacon. Stacey put the triplets to work laying the table, watching to make sure that everybody got the right amount of cutlery. You'd be surprised how much planning goes into breakfast for twelve people. Luckily, Mrs Pike is very organized (unlike my stepmother) and had everything pretty much under control.

"I think it's going to be cloudy all morning," Mrs Pike said, looking at the overcast sky. "What do you kids want to do today?"

"The beach!" Adam shouted. "What else?" He was polishing off a stack of pancakes at record speed. I noticed he was dressed for swimming, ready to go.

"Not the beach," Mal wailed. "There's no sun today."

"Who cares?" asked Vanessa.

"I do. I want to get a tan." Mal grinned at Stacey and me. "Maybe I'll find a gorgeous boy to impress."

"Only girls care about silly stuff like tanning," Jordan said. He was practically inhaling a bacon sandwich, fidgeting in his chair. "We're going snorkelling today. Right, guys?" He was holding a pair of goggles and a plastic breathing tube on his lap.

"We are?" Nicky said hopefully.

"I meant Adam and Byron," Jordan told him breezily. "You can do something with Margo and Claire. Maybe you could go into town."

Nicky looked crushed. "Oh."

"That's right," Vanessa said brightly. "We can divide up into two groups and that way everyone can do what they want. Will you take us into Sea City, Mary Anne?"

I glanced at Mrs Pike, and she nodded. "Of course, if Stacey will take the boys swimming."

Mal and the girls and I set out half an hour later (after we'd persuaded the triplets to let Nicky join them on the beach). Mrs Pike needed a few things from the grocery shop, so we decided to make that our last stop. We walked along the main street, looking out for familiar landmarks.

"Look, Gurber Garden," Claire shrieked. "My most favourite place in the world."

"Gurber Garden" is really Burger Garden, the place with the Crazy Burgers.

(Claire never gets the name right.) It's a great place to eat. You sit on seats that look like mushrooms and the waiters and waitresses dress up as friendly animals. Who could resist a place where a mouse serves you dinner?

"I thought Ice-Cream Palace was your most favourite place in the world," Mal said, teasing her.

Claire thought about it for a moment. "Can I have two most favourite places?"

"I don't see why not."

It took over an hour to see all the familiar spots. We stopped at Candy Kitchen, and watched while they slid a tray of marshmallow fudge out of the oven. The smell of chocolate was so delicious, we *nearly* fainted, but we decided to save our money for Ice-Cream Palace.

After we'd had a quick look at Fred's Putt-Putt Course and Hercules' Hot Dogs (the home of the foot-long hot dog), we ended up outside a souvenir shop. There were rows of Sea City T-shirts and shelves filled with mugs, sun visors, straw hats, and beach towels. Everything in the whole shop had "Sea City" plastered over it – usually several times. I would have liked to look at the postcards, but I knew the kids were restless.

"What next?" Mal asked. She knew her sisters were getting restless, too.

"Well, we can either walk over to the

arcade, or we can save that for another day and head to—" I started to say.

"Ice-Cream Palace!" Claire and Margo yelled.

"Ice-Cream Palace!" Vanessa said, jabbing the air with her fist like a drum major.

"Ice-Cream Palace then," Mal said authoritatively.

I'm not really sure if Ice-Cream Palace has the best ice cream in the world, but it certainly seems like it. Maybe it's just because they have flavours you can't find in Stoneybrook. Sometimes they go a bit *too* far trying to be different. (Would you really want to eat something called Banana Bubble-Gum?) But most of the flavours are great.

It always takes the younger kids ages to make up their minds, so we hung over the counter for ages. I decided on two scoops of Rocky Road Delight, since it has all my favourite things – chocolate, marshmallow, and peanuts. Mal chose a strawberry sundae straight away. But Margo, Vanessa, and Claire pondered for about ten minutes before they decided what they wanted – a chocolate chip for Claire, and hot-fudge sundaes for Margo and Vanessa.

Meanwhile, I saw a boy behind the counter eyeing either Mal or Vanessa, sneaking a look every now and then as he put together my cone. He was about twelve, with dark eyes and curly black hair, and I noticed that Vanessa was eyeing him *back*.

At least I think she was, although Vanessa has been acting so weirdly lately, it's hard to know what she's up to. Sometimes her eyes get this hazy, unfocused look, and she's not really watching anything – she's just writing poetry in her head.

Later, when he leaned across the counter to hand Claire her chocolate chip and a drink, I saw that his name tag read "Chris".

"Yummy," Claire said, reaching for her drink. Then it happened. One moment she was clutching the drink in two hands and the next moment she was swimming in chocolate.

"Oh, no," she moaned, looking at her shorts and T-shirt.

"Don't worry," Mal said, reaching for a roll of paper towels. "It will come off with a little cold— "

She never got to say "water", because at that second, Chris reached for the paper towels, and he and Mal bumped heads. It was like a scene from a slapstick film.

"Gosh, I'm sorry," Chris blurted out, just as Mal started apologizing.

"Wa-a-a-a-ah!" A long wail from Claire got everyone's attention. "I want another drink," she sobbed.

"Don't worry, you'll get one straight away," I said, trying to soothe her. Chris went back to doing our order while Mal and I mopped up Claire. Finally, everyone had been served, and after passing round extra paper napkins, I started on my ice cream.

I had only taken two bites when another disaster happened. Chris was adding extra whipped cream to Mal's strawberry sundae when he looked over his shoulder at us. His timing couldn't have been worse. The whipped-cream machine went crazy! Instead of spurting out whipped cream in neat little puffs, it blasted out clumps of cream the size of tennis balls. And it wouldn't stop.

"Oh, no!" he yelled, looking desperately around the counter for a towel. By this time, the sundae – dish and all – had turned into a giant white blob. There was whipped cream all over the counter, and a pool of whipped cream was sliding down to the floor.

"Turn it off! Pull the plug out of the wall!" someone yelled. Chris looked blankly towards the wall socket and then sprang to life. He yanked the plug just as another torrent of whipped cream buried the napkin holder.

"Wow, I don't know how that happened," he said, looking shaken. Margo and Vanessa were giggling, and Claire was laughing hysterically. Mallory looked mortified, though.

"That's okay," I said grimly, wishing we had never come into Ice-Cream Palace.

We waited while Chris made *another* sundae, and I asked him to make it a take-away. (I had already decided not to sit there a minute longer than I had to.) I was drumming my fingers on the counter when I noticed that Vanessa looked very upset.

"What's the matter?" I asked her. "That wasn't your fault."

"I know," she said in a quavery voice. I could tell that she was very close to tears.

What was going on? Why would Vanessa think she was responsible for all the problems Chris was having? I didn't have time to think about it, because people were staring at us, and I wanted to get outside as quickly as possible. The minute Mal got her sundae, I slid off the stool and we herded Claire, Margo, and Vanessa towards the door. I left my dish of Rocky Road melting on the counter, but I didn't care. For some reason, I had completely lost my taste for ice cream.

6th CHAPTER

Monday

I'm putting everyone on alert. I sat with the Rodowsky boys today, and Jackie Rodowsky hasn't changed a bit. That kid should come with a survival manual! We spent the day at the pool, which sounds harmless but wasn't. Everything that could go wrong, did go wrong, thanks to you-know-who. Poor Jackie. It's not really his fault. The kid is a walking disaster! All BSC members should be on their guard. Jackie Rodowsky is hazardous to your health....

It's times like these that make you realize how important the BSC notebook is. The "notebook" is different from the record book, in case you've forgotten. All of us are responsible for writing up about every single babysitting job we go on. Then, once a week, we're supposed to read about the jobs in the notebook. It was Kristy's idea, and even though we complain about it, it's really very helpful. We can find out if the kids we sit for are having problems the rest of us should know about, and we can learn how to deal with sticky situations (such as Kristy's problems with Jackie Rodowsky). Writing in the notebook is one of the few rules in the BSC.

Kristy's day with the Rodowsky boys started out innocently enough. (Of course, even hurricanes and monsoons start out small.) Kristy was happy to take the job, because things were getting pretty boring in Stoneybrook, and Mrs Rodowsky offered her a whole day's work. How could she know that a day at the community swimming pool would turn into a scene from a babysitting horror film?

"Are you sure you've got everything?" Mrs Rodowsky asked. She was double-parked at the entrance to the pool, while Kristy and the boys piled out of the car. The Rodowsky boys are Archie (who's four), Jackie (who's seven), and Shea (who's nine). All three boys have flaming red hair and plenty of freckles.

Kristy did a quick check and nodded. The kids were armed with towels, suntan lotion, and lunch money.

"We didn't bring Hilda," Archie complained. Hilda was a lime-green lilo with a head like the Loch Ness monster.

"You know we can't bring Hilda to the pool," Kristy explained. "They don't allow lilos or rafts because they take up too much room."

"Lilos are for babies," Shea said firmly.

"They are not!" Archie's freckles stood out on his pale skin when he was angry.

Shea shrugged and decided it wasn't worth continuing the argument. Who wanted to argue when a day at the pool stretched ahead of them?

The pool complex is much bigger than it looks from the outside. There are actually three pools – an Olympic-sized swimming pool, a wading pool, and a diving pool – and a playground and snack bar. A first-aid booth is off to one side, right next to the toilets and showers.

"I'm starving!" Jackie announced. "Can I buy one of those big chocolate chip cookies?" It was ten-thirty in the morning, and they'd just walked through the gates.

"You're hungry already?" Kristy said doubtfully.

"Yes." Jackie rubbed his stomach as if hadn't eaten in days.

"I suppose so." Even as she said the words, Kristy felt a little tingle of dread go through her. Something will go wrong, she thought. Something always goes wrong when Jackie is involved. She settled herself on a towel, watching as Jackie headed for the snack bar. So far, so good. Archie and Shea were playing in the shallow end of the pool, right next to her, so that was no problem. But Jackie? She just couldn't shake the nagging feeling that something was about to happen.

A few minutes later, Jackie returned, carefully unwrapping his cookie. It looked crumbly and delicious, the size of a small dinner plate.

"Look, what I've got," he called happily to his brothers.

"Hey, gimme a bite!" Archie yelled.

"No way, José." Jackie stood at the edge of the pool, waving the cookie playfully in front of Archie's nose. Archie made a grab for the cookie, Jackie stepped back, and then – the cookie fell into the pool!

"Aw!" Jackie wailed.

Kristy jumped to her feet and stared at the huge cookie, which was dissolving into a zillion pieces. She felt like crying. "Quick, get one of the lifeguards," she yelled to Shea. She knelt at the edge of the pool, trying to scoop up the floating mess in her hands, but it was hopeless. Jackie had dropped the cookie right next to a large circulation vent (naturally!) and goo was spinning everywhere.

"Yuck! What a mess," a male voice said.

Kristy glanced up to see a lifeguard standing next to her with a net. He made a face as he tried to capture some of the floating debris.

"I'm sorry. It was an accident." Jackie's voice sounded very small, and his lower lip was trembling. Kristy put her arm around him. No wonder he was upset. Being a klutz isn't much fun.

"You're not supposed to have food in the pool area," the lifeguard said.

"I know," Jackie said. "I wasn't going to eat it here. I was just unwrapping it here."

The lifeguard gave Kristy an I-don't-believe-a-word-of-this look, and walked away.

"I want to go to the diving pool," Shea announced. "I want to try a somersault."

"I want to do somersaults, too," Archie said, tugging at Kristy's hand.

"You can't do somersaults without a diving board, and you're too small to go in the diving pool," Kristy said. Things were starting to get complicated.

"I'm not too small!"

"Yes, you are. They have a height requirement. How about if I take you to the wading pool?"

"That's for babies!" Archie wailed.

Shea sniggered, but Kristy stopped him with a look. "No, it's not," she said quickly. "There are a lot of older kids there. You'll see. It'll be fun. You can practise keeping your eyes open underwater."

Shea picked up his towel and headed for the diving pool while Kristy walked Archie to the wading pool. Jackie tagged along, humming to himself. It was a bright, sunny day, and just for a moment, Kristy let herself relax. Maybe things would be okay after all. Maybe there would be no new disasters.

"Aughh! Ow! Ow! OW!" Jackie was shrieking as if he'd stepped on a piece of glass.

"What is it?" Kristy made him sit on the concrete while she looked at his foot. "Did you step on something?"

"O-o-o-o-o-w!" (a long drawn-out wail from Jackie). Kristy was puzzled. He had a small red spot on his foot, but apart from that, he looked okay.

And then she saw the dead bee.

"Look," Archie said, turning it over with his toe. "Jackie squished it."

Jackie stopped howling long enough to follow the conversation. "A bee? Oh, no! I've been bitten by a bee!" Another high-pitched shriek.

"It's all right," Kristy said soothingly. She had read up on bee stings and knew that if the wound was clean and there was no stinger inside, it was okay. Just to be on the safe side, though, she decided to march Jackie over to the first-aid office.

The nurse took charge of the situation immediately. Jackie stopped crying the minute he sat on the examining table, and ten minutes later, they were back out at the pool area. Jackie was fine.

Now what? Kristy thought. It was only eleven-thirty, and she was exhausted.

"Can we eat lunch, Kristy?" Archie was pulling on her arm, and she didn't have the energy to resist. It was a bit early to eat, but maybe it was safer to have everyone sitting down together. Surely nothing could happen over a plate of cheeseburgers. She rounded up Shea from the diving pool, and the two of them looked for a table, while Jackie and Archie went to the snack bar.

Then Kristy and Shea waited. And waited. Shea shifted restlessly on the wooden bench, and Kristy glanced at her watch. What was keeping Jackie and Archie?

"Hey, Kristy, what's going on over there?" Shea pointed to a commotion at the snack bar. It looked as if someone was holding up a long line of people.

It had to be Jackie. Kristy was sure of it. "Stay here," she ordered Shea, and headed for the snack bar. She spotted Jackie at the cashier, emptying his pockets while Archie nibbled on a bar of chocolate.

"What's going on?" she asked, trying to keep cool.

"Oh, Kristy, I'm glad you're here." Jackie gave her a winning smile. "I suppose I bought too much, because I've run out of money."

She looked at his tray. It was overflowing with Mars Bars, M&M's, peanuts, and crisps. Somewhere under the mess, she saw the cheeseburgers and chips she'd told him to order. "I'll say," she muttered.

Without another word, she took all the chocolate and crisps off the tray and then turned to the cashier. "Please just ring up the burgers and chips."

"Kristy!" Jackie howled. She ignored him, paid the cashier, and picked up the tray. Archie gulped down the last of his chocolate bar – probably afraid he would have to give it back – and hurried after her.

It was much later in the afternoon when Kristy breathed a small sigh of relief. The day was almost over, and nothing else had gone wrong. Or had it? Suddenly she realized that someone was missing. Her heart hammered in her chest. There was Archie, kicking in the wading pool . . . and there was Shea, showing off in the diving pool, and Jackie . . . wait a minute . . . Jackie was missing!

Frantically, Kristy scrambled to her feet and ran a few steps to the diving pool. The crowd had thinned out since lunchtime, and it was obvious that Jackie wasn't there. She dashed to the edge of the Olympic-sized-pool.

"Jackie!" she called. A few kids stopped swimming to look at her, but she knew she was wasting her time. Don't panic, don't panic, she thought. She forced herself to slow down and take a deep breath. Racing around the pool complex was pointless. The right thing for a babysitter to do in a situation like this is to notify a lifeguard. Immediately.

"Don't worry, he's around somewhere," said the nearest lifeguard encouragingly. "We'll page him over the loudspeaker."

"Thanks." Kristy leaned against the lifeguard's office, noticing for the first time that her legs were shaky. *Will Jackie Rodowsky please report to the lifeguard station?* The voice boomed over the address system every few seconds, with no results. Five minutes passed, then ten. Kristy felt as if her heart was playing leapfrog in her chest. Where was Jackie? What would she tell Mrs Rodowsky?

In the end, it was Shea who found him. "Here he is!" Shea said triumphantly. He was leading a puzzled-looking Jackie to the lifeguard's office. "Boy, are you in trouble!" he said happily to his brother.

"Where were you?" Kristy blurted out. Her voice was so quavery she barely recognized it. Even Jackie looked surprised.

"I was having a shower. I wanted to get some of that chlorine out of my hair." He was looking at the lifeguard, who was going back to his post. "Were you all actually *worried* about me?"

"We were paging you. For ten whole minutes."

"I couldn't hear you with the water running."

Kristy stared at him for a moment. There were a million things she *could* say to him, but what would be the point? Jackie was Jackie. A walking disaster!

"Look, there's Mum!" Shea yelled. "She's parked outside."

Kristy ordered everyone to pack up their beach towels and head towards the car. Four-thirty. It was hard to believe that only a few hours had passed. She stifled a yawn and helped the kids pile into the back seat. Another day with Jackie Rodowsky was finally over.

7th CHAPTER

Tuesday

Dear Dad and Sharon,

This is a super holiday! We spend practically every minute at the beach, and the Pike kids are into snorkeling. We've had just one cloudy day, but nobody minded. Stacey has a terrific tan, and I've already gone through a whole bottle of sunblock. Give Tigger a kiss for me and tell him I'll bring him back a toy!

Love You Lots,
Mary Anne

I reread my postcard and decided that it was extremely boring. It was also totally impersonal – if you knew what was *really* going on. It didn't give a clue about the exciting something in my life. Why? I'm not sure. Maybe because I wasn't exactly sure what was going on myself. I felt confused and happy at the same time, and it's all because of what happened at the beach today. . .

The day started out in a very ordinary way. Stacey and Mal and I had just spread out our blankets on the sand, and the younger Pike kids were getting ready to hurl themselves into the water. The Pikes may be a laid-back family, but there is one hard and fast rule – no one can go in the water before nine A.M. or after five P.M. That's because those are the only hours the lifeguards are on duty.

The moment the lifeguards climbed into their seats, the kids raced down to the ocean. I put another coating of zinc oxide on my nose and pulled my straw hat down over my face. Then I put sunblock on my arms and legs, and made sure my caftan covered my knees.

While I was going through all these contortions, I noticed that Stacey and Mal were doing just the opposite. I was wrapped up like an Eskimo settling in for the winter, and they were getting ready to soak up the sun. Stacey slipped out of her cover-up and stretched out in a skimpy blue bikini. I had to admit she looked great. Her skin was the colour of maple sugar, and her sun-streaked hair tumbled half-way down her back. And Mal, in a bright two-piece suit (blue bottom and striped tank top), was turning a golden brown colour. Her skin was catching up with her freckles.

Stacey was busily applying SunLite to her hair (can you get any blonder than blonde?) when we heard the shout.

"What in the world—" Stacey began.

I turned around just in time to see two teenage boys and half a dozen little kids racing towards us. The kids looked young – even younger than Margo – and I couldn't work out who they were. Then I recognized the boy in the white cut-offs and the green-and-white-striped top. "Ohmigosh!" I cried. "It's Alex."

"And Toby," Stacey added, scrambling to her feet. "Wow," she said softly. "Doesn't he look gorgeous?"

He did. Except I couldn't really concentrate on anyone except Alex. I hadn't thought of him a lot since we'd said goodbye, but I felt a jolt when I saw him now. He looked *wonderful*.

"Mary Anne! How are you?" He was at my side then, a little out of breath. He was tall, with brown hair, and had a great smile. How could I have forgotten that smile?

"I'm fine. How are you?" I smiled back. Alex took a step towards me, as if he wanted to sweep me into a big bear hug, and then he seemed to remember we were *surrounded* by kids. It was like the Munchkin scene in *The Wizard of Oz*.

"Toby and I are working together for a whole month as mother's helpers."

"Really?" I felt incredibly happy. A whole month! I'd be able to see Alex every single day.

Alex nodded. "We found two families who were holidaying together, and they wanted two sitters for all the kids." He glanced over at Toby, who was already deep in conversation with Stacey. I noticed she had tucked the SunLite bottle out of sight and was trying to dry her hair with a towel.

"Nice kids," I said, eyeing a little red-haired girl who had wrapped her arms around Alex's tanned leg.

"This is Sheila," he said, swinging her up on his shoulder. "She's two years old, and those boys are her brothers. They're twins. The other three kids are their cousins."

"And this is Mal," I said. "You remember Mallory?" Mal and Alex smiled at each other.

Claire came out of the water just then and glared at Sheila. "What's that baby doing here?" she demanded.

"Claire," I said, "that's not very nice."

Claire put her hands on her hips. "Silly-billy-goo-goo," she said to Sheila, who stuck her thumb in her mouth.

Alex laughed. "Is that some sort of code?"

"No," I said, embarrassed. "Claire just says that when she gets in one of her moods."

Alex didn't seem the least bit annoyed and knelt down so he was on eye level with Claire. "I've got a great idea," he said very seriously. "Want to hear it?" (Claire didn't say anything and looked totally unimpressed.) "Why don't we all build a sand castle?"

Claire scuffed her big toe in the sand for a full thirty seconds before answering. "That's a stupid idea," she said flatly.

"Claire!" I was shocked. Maybe Claire was feeling a bit jealous of Sheila, but that was no excuse to be rude.

I started to tell her so when the other Pike kids trooped curiously out of the water, and we introduced everybody.

"Fourteen kids," Alex said, counting heads. "Definitely enough to make a monster sand castle. Anybody interested?"

"We are!" Jordan said, speaking for the triplets. "Come on, let's start on the base. He turned to Sheila's twin brothers. "You can be helpers," he said generously.

We all walked down to the water's edge, and I noticed that Stacey and Toby never took their eyes off each other. Stacey seemed thrilled to see Toby again, but I reminded myself that she had acted exactly the same way with Pierre, a boy we'd met at a ski lodge. And there'd been Scott, the Sea City lifeguard, too. Toby was at the top of the list for the moment, but who knew if it would last?

I noticed that Sheila looked a bit left out, so I took her by the hand. "I'll show you how to decorate the sand castle," I said, putting some wet sand in her hand. "Just let it dribble out slowly."

At first Sheila didn't want to touch the sand, but then she tried it and shrieked with delight. "Birthday cake," she said loudly, and Alex laughed.

"That's right. It's just like the decorations on your birthday cake."

Everything went smoothly for the next few minutes, but then Sheila's foot slipped and she accidentally kicked the castle. A portion of the wall fell away and Claire hooted.

"Stupey-silly-billy-goo-goo," she shouted, and Sheila began to cry.

"Claire!" I said sharply. "It was an accident." Then I bent down and handed Sheila a plastic shovel. "Here," I said. "I've got a very special job for you to do." She stopped crying and looked at me. "You can make a tunnel that will lead all the way to the castle." I led her to a spot a few feet away, and she started digging happily. I watched her for a moment and then stood by Alex.

"I'm really glad we ran into each other again," he said quietly.

"I'm glad, too." The understatement of the year! There were a million things I wanted to say to Alex, but I knew the beach wasn't the time or place. Particularly with fourteen kids around. I wondered if he remembered the last night we'd spent together in Sea City, and if he still had the ring I'd given him. (I know he wasn't wearing it, because I looked.) I even found myself wondering if he had a girlfriend back home, and if he planned on seeing me when he was in Sea City. Of course we'd see each other at the beach, but I was already hoping for more than that.

The sun was setting when Stacey and Mal and I finally rounded up all the beach towels and kids and equipment. Then Stace and I said goodbye to Alex and Toby.

"That was fun, wasn't it?" I said to Stacey as we plodded through the sand back to the house, Mal at our side, the others in front of us.

"It was fantastic," she said dreamily. "Who ever thought we'd see them again? It's just *perfect*." She paused. "Do you think they'll ask us out?"

"I don't know. I suppose it depends on whether they can get any time off."

Mal looked aghast, and I had a feeling she was thinking of Logan. I shook off pangs of guilt.

Stacey stretched out her arms to inspect her tan. "From the look on Toby's face, he'll *make* the time."

I could feel the heat rising in my cheeks. I blush *very* easily, as any of my friends will tell you. "I'm not so sure about Alex."

"Ha! Believe me, I am. He was staring at you so hard, I thought his eyes were going to fall out of his head. If I were Logan, I'd be worried right now."

"Logan has nothing to worry about," I said stiffly. (Mal raised her eyebrows.)

Stacey considered what I'd said and then giggled. "Do you mean, what he doesn't know won't hurt him?"

I turned to look at her. "No, I mean Logan doesn't have to worry because I will *always* be true to him. He's my boyfriend and always will be."

I raised my voice without meaning to, because I was feeling so confused. It was amazing, but I hadn't even *thought* of Logan until now. I'd meant what I'd said about Logan being my boyfriend. But could a visit from Alex change all that? I didn't have an answer. Suddenly nothing was making any sense at all.

8th CHAPTER

Friday

Dear Claudia,
You're not going to believe this, but Alex and Toby are back in Sea City! They're working as mother's helpers, and we ran into them on the beach. This is turning out to be a very interesting holiday, and I have no idea what will happen next. Suddenly there are so many boys around here, we're practically tripping over them. Even Vanessa

met a boy she likes at Ice-Cream Palace. Furthermore, Stacey and I had sort of a fight....

Love,
Mary Anne

There was a big mix-up on Friday night. It wasn't Stacey's fault, but it wasn't my fault, either. (And I'm the one who got stuck.) This is the way it happened. Mr and Mrs Pike said that Stacey and I could have one evening off each week, but they asked us to take the evenings *separately*. I could see their point. That way they could go out every evening if they wanted to, knowing that Mal and either Stacey or I would babysit. Stacey and I were a little disappointed with the arrangement because we liked evenings off together, but we didn't say anything. We didn't even talk about it, which was a shame, because we should have agreed on our nights off at the beginning.

The first inkling I had that something was wrong was when I saw Stacey drag out the iron. It was six-thirty on Friday evening, and we had just cleared up the kitchen after an early supper. Stacey *hates* ironing, and I was amazed to see her spread a white cotton sundress over the ironing board in the corner of the kitchen.

"You're ironing?" I said incredulously.

Stacey touched her finger to her nose like you do in charades when someone guesses the right word.

I felt a little silly. It was pretty obvious that she was ironing, the question was . . . why? "I meant, why are you doing that now?"

Stacey looked up, her blue eyes very bright against her tanned face. "Well, I can't go out on a date with a wrinkled dress, can I?"

"A date?"

"With Toby." She bent over the sundress, humming a little song. She suddenly looked a little pale, even under her suntan, and I wondered if she felt okay. Stacey's diabetes is under control, but she has to watch her diet and medication. "We're going to the arcade tonight. You don't think this is too dressy, do you?" she asked worriedly. She didn't wait for me to answer, which is just as well, because I was standing there with my mouth hanging open. "I want to wear white because it will show off my tan."

"You're going to the arcade?" I blurted out. "Tonight?"

"It will certainly bring back memories," she said with a sigh. I knew exactly what she meant. The last time she went to the arcade, she and Toby had had what you would call a very romantic evening. He won a stuffed teddy bear for her, which she immediately named "Toby-Bear." But the really *big* news was that they went through the Tunnel of Luv, where Toby gave Stacey her first kiss.

"I remember the last time we went to the arcade," she began. "It was such an *incredible* evening—"

I could tell Stacey was about to launch into a lot of slushy memories, but I had something more important on my mind. If Stacey was going out with Toby that night, I had to say something – fast!

"Um, Stacey," I said, "I'm afraid there's a problem."

"A problem?" She blinked and put the iron on its end. At last I had her full attention.

"I'm going out tonight. With Alex."

"What?!" She managed to put a lot of emotion into that one word, and it wasn't surprise. It was outrage.

"That's right. Alex. Tonight. At eight." I didn't want to mention that we were planning on going to the arcade. There was no point in making her feel worse than she already did.

I thought she'd head straight for the phone to cancel with Toby, but she surprised me. She went right back to ironing!

"Stacey, did you hear me?"

"Of course," she said smoothly. "You'll just have to cancel with Alex. What a shame." She was very matter-of-fact about it.

Now it was my turn to be outraged. "Why should I cancel?" I demanded. "You had no right to make a date without asking me."

Stacey's eyes widened. "I don't need your permission to go out with Toby."

"You mean you just took it for granted that I'd stay at home with Mal and the kids?"

"Well, one of us has to be here," she said reasonably. "And anyway, all you have to do is tell Alex you'll see him tomorrow night."

She flounced up to our room to get changed and left me fuming in the kitchen. I couldn't believe that Stacey was being so selfish.

I was still thinking about our fight as Mal and I helped the kids get ready for bed that night. I went into Vanessa's room to close the window, while Mal helped Claire and Margo.

"Mary Anne," she said, "can you stay and talk to me for a minute?"

"Of course." I sat down on the edge of the bed. "What's up?"

"I've been doing some writing," she said.

She reached under the bed and pulled out a notepad and a ballpoint pen.

"Poems?" I asked.

"Well," she said, "yes. But different from the usual ones. I'm writing some poems for Chris. You know, the boy at Ice-Cream

Palace." I must have looked surprised because she added, "I have this big crush on him. I think he's adorable, don't you?"

"Well, yes."

"Here, read them and tell me what you think." She shoved the notebook at me and I quickly scanned a page. It was obvious that Vanessa was stuck on Chris. How could this have happened? I wondered. She didn't even know him!

> An accident brought us together,
> And I know we will never part.
> Please say you'll love me forever,
> You've totally stolen my heart.

"Very nice." I handed her the notebook. What else could I say?

"I wrote eight altogether. I just hope he likes them." She snuggled down under the covers.

"You're going to show Chris the poems?" A little warning bell went off in my head. Somehow I knew this wasn't such a great idea.

"Of course not," she said with a laugh. "I want to be his secret admirer. It wouldn't be much of a secret if he knew who wrote them, would it?"

"I suppose not." I paused. "What exactly are you going to do with them?"

"I thought I'd leave them on the counter at Ice-Cream Palace, where he'll be sure to find them." She yawned and started to close her eyes. "He'll be so surprised," she said, her voice already trailing off.

"I'm sure he will be," I replied. I got up quietly and tucked the quilt around her. First Alex and Toby (not to mention Logan and Pierre) and now this. Things were getting too complicated and the reason was obvious. There were just too many boys!

9th CHAPTER

Saturday

Last night I had a "surprise" baby-sitting job. It was all my father's idea. His girlfriend Carol turned up with an eight-month-old boy and a three-year-old girl. They were very cute, but I wasn't thrilled when Dad asked me to sit for them so he and Carol could go to a play. How could I refuse, though? It's lucky Jeff was home, because he turned out to be a great babysitter. By the way, if any of you BSC members have advice on what to do for colicky babies, I hope you'll write it in the notebook....

Dawn had almost forgotten how relaxing it was in California. She loved everything about the place. The sunny climate, the sparkling ocean, the big roomy house with the tile floors and slanted skylights. Life was so . . . carefree, she decided, stretching out on a sun lounger on the redwood patio. Her father had a great housekeeper, Mrs Bruen, who looked after everything and cooked all Dawn's favourite foods. And Dawn enjoyed seeing her younger brother, Jeff, again. He was *much* happier since he'd left Stoneybrook to live in California with his father.

Life was almost perfect, she decided, munching on an avocado salad that Mrs Bruen had prepared for lunch. There was only one nagging problem that wouldn't go away, and her name was Carol. Carol was her father's girlfriend, and she rubbed Dawn up the wrong way. Dawn couldn't say exactly why she didn't like Carol, but there was something about her that was very annoying. For one thing, she was always *there*. She spent so much time at the house, you'd think she was part of the family. And Dawn didn't like it one bit.

The doorbell rang later that afternoon, just as Dawn was going inside to have a shower. She'd spent the whole day soaking up the rays in her bikini, and she was covered in baby oil.

"Sunshine, get the door, will you?"

Dawn's father called from the kitchen. Sunshine was his nickname for her.

Dawn threw open the front door and felt as if someone had doused her with cold water. Her good mood vanished as she tied her beachrobe round her.

"Hi there!" Carol said brightly. "Look what I've brought!" She was holding a baby in her arms, and a solemn-looking little girl clung to her leg.

Dawn's father hurried into the foyer.

"Well, well, what do we have here?" Dawn knew he was surprised but was trying hard not to show it.

"Aren't they adorable?" Carol said in a gushy voice that Dawn hated. "This is Gregory. He's only eight months old. And this is his sister, Julie." She pulled Julie out from the folds of her sundress. "Julie's three."

"But who *are* they?" Dawn said pointedly. She knew they weren't Carol's children.

"That's a long story," Carol said as they made their way into the living room. She tossed a bag of nappies on the floor and settled Gregory on her lap. "One of my old friends from college is visiting California with her husband. They couldn't get a sitter, so I told her I'd watch her kids tonight so they can go out."

"That was very nice of you," Mr Schafer said slowly, "but it complicates things a little."

"What things?"

Mr Schafer sat down next to her. "Do you remember that musical you wanted to see at the Playhouse?"

"The one that's sold out?"

"Well, it's not completely sold out." Mr Schafer reached into his pocket and pulled out two tickets. "One of my clients got me two of the best seats in the house for tonight."

"Oh, no!" Carol wailed. "Why didn't you tell me?"

"I wanted it to be a surprise."

Dawn stood watching this scene, wondering how she could make a polite escape. She was sorry if her father was disappointed, but it didn't affect her, did it?

A moment later, she realized it did.

"Hey, I've got an idea," her father said suddenly. He turned round and stared at Dawn as if he were seeing her for the first time. "What are you and Jeff doing tonight?"

Dawn licked her lips nervously. She knew what was coming. "We're, uh . . . going to hire a video, I think."

"Perfect!" Mr Schafer clapped his hands. "You and the kids can all watch the video together."

Dawn looked at him. The idea of a small baby watching a video was so ridiculous she didn't know what to say. "You mean you want me to babysit for the kids?" she said tightly.

"Well, you're not doing anything anyway," Mr Schafer said, looking very pleased.

"Oh, could you?" Carol said, jumping to her feet. "That would be wonderful!"

"And I'll pay you," Mr Schafer said.

"Well. . ."

"Then it's all settled." Mr Schafer reached for Carol's hand. "Wait till you see what we're cooking on the barbecue tonight. . ."

"This is *not* my idea of a great evening," Jeff said a few hours later. He was trying to watch an Indiana Jones film, but Gregory was crying. He was making more noise than the soundtrack. "What do you think is wrong with him, anyway?"

"Carol said he's got colic," Dawn replied. She really felt sorry for Gregory, because she knew he was in pain. His legs were doubled up and he seemed to howl no matter what she did. She'd tried *everything*, rocking him, singing to him, but he cried louder than ever. The only thing that really worked was pacing up and down the floor with him.

It was a babysitter's nightmare, and she knew she wasn't being fair to Julie, who was wandering around the living room with nothing to do.

"Oh, let's watch this tomorrow," Jeff said, rewinding the video. He looked at Julie, who was staring blankly out of the window. "Hey, Julie," he said suddenly. "How about a game?"

"We haven't got any kiddie games," Dawn reminded him. Naturally Carol hadn't brought any toys for the kids.

"We've got playing cards," Jeff answered.

"She's too young for cards."

"Cards," Julie repeated, walking over to him.

"We're not going to play cards, we're going to build a *house* of cards," Jeff told Dawn.

For the next hour, Julie was fascinated as Jeff showed her how to place the cards on top of each other to make a house. "Gently, gently," he warned, as she laid the top card in place. "If you even breathe on it, it will all fall down." When they'd finished playing with the cards, Jeff made up a story about a cowardly dragon who wanted to be friends with a lion, and Julie giggled when he made funny faces. Then he showed her how to make shadow puppets on the white stucco walls, and invented animal voices to go with the shapes. Finally, a happy, tired Julie fell asleep on the rug.

Dawn was amazed. "You were great," she whispered. "I had no idea you were so good with kids."

"What can I say?" Jeff laughed. He put a blanket over Julie and looked at Gregory. "He's asleep, too."

"Can you believe it?" Dawn said wearily.

"Let's try carrying them upstairs and putting them both in my bed."

"So far, so good," Jeff said a few minutes later when they'd returned to the living room. He looked up at the ceiling, as if he expected to hear crying at any minute.

"What do you think is going to happen with Dad and Carol?" Dawn said. She curled up on the sofa, hugging a cushion to her chest.

Jeff shrugged. He minded Carol just as much as Dawn did, but he felt uncomfortable talking about her. "He likes her, that's all."

"Are you sure it's not serious? She's over here all the time."

"That doesn't mean anything. Dad's not going to go off the deep end and marry her or anything like that."

"How can you be so sure?"

Jeff shrugged. "I just know he's not. You worry too much."

Dawn was about to say something else, but Jeff reached for the remote control. In a moment, Harrison Ford's face filled the screen, and Dawn tried to put all her fears behind her.

"You did a great job tonight," Mr Schafer said a couple of hours later. He handed Dawn some money, and Dawn stifled a yawn. This had been one of the toughest babysitting jobs she'd ever had.

"Thanks," she mumbled, heading for the stairs. She was halfway to the landing when she stopped and walked back to the kitchen. Jeff was at the counter, making himself an enormous sandwich of Swiss cheese and beansprouts. "Here," she said, offering him half of the money. "This is for you."

"That's okay." He grinned and waved his hand.

"No way," she said, tucking the bills into his shirt pocket. "You earned every penny of it." As she headed for bed, a funny thought crossed her mind: Maybe one day Jeff would be a babysitter, too!

10th CHAPTER

Saturday

Dear Logan,
More of the same. Perfect weather, great swimming, and the kids are still getting along with each other. What could be better? Wish you were here.
Love,
Mary Anne

Talk about a guilty conscience! I had a terrible time trying to work out what to say to Logan, because I was afraid he would read between the lines. I finally decided that the less said, the better. You'll notice I didn't mention Alex. How could I? I felt silly leaving him out, but I didn't dare tell Logan what was really going on. . .

I was so excited on that Saturday afternoon I was practically floating. This is what happened. When I phoned Alex to explain that I wouldn't be able to see him on Friday night (all because of Stacey), he immediately asked me out for Saturday. We were going to have dinner at a seafood place, and I spent half an hour trying on every single outfit I'd brought with me. Nothing looked right. I had plenty of casual clothes, but we were going to a "real" restaurant (unlike Burger Garden), and I wanted to dress up.

I had just decided to ask Stacey if I could borrow her red sundress when she walked into the bedroom, drying her hair. You can imagine how surprised I was when she pulled the red sundress out of the wardrobe and tossed it onto the bed!

"Wow, you must have read my mind," I told her.

"Why's that?" She ran her fingers through her damp hair.

"I was just going to ask you if I could borrow that."

Stacey shrugged and peeled off her

T-shirt. "Normally I'd say yes, but I need it myself tonight."

"Oh, of course," I said quickly. "I understand." I really hate borrowing things, and I didn't want to put her on the spot. Then it hit me! "Wait a minute," I said, taking a step towards her. "Why do you need a dress for tonight?"

Stacey plunked herself down at the dressing table and started fumbling with bottles of nail polish. "I'm wearing it out to dinner." She was absolutely calm. I couldn't believe it.

"You're going out to dinner? On a *date*?" I squawked.

She hesitated, just for a second. "Um, yes, that's right."

"Stacey McGill, you're unbelievable!" I sat down on the bed and just stared at her. She refused to look at me and starting painting her long fingernails with a base coat. "You went out last night, remember?" Stacey opened her mouth to say something, but I didn't give her a chance. "Here's a news flash for you. I am going out tonight." I paused. "You are staying at home with the kids. That was our arrangement."

I picked up my towel and headed for the shower, my face flaming. Stacey caught up with me in the hall, and I was glad to see she had ruined her nails by jumping up so fast.

"Look, Mary Anne," she said in a wheedling tone, "I didn't mean to upset you. It's just that Toby and I had such a *fantastic* time last night that I thought you wouldn't mind if I went out with him again."

"You thought I wouldn't mind?" I said coolly. My heart was pounding in my chest, but I stood my ground.

"You can take off two nights *next* week," she said. You'd think she was doing me a big favour. "That would be fair, wouldn't it?"

"No, Stacey. It would *not* be fair. I'm going out tonight, and if you'll excuse me, I need to get ready." I brushed by her and headed for the shower without another word.

"This is very nice," I said later that evening. Alex and I were sitting at a table in the restaurant, looking at the menu. The menu was enormous – and I had no idea what to order. The truth is, I felt a little nervous sitting opposite Alex. Going to the boardwalk was one thing, but being all dressed up in a restaurant made everything seem different somehow. As if we were on a real date. The more I thought about it, the more confused I got. This was what I wanted, wasn't it? A "real" date with Alex? But what about Logan?

Alex interrupted my thoughts. "Earth to Mary Anne," he said playfully. The waitress was standing over us, order pad in hand. Ready or not, I *had* to order something!

"Um, I think I'll have the fish cakes," I said not, really caring. "With chips and iced tea."

The minute the waitress left, we just stared at each other. In dead silence. What in the world were we going to talk about?

"Wow, we got here at a good time," I said at last.

Alex looked blank. "A good time?"

"It's not crowded now. You know, it's not too early and it's not too late." I stammered a little, feeling nervous.

Even Alex couldn't think of anything to say to *that* stupid remark, and he gazed at a point somewhere over my head. I was very tempted to turn round, but I knew that there was nothing behind me except a giant flounder that was mounted on the wall.

Another long pause. "They certainly have a lot of fish on the menu," I said, thinking of the flounder. I could have bitten my tongue the minute the words were out. Of course they had a lot of fish on the menu. What did I expect at a seafood restaurant – pizza?

Alex nodded politely, but I knew he must think I was incredibly boring. Why couldn't I think of anything interesting to talk about like other girls could? I made a mental note to ask Stacey what *she* talked about on dates, and then I remembered that she was probably still annoyed with me. She was babysitting for the Pike kids with Mallory, instead of having dinner with Toby in a restaurant – and just for a moment, I envied her!

I think we would have gone on this way *for ever*, except that something really funny happened, and we both cracked up. When the waitress served Alex his lobster, she put a *bib* on him! It was just like the kind babies wear, except it was adult-sized and had a giant lobster printed on it. Alex didn't look surprised (I suppose he had ordered lobster before and knew what to expect), but I was so amazed I burst out laughing! I didn't even try to keep a straight face, and when Alex saw me laughing, *he* started laughing, and everything was okay. After the bib incident, we had a million things to say to each other, and we talked nonstop for the rest of the meal.

Later, we hit the boardwalk, where Alex played a Hoopla game, trying to win a stuffed animal for me. After about twenty minutes (and a lot of small change) he finally *did* win, and I chose a big purple hippopotamus as my prize.

"You're sure you don't want a panda?" he said, eyeing the hippo. "Or maybe one of the chimpanzees?"

"Nope." I clutched my prize. "A purple hippo is just the thing."

I don't know what to tell you about the rest of the evening, except that it was wonderful. We spent another hour or so wandering up and down and finally had a ride on the Big Wheel. Alex grumbled because I had the purple hippo wedged on the seat between us, but I knew he was only kidding.

It was a beautiful starry night, and we pointed out the constellations to each other as we walked back to the Pikes'. (He picked out the Seven Sisters, but I found the Little Dipper.) Neither one of us wanted the evening to end, and Alex made a joke as I went up the porch steps.

"Oh, Mary Anne," he said seriously. "Can I ask you a favour?"

I turned around, surprised. "Of course, what is it?"

He grinned. "The next time we go out, would you mind leaving your friend at home?"

I hugged the hippo tightly to my chest and waved goodnight. When I got upstairs to my bedroom, I sat in the window seat and stared out at the ocean for a long time. *The next time we go out...* This was what I wanted, wasn't it? Alex was so funny and sweet – of course I wanted to see him again! Then why did I feel so guilty? *Because you said you would always be true to Logan*, a little voice nagged me.

I heard Stacey moving around downstairs in the kitchen, and I quickly slipped into my nightdress and got into bed. I didn't feel like talking to anyone. It had been a wonderful, exciting, confusing evening, and there was so much to think about. . .

11th CHAPTER

Wednesday

Dear Jessi,

Everything here has gotten very complicated, and it's all because of a boy, a bunch of love poems, and a case of mistaken identity. It sounds just like something out of Shakespeare, but I swear that it's true. I have no idea how everything will turn out, but I have the feeling that it will get worse before it gets better. I will keep you posted! Love to everyone in Stoneybrook,

MaryAnne

"You're sure you want to go into town today?" It was nine-thirty in the morning, and Stacey and I had just finished clearing up the breakfast dishes.

"Of course we're sure!" Vanessa said impatiently. "We *love* Sea City, don't we, Margo?"

Margo nodded, eager to escape a boring game of Candy Land with Claire.

"So can we? Can we *please*?" Vanessa chanted, practically jumping up and down in excitement.

"Go ahead," Stacey said, seeing my hesitation. "I'll take the boys to the beach as soon as they get changed."

"I'll go with you," added Mal. "My tan's not nearly good enough yet."

"Yippee!" Vanessa hooted, throwing her sun visor in the air.

Looking back, I'm surprised I didn't catch on to the *real* reason that Vanessa was so eager to go into town. (If you've already guessed that it was because of a certain boy called Chris, you're right.)

It was almost eleven by the time all four of us – Claire, Margo, Vanessa, and myself – stepped onto the boardwalk. It was a cool day, and Sea City was crowded with tourists.

"Can we look at souvenirs?" Margo asked. "I brought my money with me."

We made our first stop at a little shop that sold hundreds of souvenirs made of seashells. There were jewellery boxes decorated with pearly pink shells that looked like fans, and mirrors ringed with tiny white shells no bigger than a dime. There was a music box shaped like a clam shell, and dozens of shell key rings. Everything seemed a bit expensive for Margo, so I tried to persuade her to buy a plain conch shell.

"But it doesn't say Sea City on it," she said.

"But it's pretty, and every time you look at it, you'll think of the ocean," I pointed out.

Margo looked unconvinced, and Vanessa was getting impatient with her. "Don't make such a big deal out of it, Margo. Do you want to buy a seashell or not?"

"But that's just a plain old shell. I can find one of those on the beach."

"But you haven't found one yet," Vanessa said reasonably. "How about this?" She picked up a beautiful white sand dollar and handed it to Margo. Someone had drilled a hole in the top and tied a strand of ribbon through it.

"Ooh, that's pretty," Margo said. "What is it?"

"It's a Christmas tree ornament," I told her. "You can hang it on the tree every year, and when it's snowing in Stoneybrook, you can dream about Sea City."

"I love it!" Margo cried. She had exactly enough money to pay for it, and Vanessa took her to the cashier while I wandered around the shop for a few more minutes. I saw a black T-shirt that I knew Dawn would love. "Sea City" was scrawled across it in bright pink letters that looked as if they were written in lipstick. It was exactly right for Dawn – but not for me – and I finally bought two coffee mugs, one for my father and one for Sharon. They looked handmade and said SEA CITY in *very* small letters at the bottom. I even found a toy for Tigger.

Our next stop was Trampoline Land, which is one of Margo's favourite spots in town. She immediately pulled Claire onto a giant trampoline with her, while Vanessa and I watched from the sidelines. I always feel a little dizzy when I watch people jump up and down on a trampoline, and I can't understand why Margo likes it so much. What's even stranger is that Margo gets seasick just from travelling in a car, but trampolines don't seem to bother her.

Except this time.

Margo had been jumping like a human pogo stick for almost twenty minutes when I noticed that she looked a little pale. "She looks sort of . . . white, doesn't she?" I said to no one in particular.

Vanessa gasped. "White – she looks green!" She grabbed my arm. "Mary Anne, we have to do something fast. She's going to be sick!"

"Oh, no," I moaned. I looked at Margo's head bobbing up and down and I realized that Vanessa was right. Margo's eyes were glassy, and her skin was suddenly flushed. She *definitely* looked ill, and in a moment or two, everyone would know about it. "But what can we do? Why doesn't she stop?"

Vanessa shook her head. "She can't stop. She's probably trying to work her way over to the edge right now, but all those other kids are in the way. You can't just walk off a trampoline, you know."

Vanessa was absolutely right. When you're on a trampoline, you bounce up and down, even if you don't want to. Sometimes parents go on the trampoline to get their kids, and they bob up and down just like everybody else.

"I'm going to get her," I said, coming to a decision. I felt pretty silly bouncing like a kangaroo towards Margo, but after all, I was the babysitter. I knew I had to get her. "Hang on, Margo," I said when I finally caught up with her. I grabbed her arm to guide her off the trampoline, and she stood on the sidelines for a few moments, swaying back and forth. Claire stood next to us.

"As soon as she feels better, we'll leave," I said to Vanessa and Claire.

"Good," Vanessa spoke up. "I want to go to Ice-Cream Palace."

I was shocked. "Vanessa, give Margo a few minutes to recover. She *was* nearly sick."

Vanessa rolled her eyes. "Ice cream settles

your stomach," she said. No one believed her, and we headed for Fred's Putt-Putt Course to watch the miniature golf.

"*Now* can we go to Ice-Cream Palace?" Vanessa asked half an hour later. I've never known Vanessa to be so incredibly whiny.

"I suppose so," I said. "Margo seems to be feeling better, and—" I never got a chance to finish the sentence because Vanessa raced ahead of me. What was the big deal about going to Ice-Cream Palace? (I should have known!)

"There he is," Vanessa said happily when we caught up with her at the Palace. She was speaking very quietly so only I could hear her. She nodded towards the counter and I saw that Chris was on duty. "I've left him three poems," she said proudly.

"You did what?"

"I managed to come here three times since last Friday," she whispered. "And I left him a note on the counter each time."

"I didn't think you were really going to do that." I felt awful and wished I'd spent more time trying to talk Vanessa out of it.

"I told you I was," she said flatly. "That's the only way he'll know how I feel about him." She smiled. "And pretty soon, I'll know how he feels about me."

Chris caught sight of us then, and to my surprise, he started a conversation with Vanessa. Could he really be interested in her? I wondered. He seemed *very* curious about where we lived, and how long we were staying in Sea City. In between all the questions, he managed to make four hot fudge sundaes for us, and this time, there weren't any accidents. I noticed that his boss was keeping an eye on him, so I think he was being extra careful.

Vanessa dawdled over her sundae *for ever*, probably hoping to hear more from Chris, but finally it was time to leave. We were almost out of the door when Chris came dashing over, wiping his hands on his apron.

"Hey, Vanessa?" He kept his voice so low, I had to strain to hear him.

"Yes?"

"Do me a favour, will you?"

"Of course!"

"Tell Mallory I'll be able to go out with her on Saturday night."

Vanessa was speechless, and so was I. He was going out with Mallory on Saturday night? How in the world had this happened?

He didn't even *know* Mallory. And Mallory probably didn't like him, so why did he think – then it hit me. The poems! Somehow Chris had misunderstood the poems. He must have thought they were from Mallory. I struggled to remember the one I'd read. Something about "an accident brought us together." Of course! He remembered bumping heads with Mallory, so naturally he thought of her when he read that line. What a mess!

In a strange way, it made sense. After all, Chris is twelve, and Mal is eleven. Vanessa is only nine, and at that age there is a big difference. Chris probably thinks of Vanessa as a baby – but of Mal as a cute girl.

I waited until we were on the boardwalk before whispering to Vanessa, "What are you going to do?"

Vanessa shook her head, her eyes very bright. "I don't know," she said sadly. "How could I have been so stupid?"

Claire interrupted us then, and we didn't get a chance to continue the conversation. Things were really busy at the Pikes' when we got back, and when I finally had a free moment, Mrs Pike said Vanessa was having a nap.

A nap at four-thirty in the afternoon? I tiptoed upstairs and stood for a minute outside her closed door. There was no sound coming from inside, and after a moment I went back downstairs. I was very worried about Vanessa.

12th CHAPTER

Thursday

It started out as the world's easiest baby-sitting job and turned into a manhunt. Or I should say, a hamster hunt! I was sitting for Becca and Squirt, and it was so hot we decided to stay indoors with the air-conditioning. Becca and Charlotte Johanssen were playing Sweet Shop, Squirt was toddling around the house as usual, and I was stretched out with a book. And then it happened! Becca and Charlotte discovered that

Frodo, the Pikes' hamster, was missing from his cage. I told myself not to panic and tried to think of all the places a hamster might hide. Losing a pet has got to be one of the worst things that could happen to a baby-sitter, and I just hope it doesn't happen to anyone else....

It was one of those days when you're sure that nothing interesting will ever happen, and then, pow! Something zaps you right out of the blue. Jessi Ramsey was babysitting for Becca and Squirt while her mother was at a job interview and her father was at work. She was happy when Charlotte Johanssen came to the door and asked if she could play with Becca. Charlotte is an only child and a favourite with the BSC members, especially Stacey. She's one of those good-natured kids, bright with a serious, adult side to her. She and Becca get along very well together, and both have good imaginations.

"Want to play Snakes and Ladders?" Becca asked. "Or Junior Scrabble?"

"I don't really feel like a board game, do you?" Charlotte said, curling up on the window seat. "Let's act out something."

"Okay!" Becca said eagerly. Becca loves to pretend and can imitate any animal you can name. For instance, when she's a cat, she meows and rubs her head against your leg until you reach down and pet her. "Let's play sweet shop," she suggested.

Sweet shop is a game that can go on *for ever* because Becca and Charlotte each take turns being the shop owner and the customer – and they both like sweets.

"What kind of licorice twists do you have?" Jessi heard Becca ask. Charlotte was kneeling behind the coffee table, pretending it was a sweets counter.

"We have some new cherry-flavoured twists," Charlotte said, pointing to a blank spot on the coffee table. "They're absolutely delicious. And of course we have our ordinary black licorice ropes. Would you like to try one? We give free samples."

"I can't make up my mind," Becca said, rubbing her chin. "I came in here because I wanted something really different."

"Something *really* different? Well, you've come to the right place." Charlotte reached down under the coffee table and pretended to lift out a tray of goodies. "These just came in today."

"What are they?"

"Licorice root-beer barrels! See, they're

shaped like little barrels but they taste like licorice."

"Wow, that *is* different."

Charlotte looked pleased. "We're the only shop in Stoneybrook that stocks them. . ."

Jessi let snatches of the girls' conversation drift in and out of her head while she kept an eye on Squirt and read a horse story. Squirt is a pretty steady walker and the Ramseys' house is completely baby-proofed, so she didn't worry when he wandered out to the kitchen and didn't come back for a few minutes.

She kept one of his favourite children's programmes on TV, in case he decided to come back to the study and settle down with her. She liked to watch the programme herself, because it had very good actors and some interesting sketches. She idly watched as two little boys became friends, and then went back to her reading when they talked about the letter S.

Soon a jingle caught her attention, and she looked up to watch a matching game. The neighbourhood kids were asked to identify which things were alike and which things were different. It was fun, and there was a lot of giggling as the kids decided that an egg-beater didn't belong with a dog and a cat and a pig.

"Why not?" asked the host.

"Because it's different," the kids shouted.

"And what *should go* with the dog and cat and pig?"

"The goat!"

"Why?"

"Because those things are the *same*. They're all animals."

"You're absolutely right!"

Jessi heard someone clapping enthusiastically behind her and turned to see that Squirt was sitting on the floor. "Hey, Squirt, did you like that?"

Squirt didn't answer. He wandered back to the kitchen then, and Jessi returned to her book. Twenty minutes later, disaster struck. Becca and Charlotte came flying into the study.

"Jessi!" Becca cried. "Frodo's missing!"

Jessi jumped to her feet. "Frodo? That's impossible. I fed him this morning and he was curled up in his cage."

"Not any more," Charlotte piped up.

Jessi ran out to the kitchen and saw the empty cage. "Oh, no!" she wailed. She had been looking after Frodo for the Pikes, and she'd been *very* careful with him. She knew a lot about hamsters because of Misty, and she knew that you have to keep them in their cages unless you're changing their litter or playing with them. You can't just let them run around the house, or they're bound to get lost.

"What should we do?" Becca asked.

"Start searching!" Jessi said. "Let's split

up. We'll have to cover the whole house. He could be anywhere."

"But where should we start?" Charlotte looked around the kitchen.

Jessi thought for a moment. "I'm pretty sure he's hiding somewhere in the house." (She wouldn't even let herself *think* that he might be outside.) "We'll have to look under all the tables and chairs. Hamsters like to hide, so you'll have to check any place that he could fit under. And don't forget the cupboards."

Fifteen minutes later, Becca yelled down the stairs, "Jessi! Come up to my room. I've found him!"

"Thank goodness. Where was he?" Jessi rushed upstairs to find Charlotte and Becca both kneeling down in front of Misty's cage. She was amazed to see *two* furry bodies munching on hamster pellets. "He's in Misty's cage!"

"Yeah, but how did he get there?" Becca reached to pet him.

Jessi shook her head. She was baffled. "I have no idea. He certainly didn't open the cage door himself."

Becca and Charlotte laughed at the idea.

"Now what?" Charlotte asked.

Jessi opened the cage and carefully lifted out a wriggling Frodo. "He's going right back where he belongs," she said firmly. "Back to his own cage in the kitchen."

On the way downstairs she started

thinking over what had just happened. There was only one explanation: Becca. Maybe Becca had thought it would be funny to put Frodo in with Misty, or maybe she thought Frodo was lonely. She decided it was time to speak up. "Becca," she said, "I know you didn't mean to do anything wrong, but it wasn't a good idea to put Frodo in with Misty—"

"But I didn't!" Becca protested. "I didn't go anywhere near him."

"Now, Becca," she said gently, "Frodo didn't *let* himself in the cage."

"But I didn't do it!" Becca repeated. "I would never do something like that. Maybe they wouldn't like each other, or maybe Frodo would eat Misty's food. You know I would never do anything that might hurt Misty."

Jessi knew that this was true. Then what had really happened?

A few minutes later, she was carefully putting Frodo back in his own cage when Squirt started yelling. "No, no! Same! Same!"

Jessi looked up. "What's the matter, Squirt?" She shut the cage door and went to the sink to wash her hands.

Squirt rushed to the cage and tried to open it. "Open!" he demanded.

Jessi knelt down so she was at eye level with him. "Frodo belongs in his own cage," she said, but Squirt went right on yelling.

"Same, same!"

Finally Jessi got it. Squirt had put the two hamsters in the same cage because they were the same! He'd really been paying attention to the TV show.

"Wow," she said softly. Squirt was obviously a genius. She could hardly wait to tell her parents that her baby brother was *much* brighter than anyone had guessed.

13th CHAPTER

Friday

Dear Kristy,
I never thought I'd say this, but Stacey is driving me crazy! She's going through a bad time, and she's taking it out on me. In case you're wondering, it's all because of a boy. Boys really complicate things, don't they? I can't believe that we're leaving Sea City tomorrow. It's been fun, but in some ways I can hardly wait to be back in Stoneybrook.

By the time you get this postcard you'll probably know the whole story.
Love,
MaryAnne

I didn't want to say too much in the postcard, but Stacey and I haven't been getting on very well. It's all because Toby *dumped* her on Thursday night. I didn't find out about it until Friday morning after breakfast.

Stacey came charging out of the bathroom, her face like a thundercloud. "You've used my towel – again!" she yelled.

"I did *not* use your towel," I said quietly. I hate it when people shout at me, but I wasn't going to confess to something I hadn't done. I've found that the best thing to do when Stacey gets in one of her moods is to ignore her, and that's just what I did.

"How can you stand there and deny it?" she demanded. She walked right up to me, so close our noses were practically touching.

"Stacey," I said, trying to keep my cool, "*my* towel has blue flowers with yellow centres. *Your* towel has yellow flowers with blue centres."

She frowned. "Yellow flowers with—"

"That's right." I turned away and started folding my shorts and T-shirts into a pile.

I knew it would be hectic tomorrow when we had to close up the house.

"Humph," she snorted. "Well, maybe you're right about the towel," she admitted. She stood staring at me, and I could practically see the wheels turning. She was *looking* for something to argue about. "I can't believe you're doing this *now*," she said, pointing to the stack of clothes.

"I like to be organized," I said, sighing, "and things will be really busy in the morning."

"You're *always* organized," she said coolly. "I would find it *very* boring to live like that."

"Uh-huh." I looked at Stacey's make-up strewn all over the dressing table. Not much danger of that, I thought.

She ran her finger lightly along the edge of my T-shirts. "You're so neat, I'm surprised you don't iron your underwear." She paused. "Or maybe you do when we're all asleep." She flounced out of the room before I could think up an answer to that one.

I didn't find out about Toby until that evening. Stacey had calmed down a bit after dinner, and she and Mal and I were sitting on the porch swing. It was dusk, my favourite time of day, and a salty breeze was blowing off the ocean.

"I suppose tonight is the time for good-byes," I said quietly.

"Toby's already said goodbye. Last night," she sniffled. She buried her face in her hands, just for a minute.

"Stacey?" said Mal, glancing at me.

Stacey looked up, her blue eyes misting over. "He *broke up* with me. Can you believe it?" (Mal's eyes widened.)

"Why? Did you two have a row?" I asked.

"Of course not." She ran her hand very quickly over her eyes. "We never argue."

"Then what happened?"

"She shrugged. "I can't work it out. He just said that these past two weeks have been great, but that it's over. He wants to go home and see other people. He doesn't want to be tied to me."

"Gosh," said Mal breathily.

I thought guiltily of Logan. "But couldn't you date other people and still stay in touch with each other?"

Stacey shook her head. "He doesn't see it that way." She stood up and leaned against the railing. "You're really lucky you've got Logan waiting for you back at home, Mary Anne. As you always say, he's your one true love."

Oh, yes. I had been saying that, hadn't I?

Stacey gave a long sigh. "It must be nice to have someone to count on."

Mal looked from Stacey to me with interest. She's just beginning to think that not all boys are jerks.

Margo and Claire came out on to the porch then, so the conversation was over, but I couldn't stop thinking about Logan and Alex and how confused I was. Whenever I was with Alex, I had a wonderful time. Maybe I was even in love with him. I wasn't sure. And when I thought of Logan – that sweet smile, that deep voice – I thought I was in love with *him*! You can't be in love with two boys at once, can you? I just didn't know.

Alex and I decided to spend our last night together at the "real" restaurant, since we had had so much fun there before. As it turned out, it was a big mistake. Everything seemed different this time, and I couldn't put my finger on it.

For one thing, Alex had absolutely nothing to say. Naturally that made me very nervous, and when I get nervous I clam up. So both of us were sitting there like ventriloquist's dummies, waiting for someone to make us talk.

I *had* to break the silence or I would go mad, so I made a big deal out of choosing dinner. "Let's do something wild and *not* order fish," I said gaily. "That's the rule tonight. You can order anything but fish or shellfish."

Alex smiled politely. He must have thought I was mad. "Whatever you say." He glanced at the menu. "There won't be much of a choice, though. After all, this is a seafood restaurant."

"Oh, there will be enough to choose from. It will just be a challenge." I tried a little laugh that didn't quite come off. Why had I started this?

"I suppose we could try the spaghetti." Alex smiled, but his heart wasn't in it.

"No way," I said. I shook my finger at him. "It has clam sauce."

"Oh, sorry." He stared at the menu for a long time. "Well," he said finally, "we could try the giant sub sandwich. I'm sure that doesn't have any fish in it."

"Sounds good to me!" I laughed like I was having the time of my life. When the sandwich arrived, I felt like crawling under the table. In the first place you should never order a sub sandwich when you're eating out because they are incredibly messy. Tomato slices slide down your chin, mayonnaise squirts out of both ends, and salami slithers into your lap. Not a pretty sight. In the second place, they're *huge*. This sandwich looked bigger than my head. I realized too late that we should have split one between us.

The only good thing was that now we had an excuse not to talk. We were too busy working our way through a mountain of meat and French bread. I told Alex a little more about the Pike kids, and he talked about his softball team, but somehow the conversation never really got going. We weren't really talking, we were "saying lines", just as you do in a school play. Except it felt as if we were in *different* plays, because the lines didn't sound right.

I thought the meal would *never* end, and when it finally did, I reached for the bill.

"You can't do that," Alex said, making a grab for it.

"Why not?"

"Girls don't pay for dates."

"Of course they do. Logan and I always take turns paying."

"Who's Logan?"

Uh-oh. "He's my, uh, boyfriend. Back in Stoneybrook." The truth was finally out!

Alex didn't seem too upset. "I've got a girlfriend back home, too," he said casually.

"That's nice," I said. What was I talking about?

"What is?"

"That you have a girlfriend. And I have a boyfriend."

Alex looked at me and burst out laughing. "What's so funny?" I asked.

"I can't believe we're having this conversation, can you?"

I started laughing. "Not really. It certainly beats hearing about your pitching arm, though."

Alex laughed even harder then, and I knew that everything would be okay. Suddenly he was the warm, funny Alex I knew, and we talked until it was time to go. (He ended up letting me pay the bill.)

Later on, when we walked along the boardwalk, I thought about how much I liked Alex, and how much fun we'd had at Sea City. We were pals – friends – and it was much nicer than being boyfriend and girlfriend. After all, we each *had* a romantic relationship back home. Why complicate things?

"You know what?" Alex said, walking me up the Pikes' porch steps. "This has been one of the best nights of my life."

"You know what? I feel exactly the same way!"

"Friends?" He leaned forward and gave me a big hug.

I nodded. "For ever."

14th CHAPTER

Friday

Dear Dad and Sharon,

Sometimes kids are amazing! Vanessa surprised me by coming up with a very grown-up solution to a tough problem. I can't believe I'm going to see you and Dawn tomorrow before you even get this card! This holiday has been fun, but I can't wait to get home.

Love,
Mary Anne

Mr and Mrs Pike were sitting in the kitchen when I got home from my evening with Alex.

"Did you have a good time?" Mrs Pike asked.

"I had a *wonderful* time." We were speaking in low voices, because everyone else was in bed.

Mrs Pike smiled. "Mmm, sounds serious," she said teasingly. "Maybe you'd better sit down and talk about it over a piece of apple pie."

I laughed. "No, that's the great part about it. It's not serious at all." I realized they had no idea what I was talking about and decided to leave it that way. "And thanks for the pie, but we had a big dinner, and I'm stuffed. I think I'll just go to bed."

"Sleep well," Mr Pike said. "Tomorrow's a busy day."

I tiptoed up the stairs, suddenly very tired. I was all ready to open my bedroom door when I saw a faint light at the end of the hall. It was coming from under the door to the room Mal and Vanessa were sharing. I decided to check on things.

"What's up?" I whispered, sticking my head in the door. Mallory was sound asleep, but Vanessa was sitting up in bed, her notepad balanced on her knees, a small reading light on.

She motioned me over to the bed. "I'm writing to Chris," she said quietly.

I sat down carefully on the edge of the bed. "What did you decide to tell him?"

"Well," she said, "I tried to look at the problem from every angle, and I decided there was only one solution."

I was impressed with how grown-up she sounded. I'd been thinking about the problem all day and didn't have a clue what to do. I was totally stumped.

She took a deep breath. "This is what I've come up with. Chris thinks Mal is his secret admirer."

"Right."

"And he wants to take her out on Saturday night." She paused. "So the answer is obvious."

"It is?" I had no idea what she was going to say next.

"It's very simple. We won't *be* here on Saturday night. We're leaving tomorrow. So all I have to do is write Chris another poem and tell him how disappointed I am that we'll be back in Stoneybrook."

"You're not going to tell him that *you*, and not Mallory, were the one who fell in love with him and sent him those poems?"

She shook her head. "What good would it do? Mallory is the one he likes. This way is much better. He'll never know the real story, and neither will Mallory."

It was pretty hard to believe that a nine-year-old kid could come up with such a good idea.

"I'll read the poem to you if you like, but you've got to promise me something. If you think it's silly, please tell me. I don't want to make a *total* idiot of myself."

Just then, Mallory made a funny snuffling noise in her sleep and rolled over. Vanessa and I froze for a minute and then relaxed. "It's okay. She's a very heavy sleeper. She's just dreaming," said Vanessa.

"Read the poem," I whispered.

" '*Dear Chris,*
I'd love to see you tonight,
but the timing just isn't right.
We're leaving Sea City today,
and going far away.
I'll always remember your smile,
please think of me once in a while.
I ♥ you for ever, your secret admirer.' "

Vanessa's voice choked a little on the last line, and I had a lump in my throat. "It's a beautiful poem," I told her. "You've said just the right thing, and it's not silly at all."

"Are you sure?"

"I'm sure." I leaned over and hugged her. "I'm so proud of you, Vanessa. I know this must have been really hard to do."

"It was one of the hardest things I've done in my whole life." She hugged me very tightly, and I knew she was trying not to cry. "Will you help me deliver it to Ice-Cream Palace tomorrow?"

"Of course I will." I could hardly get the words out because I had started to cry myself. All I need is to see someone sad or in trouble, and I immediately start bawling.

"Don't cry, Mary Anne," Vanessa whispered against my shoulder. That only made things worse, and before you know it, both of us were crying.

"I'd better go to my room," I said finally. "You need to get some sleep."

"Okay," she said, turning off the light and snuggling under the covers. She managed to smile at me, even though she looked a bit weepy. "Thanks for helping me out."

"Any time." I was heading for the door when a noise made me turn round suddenly.

"I told you I want sunscreen, not sunblock!" Mallory was sitting straight up in bed, pointing a finger at me. I felt like a criminal.

My heart stopped. "What – what did you say?" I stammered. I looked at Vanessa, who flipped the light back on. I knew my face must be flaming red.

"Lie down, Mallory. You're in the middle of a dream," Vanessa said calmly.

I was amazed. "She is? She looks like she's wide awake."

Vanessa nodded. "She does this all the time. She's sound asleep but she talks to herself. It's pretty creepy, but I'm used to it by now."

Vanessa hopped out of bed and gently pushed Mallory's shoulders until she was lying down again. Mallory's eyelids fluttered a few times and then closed.

Vanessa smiled as she got back into bed. "She won't remember a word of this in the morning," she said, as I tiptoed out of the room.

I was dying to crawl into bed, but there was one more hurdle to cross. Stacey. She was in bed, but she wasn't asleep. In fact, she was sitting up with a book. She closed it when I came into our bedroom, though.

"I'm glad you're back," she said. "I've been waiting up for you."

I felt exhausted. "Look, Stacey," I said wearily, "if you're ready for another argument, it'll have to wait till morning." Stacey had seemed saner – almost nice – earlier in the evening, but I still didn't trust her. People who've been dumped like to pick arguments.

"No, I don't want to argue with you, Mary Anne." She hesitated. "Just the opposite. I've been such a jerk. I want to apologize for the lousy way I've treated you."

I could feel tears welling up in my eyes. Oh, no. Not again! I thought.

"Do you think you can ever forgive me?" Stacey asked in a quavery voice.

"Of course I can," I told her. "But please don't say another word about it, or I'll start crying."

"Okay," she said, laughing a little. "I don't want you to turn on the waterworks or we'll be drowning in here." She quickly changed the subject. "How was your evening?"

"It was great." I could feel myself breaking into a grin. "A really super night."

Stacey looked surprised. "No sad goodbyes?"

I shook my head. "No, everything was wonderful. Because I've finally realized something."

"You have?"

I nodded. "Alex is a good friend, but Logan is my boyfriend. The love of my life," I added, blushing a little. "Once I'd worked that out, everything fell into place. I don't feel confused any more."

Stacey leaned back against the pillows. "I'm glad things have worked out for you."

"I'm sorry they didn't work out for you," I said, reaching for my pyjamas.

Stacey sighed. "Well, at least it's been an interesting holiday. Never a dull moment."

"Never a dull moment," I repeated.

"You know what, Mary Anne? I think I'll be quite glad to get back to Stoneybrook."

"Mmm, me, too." I pulled on my pyjamas and fell into bed.

"Do you think Stoneybrook will seem

dull after Sea City?"

I yawned and buried my head in the pillow.

"No," I mumbled. "I think it will seem . . . peaceful." Stacey said something else, but I had already pulled the quilt over my shoulders and was heading for a dream.

15th CHAPTER

"Who's got the beach towels?"

"My swimming costume's still wet!"

"My inner tube's got a leak."

"Good, it has to be deflated anyway."

Moving out of the Sea City house was just as hectic as moving in. Maybe more so. Let's face it, packing up to go home is never as much fun as unpacking in a new place. The excitement just isn't there. The house looked empty now that most of our belongings were stashed in the cars.

Mr Pike was cooking an early breakfast, while I helped Mrs Pike clean out the refrigerator.

"At least we don't have many leftovers," she said, tossing some cold meat into a cool box. "How about the pantry?" she said to Stacey, who was opening cabinet doors all over the kitchen.

"It's almost bare," Stacey said. "So far all

I've found are some stale crisps, a piece of bubble gum, and three biscuits." She peered at something moving on one of the shelves. "Yuck! And a few ants."

"You don't have to pack those," Mr Pike teased her.

All the kids wanted to take one last swim after breakfast, but the sky was overcast, and they finally decided against it. I was glad. Now that our holiday was over, I was eager to get back to Stoneybrook. Of course I had one important thing to do before we left. I had to keep my promise to Vanessa to take her to Ice-Cream Palace.

"It would have been nice if the sun was shining on our last day here," Stacey said, sitting down to breakfast. "I could have done with another hour on the backs of my legs."

"The backs of your legs look fine," Mal told her. Stacey had been aiming for the perfect tan for the past two weeks. She brought her watch to the beach and carefully turned over every half hour so her tan would be even. She reminded me of a chicken rotating on a barbecue, but I didn't tell her so. (I still looked as pale as ever, because I'd worn my caftan and hat every single day.)

"Can we play on the beach before we go, Dad?" Adam asked.

"Yeah, let's build one more sandcastle," Jordan chimed in.

Mr Pike looked at Mrs Pike. "I'll leave it up to you."

"Well, I don't know," Mrs Pike began, "the swimsuits are packed now."

"We don't need them to play in the sand," Nicky said.

"You win." Mrs Pike got up and started to clear the table. "I want to get going by eleven, though." She looked at Stacey and me. "We seem to have everything under control here. Is there anything you girls would like to do before we leave?"

"I think I'll play with the kids on the beach," Stacey said. "Who knows? Maybe you can get a tan on a cloudy day."

I caught up with Stacey as she was heading towards the porch. "There's something Vanessa and I have to do in town," I said quickly. "Can you and Mal cope with things here while we're gone?"

"Of course." Stacey looked puzzled but didn't ask any questions.

I told Mrs Pike that Vanessa wanted one last trip into town. Then I nodded to Vanessa, who was clutching her poem in her hand, and we headed for Ice-Cream Palace.

I was feeling a little nervous by this time, but Vanessa was very cool as we walked along the boardwalk. I found out that she had planned everything down to the second.

"Slow down a little," she said. "I want to get there at exactly ten-fifteen."

"You do? What happens at ten-fifteen?"

"That's when the other boy behind the counter takes his break. Chris is really busy then because he has to cope with all the customers himself."

I was amazed at the way she'd thought things out. "What are we going to do exactly?"

She smiled. "You'll see."

We peered in the window just as a sandy-haired boy flung his cap on the counter and headed out of the front door. Right on cue, a bunch of giggling girls poured *into* Ice-Cream Palace and nearly collided with him.

"Perfect," Vanessa said under her breath. "Chris will go mad trying to wait on all those kids at once."

She grabbed my hand, and we sneaked in behind the girls. Chris was facing us, scooping out ice cream. Vanessa hung back for a moment, staying out of sight. She waited until he turned around to use the whipped-cream machine, and then she darted forward to toss the note on the counter. Before I knew what had happened, the whole thing was over and we were outside.

Hearts pounding, we took a few steps and then stopped to hug each other. "We did it!" Vanessa cried.

"We did it," I echoed. I was glad to see she could smile about it.

Later that day, we were back in Stoneybrook. I was practically bouncing off the seat when Mrs Pike pulled into my drive.

"You did a great job, dear," Mrs Pike said, handing me an envelope. I knew it contained a nice cheque, but that was the last thing on my mind. I wanted to run straight inside and see everyone.

"Goodbye, Mary Anne!" shouted Stacey and the Pikes as I raced for the kitchen door.

When I burst into the kitchen, Sharon was standing at the sink. "Oh, I'm so glad you're back!" she said, giving me a big hug. "We really missed you."

"I missed you, too."

A moment later, Dad hurried in to hug me, with Tigger at his heels. "He's been meowing since you left," Dad said. "I think he was lonely."

I scooped up Tigger and cradled him in my arms. He started purring like a motorboat and I knew he was happy to see me. And I was happy to be back. I looked around the kitchen as if I'd never seen it before. Sea City had been fun, but it was great to be home.

"Where's Dawn?"

"She's upstairs lying down," Sharon said. "But she asked me to wake her up the minute you got back."

Dawn was asleep in the middle of the day? "What's wrong? Is she ill?" I asked.

"She flew in from California yesterday and she has jet lag. She's been acting like a zombie. If you want to relax for a minute, I'll go and get her."

I decided to make a quick phone call while I waited for Dawn to make her appearance. A moment later, Logan's warm voice came flowing through the phone wires.

"Hi, it's me," I said softly. I was trying to sound cool, but I couldn't keep the excitement out of my voice.

"You're back!" Logan exclaimed. He sounded *really* pleased, and I could feel myself grinning from ear to ear.

"I just got here."

"I missed you."

"Me, too," I assured him.

We made plans to see each other after dinner and said goodbye just as Dawn staggered down the stairs in her bathrobe. She looked as if she'd been awake for forty-eight hours. Her face was pale, her eyes were glazed over, and her long hair was lifeless. "Hi there," she said.

"Hi yourself." I put my arms around her and squeezed her tightly. "Are you sure you're okay?"

Dawn opened her mouth in a jaw-breaking yawn and then collapsed on the sofa. "I'm okay. I just feel as if I want to sleep for a year."

"I'll make you girls some cinnamon-apple tea while you catch up on things," Sharon offered.

"That would be nice, Mum." Dawn yawned again. When we were alone, she tucked a pillow behind her head. "Okay," she said. "You go first. I want to hear *everything* about Sea City."

"Everything?"

"You can start by telling me about Alex. And Toby – is that the boy Stacey was going out with? And I want to hear what happened with Vanessa." Dawn had obviously paid close attention to the postcards I'd sent her.

"This is going to take a while," I said, settling down on the floor. Tigger immediately jumped into my lap. "The problem is there were just so many boys. Things got so complicated."

"That's okay," Dawn said, waving her hand. "Start at the beginning and don't leave anything out. I'm not going anywhere."

I took a deep breath and plunged in. "It all started when we saw Alex and Toby on the beach. Or I should say, when they saw us. . ."

Dawn and I talked until dinnertime, and afterwards she sat on my bed while I unpacked.

"So you think Vanessa is over her broken heart?" she said.

"I'm sure of it. She handled it very well. I'm proud of her." I reached for a pile of T-shirts, and something white caught my eye.

A piece of notebook paper was tucked between my shirts.

It was a poem from Vanessa, and my eyes misted over when I read it.

> Dear Mary Anne,
> Love can hurt, love can sting,
> a broken heart can never sing.
> Boys will come, boys will go
> but a friend is forever, this I know.
> A friend is rare and hard to find
> everyone knows it's true.
>
> You helped me through a very bad time
> I'll always be grateful to you.
> Thank you, Mary Anne.   Love, Vanessa

"Yes," I said softly. "I think Vanessa will be just fine."

The Babysitters Club

STACEY AND THE
MYSTERY OF
STONEYBROOK

The author gratefully acknowledges
Ellen Miles
for her help in
preparing this manuscript.

1st CHAPTER

As the train pulled out, I sat back in my seat, leaned my head against the window, and smiled to myself. On the surface it might seem as if I, eighth-grader Stacey McGill, had a perfect life. Most of the time I live in lovely old Stoneybrook, Connecticut. That's where my train was bound. I go to a great school, have tons of friends, and belong to the best club in the world – but more about that later.

Every now and then, though – pretty much whenever I feel like it – I get to go on a "Fun-Filled Action-Packed All-Expenses-Paid-Weekend in the Glamorous Big Apple, New York City!" as they say on the TV game shows.

That's how it looks on the surface. And I'll admit, I *had* just had a terrific weekend in New York. But as soon as you peer beneath the surface of my life, you'll see that it isn't quite as ideal as it looks. Maybe you've guessed by now that the reason I go back and forth between Stoneybrook and New York is that my parents are divorced. When they broke up, my mum and I moved to Stoneybrook, and my dad stayed in the city. The split happened pretty recently, and believe me, it was not Fun-Filled, although it was quite Action-Packed. Before they split up, my parents fought a lot – not physically or anything, but all that shouting really got to me.

How did my mum and I end up in Stoneybrook? Well, that's a bit complicated, but here goes. I grew up in New York City, and in a way I'll always consider it my home. I love all the excitement. I also love eating out, going to the theatre and . . . shopping! There's no place like New York for great clothes. I still shop there, which means I look pretty sophisticated in Stoneybrook. For example, I had dressed for my train journey in a white jumpsuit, layered over a blue tank top. I had on white ankle socks with blue hearts all over them, a wide blue patent leather belt, and a necklace made of all kinds of plastic sea creatures in a rainbow of colours.

Oops. I think I went off the subject there a little. Where was I? Okay, so I grew up in New York, but then when I was in the seventh grade my dad's company transferred him to their Connecticut office. And then, a year later, just as I'd really begun to feel at home in Stoneybrook, they transferred him *back* to New York. Can you believe it?

It wasn't long after we'd moved back to the city that I noticed how my parents seemed to be arguing all the time. And you can guess the rest of the story. *They* decided to get divorced, *I* decided to move back to Stoneybrook with my mum (instead of moving to the Upper East Side with my dad), and that's why I was on that train, thinking about my weekend in New York.

The first great thing about the weekend was that my dad had taken the whole day off on Saturday just to be with me. I know, you're thinking, What's the big deal? Nobody works on Saturday. Nobody except my dad. I suppose he's what you'd call a workaholic. That was one of the things he and my mum used to argue about: how his job was more important to him than his family, how he was never at home. . . But on *this* Saturday, I think it was important to him to show me a good time, because that's what he did.

We started the day by going out to brunch, to a little cafe I've always loved. All the waiters are really nice, and you can get any kind of omelette you want. The food is excellent, but what I really love are the cappuccinos. (That's coffee with foamy hot milk in it and cinnamon sprinkled on top. Yum.) I'm not usually allowed to drink coffee, but my dad always lets me have a little of his cappuccino.

After brunch we just walked around for a while, window shopping and people watching. You never know who or what you'll see in New York. At one point, as we were crossing Fifth Avenue, I looked to my right just in time to see Gary Rockman (he is the hottest – and most gorgeous – star around right now) jump into a taxi. I nearly died!

My dad knows that one of my favourite shops is Fiorucci, so when we got near it he suggested that we go in. He told me to choose anything I wanted. For a second, I considered taking him at his word and asking him to buy me this outrageous purple suede jacket. Was it beautiful! Cropped short at the waist and covered with fringe all up the arms and across the back. But I did the mature thing (silly me!) and chose a pair of sunglasses – heart-shaped ones, in a black-and-white checked pattern. Claudia (my best friend in Stoneybrook) will love them, I know.

We walked and shopped some more, and by 5:00 we were starving, so we decided to go out for dinner. Dad let me choose the restaurant, so I chose Hunan Supreme, a Chinese place in our old neighbourhood. We know the owner there, Mr Lee, and the food is great.

Our meal was delicious, but I have to say that dinner wasn't my favourite part of the weekend. Here's why: When our food came, I started to dig in, but Dad just sat there looking worried.

"Are you sure those noodles are okay for you to eat, darling?" he asked.

That might seem like a silly question, but he actually had a good reason to ask it. I'm a diabetic. I have to be really careful about what I eat, when I eat it, and how many calories it has. If I'm not careful, my blood sugar gets all out of control, and I can get seriously ill. I also have to take insulin every day. I give myself the injections, which sounds horrible, but really isn't a big deal once you get used to it. When I first got diabetes, my parents were constantly fussing over me. They drove me mad. But by now they understand that *I* know how to take care of myself.

Unfortunately, though, I'd recently been told by my regular doctor that I'd have to be even *more* careful with my diet and with taking just the right amount of insulin. I suppose my body is going through some changes just now that make it hard for everything to stay in balance.

So there I was, about to tuck into some more of my noodles. I *do* know that they're okay for me to eat, of course; otherwise I'd never have ordered them. Who wants to be ill? Then my dad started up again.

"I think you should arrange an appointment with Dr Werner for the next time you visit me."

Dr Werner is my diabetes specialist. I don't have to see her regularly – just when there's a special problem.

I hate it when my parents start worrying about my diabetes. I don't feel ill all the time, and I can't stand being treated like an invalid. To tell you the truth, it scares me a little when they make a big issue out of my diabetes. It reminds me that I do have a serious illness.

"Dad, it's under control. Come on! Don't you think I know how to take care of myself? I'm a big girl now, remember? I'm not your little boontsie any more." ("Boontsie" is what my dad calls kids who are at that really cute big-tummy, bow-legged stage, around two or three.)

He softened. I could tell I'd put off having to see Dr Werner, for a while, anyway.

"No, you're not my little boontsie any more, are you, Anastasia?"

He's the only one who gets away with calling me that. I know, it *is* my real name but really. Anastasia?

So that was my big weekend in New York. On Sunday I woke up late in my dad's flat. I could hear him clicking away at his computer keyboard in the room next to mine I should have known he couldn't bear to take the *whole* weekend off. I started to get a little annoyed with him – after all, it was Sunday – but just then the doorbell rang.

I threw on my bathrobe and ran for the door. It was my best-friend-in-New-York, Laine Cummings, carrying a huge, bulging bag from Zabar's. Zabar's is only the most incredible deli in the world. Everybody goes there on Sunday mornings to get bagels, fresh cream cheese, and all kinds of other goodies.

Laine and I arranged the food on the table, and proceeded to eat and gossip until it was time for me to catch my train.

I'd just started thinking again about that purple jacket, when the conductor came strolling through the carriage.

"Stoneybrook, all those for Stoneybrook, get off here!" he said.

I jumped off the last step of the train straight into my mother's arms. She gave me a huge hug.

"I've missed you so much, darling! How was your weekend?"

As we walked to the car, got in, and started home, I told her all about my visit to New York. As she listened to the details of that wonderful Saturday I could see her mouth tighten a little.

"Do you mean to tell me that he *really* took the entire weekend off?" she asked.

I hadn't told her about the computer sounds that morning, but I didn't want to go into it now, even though I could see that I hadn't made her feel brilliant by telling her all about the terrific time I'd had.

"Mum, I missed you, too. Let's go into the city together sometime soon. Remember how much fun we used to have in the cosmetics department at Bloomingdale's?"

She laughed. I bet she was thinking of the day we tried on at least fourteen different types of perfume each.

As soon as we pulled into the drive, I ran up to my room to unpack. It was good to be back – after all, Stoneybrook is really home for me now. After dinner, I phoned Claud to tell her about my weekend.

"Oh, Stace, I can't believe you didn't at least *try* for the jacket!" she cried. (Claudia loves clothes as much as I do. Maybe more.)

"But wait till you see my sunglasses. They're amazing, I'm telling you."

We talked for a bit longer until my mum called up the stairs to let me know that it was time to get off the phone.

"'Bye Stace! See you at school tomorrow," said Claudia.

"And at the meeting, too," I said.

Claudia and I, along with our other Stoneybrook-best-friends (all five of them!) belong to the Babysitters Club. The club is really a business – a babysitting business, of course – but I'll tell you more about it later.

As soon as I'd hung up the phone, I got ready for bed. I was exhausted! Those "Fun-Filled Action-Packed Weekends" certainly take a lot out of you.

2nd CHAPTER

I'd been planning to walk over to Claudia's for the Babysitters Club meeting the next day, but for some reason I'd been running late from the moment I'd got up that morning. I suppose I'm not used to going back and forth between my two "worlds" – New York and Stoneybrook. It takes me a while to readjust every time I come back from a weekend away.

I started out the day by oversleeping. I gobbled my breakfast, threw on any old outfit I could find (the same white jumpsuit with a *pink* shirt and – oops! – red socks), and practically ran all the way to school. It seemed as though I was rushing around all day, and now here it was, almost 5:30, club meeting time, and I was still at home.

I grabbed my bike and hopped on. I knew I could still make it on time if I pedalled fast enough. As I cycled, I thought about everyone I would see over at Claud's. I'd been really lucky to find so many great friends when I moved to Stoneybrook. If it hadn't been for the Babysitters Club, my life would be quite different.

The BSC was all Kristy's idea. That's Kristy Thomas, chairman of the club. She's always coming up with excellent ideas, but this one has to be the best.

It all started at the beginning of the seventh grade. At the time, Kristy lived with her mum; her two older brothers, Sam and Charlie; and her little brother, David Michael. Her mum was divorced: Kristy's dad walked out on the family years ago. Kristy never even sees him. Isn't that awful? I thought my parents' divorce was awful, but at least I get to *see* my dad fairly often.

Anyway, Kristy and her brothers used to babysit for David Michael most of the time, but when they couldn't, Mrs Thomas would have to make loads of phone calls to try to arrange a sitter. One night as her mum was doing this, Kristy had one of her Brilliant Brainstorms. What if parents could reach a whole group of experienced sitters with just one phone call?

And so the Babysitters Club was born. Kristy got together with Claudia, as well as Mary Anne, who lived across the street and was Kristy's best friend. They immediately decided that they needed more than three people in the club, so Claud suggested me. We had met at school and were already becoming friends. Claudia was elected vice-chairman, mainly because we hold our meetings in her room. Also she has her own phone with a private line – very important for the club. Mary Anne became secretary because she's neat and organized, and I took on the job of treasurer, because I'm good at maths. We'd meet three times a week, on Mondays, Wednesdays, and Fridays. During our meetings parents would call us to arrange sitters.

The club has worked perfectly since Day One, but believe me, it's been through some big changes, and so have all its members. I'm not the only one who feels as if my whole life has been turned inside out and upside down in the last year or so. Also, the BSC has expanded a lot since it started. Besides the original members, there're now also Dawn, Jessi, and Mallory. Not to mention Logan and Shannon . . . but I'm getting ahead of myself here.

Let me go back to Kristy. Besides being brilliant, Kristy can also be bossy at times, and occasionally (I hate to say it) a little babyish. Kristy's small for her age and a bit of a tomboy. She wears the same thing every day: jeans, a sweater, and trainers. But Kristy's okay. She's had a hectic year or so, and I'd have to say she's dealing with it really well.

While Kristy was starting the club, her mum was falling in love with a real life millionaire called Watson Brewer. They got married, and Kristy moved across town to live in his – get this – mansion. She wasn't wild about Watson *or* the move at first, but she did like Watson's kids, her new stepbrother and stepsister, Andrew and Karen. And just as the two families were starting to become one, Kristy's mum and Mr Brewer decided to adopt Emily Michelle, a two-year-old Vietnamese girl. (She's *adorable*.) And then Kristy's grandmother, Nannie, moved in to help look after Emily! So it's a pretty full house just now, especially when you throw in Shannon, the Bernese mountain dog puppy, and Boo-Boo, the fat, grumpy, geriatric cat. But they all seem to be getting along well, and Kristy likes her new house, new family, and new neighbourhood better all the time.

As I mentioned before, Claudia Kishi (my best friend, remember?) is the vice-chairman of the club. Claudia is, well . . . *gorgeous*. She's Japanese-American and has L-O-N-G silky black hair, a perfect complexion (despite her incurable junk-food habit), and almond-shaped eyes. And if there's anyone in town who's a wilder, more sophisticated dresser than me, it's got to be Claud. She's a really talented artist, and she's always putting together the most outrageous outfits, then accessorizing them with even more outrageous jewellery, which, of course, she's made herself.

Claud's likes and dislikes? Likes: reading Nancy Drew mysteries. Dislikes: studying. Has a love/hate relationship with her genius older sister, Janine. Misses: her grandmother Mimi, whom she was really close to. Mimi died not long ago and actually we *all* miss her.

Mary Anne Spier, the club secretary, has brown hair and brown eyes, just like Kristy. But while Kristy is loudmouthed and always in the spotlight, Mary Anne is extremely shy and sensitive. (And I mean *sensitive*. She cries at the drop of a hat – probably because she feels sorry for the poor hat!) Mary Anne grew up with only her father. Her mum died when she was really little. For years, Mr Spier was incredibly strict with Mary Anne, but he's finally begun to relax. He even let her get a kitten!

If there's anybody, besides her father, that Mary Anne loves more than Tigger (that's her kitten), it's her boyfriend, Logan Bruno. I always think it's quite weird that Mary Anne, who is the shyest girl in the Babysitters Club, is the only one of us who has a steady boyfriend. I suppose Logan must like Mary Anne for the same reasons all of us do: she's understanding, a good listener, and a lot of fun.

Mary Anne is another one who's had a big change in her life recently, but before I go into that, let me tell you about Dawn Schafer, since she's got something to do with that change.

Dawn is the alternate officer of the club, which means that she can fill in for any of the other officers if they can't make it to a meeting. (She was treasurer the whole time I was living in New York.) Dawn moved here from California when her parents got a divorce. Her mum had grown up here, so it was natural that she'd want to come back. Their first year in Stoneybrook was quite rough. Dawn's little brother, Jeff, didn't adjust well to the move. He never stopped missing his dad and feeling homesick for California. So finally, he moved back there to live with his dad. I know Dawn misses him a lot. But she's really close to her mum and she loves the house they live in – it was built in 1795 and it has a secret passage and maybe even a real ghost. Honest.

Even though she's lived here for almost two years now, Dawn still looks like a California girl. She dresses like a real individual, and she's got long, long pale blonde hair and beautiful blue eyes. She's into health food in a big way, and it doesn't seem to bother her at all when we all make gagging noises at her tofu salads. Dawn just is who she is: she's got a lot of self-confidence and she doesn't seem to care too much about what other people think.

Now, remember when I said that Dawn

had something to do with the big change in Mary Anne's life? Well, get this: Dawn's mother recently got married. Who did she marry? Mary Anne's father! Can you believe it? They used to go out together at high school when they were growing up, right here in Stoneybrook. Then, when Mrs Schafer moved back here, the romance began all over again.

So Dawn and Mary Anne are now stepsisters! And I can't say that the transition from friends to relatives was an easy one for them. When Mary Anne, her father, and Tigger first moved into Dawn's house, things were more than a little rocky for a while. But it seems as if they're all getting on much better now.

Okay, there are still two more members of the club, our junior officers, Mallory Pike and Jessi Ramsey. They were both asked to join while I was away in New York last year and the other members couldn't quite keep up with all the jobs they were offered. Of course, they're still members even though I'm back now. They're called junior officers because they're two years younger than the rest of us – they're in the sixth grade – and aren't allowed to sit at night, except for their own brothers and sisters. But there are plenty of day jobs to keep them busy. Mallory and Jessi are both great sitters, and we were lucky to get them for the club.

Mallory's a good sitter partly because

she comes from a big family. She has seven younger sisters and brothers! The Pikes have always been big clients of ours – Mal is actually someone we used to sit for. But she was a big help even then, and now she's grown up a lot. She knows just about everything about kids – she's seen it all!

Mal loves to read and write – in fact, she's thinking of becoming a children's book author one day. Her favourite books to read are horse stories. I think she's read *Misty of Chincoteague* something like seventy-six times!

Mal's main problem is being eleven. That's right, being eleven. She feels more grown-up than her parents are ready to let her be. (That's a funny way to put it, but you know what I mean.) She wants to get contact lenses, instead of wearing glasses, and she hates her brace with a passion. At least her parents have finally let her get her hair cut and her ears pierced. As for the rest, I suppose she'll just have to be patient. That's easy to say, but I know how hard that can be.

Mallory's best friend is, guess who? Jessi Ramsey. They became best friends almost straight away, when Jessi's family moved here last year. I suppose Mal really needed somebody just then, and I *know* Jessi did. Her family had a hard time when they first moved to Stoneybrook. Why? Because they're black, and there are hardly any other black families in town. I know, it shouldn't make a difference *what* colour someone is, but it did to a lot of people. It was so unfair! I think things are better for the Ramseys now. Jessi's little sister, Becca (short for Rebecca), has a best friend, and her baby brother, Squirt (his real name is John Philip Ramsey, Jr., but Squirt fits him much better), would be happy anywhere. Also, the neighbours have seen that the Ramseys are simply a very nice family. By the way, guess where Jessi lives? In my old house!

Jessi loves horse stories, too, but her real passion is ballet. Jessi's a really talented dancer, and she puts a lot of work into practising. She takes lessons twice a week in Stamford, and believe me, they're *serious* lessons.

So, that's everyone. Oops! I almost forgot to mention our two associate members, Logan Bruno (Mary Anne's boyfriend) and Shannon Kilbourne, a friend of Kristy's from her new neighbourhood. They don't come to meetings, but they're available to fill in for us when we have too many jobs to handle ourselves.

Whew! I think that's really everyone. What a crew! As I wheeled my bike up Claud's drive, I glanced at my watch. Only minutes to spare. I would make it on time after all.

3rd CHAPTER

I pounded up the stairs, out of breath. Had I made it? Just as I got to the door of Claud's room, I heard Kristy's voice.

"And then, on top of everything, Shannon got into the dustbins. I walked into the kitchen and I saw coffee grounds and chicken bones all over the floor!"

"Ugh! You're kidding! Oh no!" exclaimed a couple of voices. I had a feeling that Kristy was talking about Shannon the puppy, not Shannon the Associate Member of the Babysitters Club.

Club meetings always start at five-thirty on the dot, as soon as Claud's digital clock flips over from five twenty-nine. The clock read five twenty-eight, so I had arrived in plenty of time. I settled onto Claud's bed next to Mary Anne, who was talking to Dawn. (Dawn was sitting backwards in Claud's desk chair.) They were in the middle of an intense discussion regarding the exact colour of Cam Geary's eyes, Cam Geary being Mary Anne's favourite star.

Most of Claudia was inside her wardrobe. She was poking her hand into every compartment of her shoe bag. I had an idea of what she might be looking for, and sure enough, when she finally backed out of the wardrobe, she was gripping a bag of M&M's in one hand and a packet of Mintolas in the other. Plus she had a Twix bar clenched between her teeth. Claudia's parents, as you might guess, don't exactly approve of her junk-food habit, so she has to hide the stuff all over her room.

I was bursting with all the things I'd done at the weekend. I couldn't wait to tell everyone about how I'd spotted Gary Rockman, but Mallory grabbed their attention first.

"Did you lot see that old house at the end of Elm Street? They're tearing it down!"

That was my street. She must mean the other end, though, *away* from Claudia's house. There weren't all that many really old houses down at this end. But what was the big deal about a house being torn down? I started to say something about Gary Rockman, but Claud interrupted me.

"You're kidding! They're demolishing that old place? I thought it was some kind of historical landmark. I thought they *couldn't* tear it down."

"I heard that some company wants to build flats there and got around that rule somehow," chimed in Mary Anne. "That house is the only one still standing in that whole area, and they're not about to let it get in their way."

I couldn't believe how fascinated everyone was with the "news" about some dumb old house. I suppose that's what happens when you live in Stoneybrook all your life. *Anything* seems exciting.

"Order," said Kristy just then, making all of us jump. I looked at the clock. Sure enough. Five-thirty had just clicked into place. Kristy sat, as usual, in the director's chair. She wore her visor (I suppose it makes her feel like the boss), and she had a pencil stuck behind her ear.

Kristy does a great job as chairman of the club, I must say. Dawn's always wishing that Kristy would miss a meeting one day – then, as alternate officer, Dawn would get to be chairman-for-a-day. But it's never happened yet. It's hard to imagine Kristy missing a meeting, and it's even harder to imagine anyone else as chairman.

"Has everyone read the club notebook?" Kristy asked. We all groaned.

"I thought you promised not to ask us that any more," said Claud. "I thought you were going to have some *trust* in your best friends!"

The club notebook is a bit like a diary of

the jobs we've been on. We're all supposed to write in it after every job and read it once a week or so. It's not really a bad idea – often it's pretty interesting to read and lots of times there's information in it that's helpful to us. But there's something about that notebook. . . Sometimes it's almost like homework – and Kristy's the teacher.

Anyway, we all said we'd read it. It's a habit by now.

"M&M's?" offered Claud, passing them round. Everyone except for Dawn and me shook out a few. I'm really glad Dawn's a health-food freak because then I'm not the only one always turning down Claud's treats.

"Oh, sorry, Stace – sorry, Dawn. Here, let me find. . ." Claud rummaged around in a box under her bed marked CHARCAOLS. (I told you she hates studying. She's an awful speller.) She came up with a bag of wholewheat crackers and tossed it to me. I caught it but handed it straight over to Dawn without even opening it. Dawn gave me a curious look, which I pretended not to notice. I didn't really want to draw attention to the fact that my diabetes seemed harder than ever to control.

"Ahem," said Kristy. "Are we all ready? May we proceed with the business at hand?"

Where'd she learn to talk like *that*? We all looked at each other and started to giggle.

Kristy looked a little put out at first, but then she cracked up, too.

Just then, the phone rang. The first call! Kristy grabbed the phone. "Babysitters Club. Can I help you?" She listened for a moment.

"No problem, Mrs Newton. We'll get straight back to you." Kristy hung up and turned to Mary Anne. "How does the schedule look for tomorrow afternoon?" she asked. "Mrs Newton needs someone to watch Jamie while she takes Lucy to the paediatrician for a check-up."

I'd have liked the job – Jamie's a great kid, and we all like to sit for him – but Mary Anne looked in the record book and reminded me that I already had a job, sitting at the Pikes' with Mallory. (The Pikes are always a two-sitter job.)

"And Jessi has ballet, and Dawn's staying late at school tomorrow, and Claud, you have an art class. That leaves you and me, Kristy," Mary Anne continued. She's incredible, the way she keeps the record book up-to-date with all of our activities. Not only that, she's also on top of all the other stuff in the record book, like our rates and customers' addresses and phone numbers. She even has a list of the names of all their pets.

"You take it, Mary Anne. I promised I'd help David Michael give Shannon a bath." Kristy went ahead and phoned Mrs Newton to let her know Mary Anne would be there. That's generally the way our club works. We rarely squabble over jobs, because there's always enough to go around.

"Don't forget your Kid-Kit, Mary Anne. I hear it's supposed to rain, and you know how Jamie can be when he's stuck inside," Dawn said.

Kid-Kits are another of Kristy's great ideas. They've been lifesavers more times than I can count, especially on rainy days or when kids miss their parents and need to be distracted. Kid-Kits are boxes filled with toys, books, and games. (We've each made our own, decorating them with scraps of cloth, sequins, or whatever else we could find in Claudia's MISSELANIUS carton of supplies. The Kid-Kits don't have all new stuff, but it's new to the kids we sit for, and it really keeps them occupied.)

"Speaking of Kid-Kits, how's the treasury? Can we afford some new stickers?" Kristy looked over at me.

I checked the manila envelope to see how much subs money we had. We each get to keep all the money we earn on every job, but we pay subs weekly to buy stuff for the Kid-Kits. We also use money from the treasury to pay Kristy's big brother Charlie to drive her to meetings – it's too far to walk since she moved to Watson's – and for the occasional pizza party, and to help Claud pay her phone bill. It only took me a second to count the money (that's why I'm treasurer).

"There's plenty for stickers," I said when I'd finished. "Anyone else need supplies?"

Everybody started to talk at once, but the phone began to ring. There were four or five calls in a row, but we dealt with each one quickly. Then, just as Kristy was getting ready to adjourn the meeting, the phone rang one more time.

Kristy answered it. She talked for ages. I could tell she was talking to Dr Johanssen, who's the mother of my favourite babysitting charge, Charlotte. But I couldn't work out what Dr Johanssen wanted. It sounded complicated.

When she hung up, Kristy pushed back her visor. "Okay, everyone, here's the story. Mr Johanssen's father has to have an operation, and the Johanssens want to be there with him. Dr Johanssen said her father-in-law isn't in any real danger – but he's pretty old, so the operation could be tough on him. So they'll be away for about a week, but they don't want to make Charlotte miss school."

I couldn't see how they could avoid that. It's not as if Charlotte's other grandparents live here in Stoneybrook. In fact, the Johanssens have no family here at all.

"So she was wondering if Charlotte could stay with either Jessi's family or with you, Stace," Kristy finished. "She said she's willing to pay well for all the time they'd be away."

This was really something new! No BSC member had ever had this kind of job before.

Straight away, Jessi said she couldn't do it. "Too bad. Becca would be so thrilled to have her best friend staying for a whole week! But we're going to New Jersey this weekend to see my cousins."

"Let me have the phone, Kristy," I said. "I bet my mum will say it's okay for Charlotte to stay with us." Mum's looking for a job at the moment (she hasn't worked full-time for years, but now that we're on our own she wants a job), and I knew she'd be glad to watch Charlotte whenever I couldn't. Sure enough, she said it was fine, as long as she could have a talk with the Johanssens first.

I called Dr Johanssen back and told her the good news. She said she'd call my mum straight away. I was so excited. I couldn't believe it! I've always wanted a little brother or sister and having Charlotte around for a whole week would be so much fun. I started to think about all the things we'd do. Where would she sleep? I thought of the guest bedroom, and how nicely I could arrange it for her. I'd use the special sheets Mum had found at a garage sale, and—

"Meeting adjourned," Kristy said. It was six o'clock. I left Claud's house without really even saying goodbye to everyone and cycled home. My head was full of plans.

4th CHAPTER

By Thursday, I'd got the guest room all ready. I'd made the bed with some great Raggedy Ann sheets my mum had found. I knew Charlotte would love them. My old teddy bear, Goobaw, leaned against the pillow. He was missing one eye and most of his fur was rubbed bare, but he'd always been a comfort to me. I had filled a shelf with some other old dolls and toys that I thought an eight-year-old might like. There were a couple of books on the bedside table: *Charlotte's Web* and *The Long Winter*, two of Charlotte's favourites. I'd even picked some flowers and put them in a little vase on the windowsill.

I stood in the doorway, surveying the room. It looked great. I was sure Charlotte would feel really at home. I walked over to smooth the sheets one more time, but just then I heard a car honking in the drive. I ran to the window and looked out. It was the Johanssens! I ran downstairs and out of the door. My mum came out behind me.

Charlotte was struggling to get out of the backseat, which was piled high with suitcases and shopping bags. A suit of Mr Johanssen's was hanging on one side of the car, and several of Dr Johanssen's blouses were on the other. Finally Charlotte stood in the drive. She was clutching a loaded shopping bag and a pillow. Her father pulled a small suitcase out of the space between the front and back seats.

"Is that everything, darling?" he asked.

Charlotte was looking down at the ground. She nodded without saying anything. Suddenly I realized that she was about to cry. I think my mum noticed, too.

"Charlotte, we're so happy to have you to stay," she said. "Stacey tells me that spaghetti and meatballs is your favourite supper, and guess what? That's what we're having tonight."

Charlotte managed a tiny smile. I put my arm around her. "What did you bring, Char? Is this shopping bag full of your special things?" I asked.

She drew away from me and ran to her father's side. She grabbed him round the waist, and the tears began. "Daddy, please don't go! I'm going to be so lonely," she cried.

I was surprised, and even though I knew

I shouldn't take it personally, I was a little hurt. This was the *old* Charlotte, the shy, clingy girl she'd been when we first met. But she'd come so far since then. The Charlotte I knew now was confident, talkative, and friendly. She was independent, too – after all, she'd been separated from her parents for two whole weeks when we'd all gone off to Camp Mohawk.

Also, I don't mean to sound conceited, but Charlotte really loves me. I've always been her favourite sitter, but it's even more than that. I think she thinks of me as kind of a big sister. She was heartbroken when I moved away from Stoneybrook and thrilled when I came back.

I suppose Dr Johanssen noticed that I was looking a little crestfallen. She took me aside and told me not to feel too bad.

"Charlotte's having an especially hard time with this separation, Stacey. She's really worried about her grandfather – she loves him so much. And even though we've told her that he's going to be fine, she's still afraid. I think she'll be okay once she settles in with you. We're *so* grateful that she can stay here where we'll know she's safe," she said.

Then she walked over to give Charlotte a hug. Charlotte *really* started crying then, but after both her parents had held her and said their goodbyes, they had to leave. I held her hand as they pulled out of the drive, and we waved until the car was out of sight. As we walked into the house and up the stairs, carrying all the stuff she'd brought, her sobs died down into sniffles interspersed with hiccuppy sighs.

When I opened the door of the guest room, Charlotte really stopped crying for the first time since she'd got out of the car.

"Oh, Stacey, this is brilliant!" she said. She walked round the room, and I could tell that she was noticing all the little things I'd done to make her feel at home. Charlotte's a pretty thoughtful kid herself, so I knew she'd appreciate my efforts.

She sat on the bed and picked up Goobaw. "My grandpa's very ill," she told him. "He might die."

"Oh, Charlotte, he's not going to die," I said. "He's going to be fine. And having your parents there with him will help him get better even faster."

I sat next to her on the bed, and this time when I put my arms around her she hugged me back. "I'm scared, Stacey," she said.

"Of course you are. But everything will be all right, and we'll have lots of fun while you're here. Tell you what: How about a game of Cluedo before dinner?" I asked. "You can be Miss Scarlet."

We played and talked until Mum told us that dinner was ready. By then I thought Charlotte had begun to feel at home. She still sniffed once in a while, and she kept asking questions about her grandpa's operation ("Does it hurt him when they cut him open?" "But if he's asleep, what if he has a bad dream?"), but she seemed much calmer. (Obviously, Dr Johanssen hadn't had time to explain the details of the operation to her.)

The spaghetti sauce smelled absolutely delicious. Mum was giving it one last stir as we walked into the kitchen.

"Charlotte, you can sit here, opposite Stacey," she said. She filled our plates and brought them to the table. It's usually my job to set the table, but I suppose I'd been let off on account of Charlotte being there. Then Mum brought her own plate over along with a huge salad.

We all dug in. All but Charlotte, that is. She just sat there, looking down at her plate as if she didn't recognize what was on it. I knew something had to be wrong, since she usually loves spaghetti.

"What's the matter, Charlotte?" I asked "Do you want me to cut up your meatballs?" Maybe she just needed a little babying.

I suppose I'm just not hungry," she said in a small voice. "It looks delicious, Mrs McGill, but. . ." She looked as if she was going to cry again.

"That's all right, Charlotte," my mum said. If you get hungry later there'll be plenty left over." Mum must have been thinking the same thing I was: Charlotte was just feeling too nervous and upset to eat much. There was no point in forcing her.

I finished my meal quickly while Charlotte waited. I'd told her she could go into the living room and watch TV, but she didn't seem to want to leave my side. She helped me clear the table, and she stuck right next to me as I stacked the dishes into the dishwasher.

"Are my parents still on the plane?" she asked. I started to work out the answer. Let's see, I thought. They left for the airport at around 4:30, their flight left at 5:30 and lasted . . . how many hours? But before I could finish my calculations, Charlotte came up with more questions.

"When they land at the airport, what will they do with all those suitcases? Will somebody meet them? Are they going straight to the hospital to see Grandpa?"

I could see that Charlotte needed some distraction. I turned on the TV. Luckily, *The Cosby Show*, one of Charlotte's favourites, was on. That kept her occupied for half an hour, but as soon as it was over, the questions started up again.

"They must be at the hospital now. Do you think Grandpa is happy to see them? Grandpa must be scared about his operation. How do they close him up again when it's all over?"

Honestly! After I'd explained how stitches work and why a zip wouldn't be practical, I suggested another game of Cluedo. But halfway through the game I could see that Charlotte was getting restless. How could I distract her before she came up with another round of questions?

"Have you ever played Snap, Charlotte?" I asked as I dug into my desk drawer for a pack of cards. She had never played that game, so I taught her how. "Look, you split the pack in half, and then we each turn over a card at the same time. And when we both turn over the same card, we say 'snap', like this: one, two, three, SNAP! The first one to say it gets all those cards. And whoever gets all the cards in the deck first, wins."

Charlotte loved playing Snap. Personally, I've always thought it was about the most boring card game on the face of the earth, but that night I played twelve games in a row, very happily. Anything to keep Charlotte's mind off her travelling parents, her sick grandpa, and her own homesickness.

After the twelfth game (which Charlotte won), I suggested that it was time for bed. I had some homework to do once she was asleep, and it was getting late. *Slowly*, she changed into her pyjamas. *Slowly*, she brushed her teeth. I could see that she was stalling. She was probably nervous about sleeping in a strange bed.

I tucked her in and gave her Goobaw to hold. And then, even though Charlotte is a great reader, I read to her from *Charlotte's*

Web. She loves that book, and I love to read to her. "I'm proud to have the same name as that spider," she always says.

After three chapters, just as my throat was beginning to hurt from so much reading aloud, I could see that Charlotte's eyelids were drooping. A few moments later, I stopped reading, and sure enough, she'd fallen asleep.

I tiptoed out of the room, leaving the door open a crack so I'd hear her if she woke up. For a moment I thought about skipping my maths homework. I was exhausted! I never would have guessed that having Charlotte to visit would take so much energy. It would probably get easier as the week went on, I thought. I hoped. I sat down at my desk and blitzed through the maths problems as fast as I could.

By the time I finally got into bed I was too tired even to finish a chapter of the book I was reading, *Summer of My German Soldier*. I turned off my light and fell asleep straight away. When I woke up the next morning, sunlight was streaming through the window. Birds were singing outside. Mum was pottering around downstairs in the kitchen. And Charlotte was sleeping, all cuddled up next to me in my bed, still clutching Goobaw.

5th CHAPTER

Charlotte and I got home from school at around the same time on Friday. Mum rushed out for a job interview just as I walked in the door. "Hi, girls! See you at dinnertime," she said as she ran out of the door. She looked pretty professional, all dressed up in a suit.

I made a snack for us (biscuits with mustard spread on them and a piece of cheddar cheese on top – yum!), but Charlotte only picked at the food.

"I don't feel very well, Stacey. My throat's all itchy and I feel dizzy," she said.

I felt her forehead, but she didn't seem hot. I thought she was probably just still having a hard time adjusting. After all, she'd made it through a full day of school – how ill could she be? Anyway, she'd survived the first twenty-four hours without her parents, and I knew it could only get easier as time went on. But I still thought she could do with some distraction, and I wasn't about to play any more games of Snap for a while.

"Let's walk down the street and have a look at that old house they're tearing down," I said. Charlotte agreed to the plan, but first we cleared up from our snack and changed out of our school clothes. (This all took some time, since Charlotte was still sticking to me like glue.) Finally we set off down the street. I wasn't all that interested in the old house, but it was something different to do.

It was only about four o'clock when we got to the house, but the workmen had already left for the day. The big old place stood there silently, looking a little forlorn with its porch railings ripped off and its front door gone. There were straggly bushes on both sides of the house and overgrown gardens in front of it. Vines climbed up the porch and twined themselves around the second-story windows. The grass in the garden was almost up to Charlotte's knees. The place seemed oddly quiet all of a sudden.

"Without that front door, the house looks like a person with a tooth missing," said Charlotte. "Let's go inside and look round!"

"No way," I said. "They've started tearing out all the fixtures inside. There could be holes in the floor, or the ceiling might start to come down. We could really get hurt."

My mum had told me that the Stoneybrook Historical Society had asked the developer to save certain parts of the house, since he was being allowed to tear it down. There was supposedly a huge marble fireplace that was in perfect condition, and the society wanted to preserve it. I wondered if they'd taken that out yet. Also, there were supposed to be some old lighting fixtures, from way back when Stoneybrook first got electricity. It was going to take a while to get all that stuff out of the house. Once they'd removed it all, they could just knock down whatever was left.

Charlotte and I walked round the outside of the house, fighting our way through the weeds and brambles. I had to admit that it was a pretty interesting old place, even if I didn't think it rated right up there with Gary Rockman as hot news. It was built on a huge scale. There was a long porch that wrapped around the front of it, and a smaller one at the back door. One of the upstairs rooms had big windowed doors that opened out onto a little balcony.

It also had several little towers sticking up here and there. Imagine having your bedroom in one of those round turrets – you could pretend you were Rapunzel or something. Charlotte liked that idea. "Or what if there was a secret trapdoor, so you could be up there and nobody would ever know," she said. One of the things I love about her is her imagination. She's so creative.

As I was looking round the towers, trying to decide which one I would choose for my room, I saw something that made the hair stand up on the back of my neck. There was a face in the window of one of the towers, and it was looking straight at me! I gasped and turned to Charlotte to see if she'd seen it, but she was examining the gingerbread trim on the porch roof. I looked back quickly, but the face had disappeared from the window. Maybe it hadn't really been there in the first place. I was probably just imagining things.

I walked on ahead to catch up with Charlotte. When I found her, her face was dead white. "Did you hear that noise, Stacey?" she asked.

"What noise? I can't hear—" Just then, I *did* hear it. Something was clanking rhythmically. It sounded like chains being dragged across the floors.

"Oh, that's just, um . . . loose pipes! Yeah, that's it. I'm sure it's just the plumbing, Charlotte."

I wasn't really all that sure, but I hoped there was no way that Charlotte would be able to tell. Anyway, I knew the workmen were also removing some of the plumbing and fixtures for preservation. Mum had said that there were antique radiators and also some of those big old bathtubs that sit on clawed feet. Maybe the men had been working on pulling that stuff out today, and some of the pipes had been left to bang against each other. That really could explain the noises we'd heard. Couldn't it?

We kept walking round the house. It was a bit sad to see it looking so shabby. Most of the windows were broken, and the shutters hung crookedly. The paint was peeling. And what was that near the back door?

I couldn't believe my eyes. It was a gigantic, and I mean *huge*, swarm of gross flies, just like in *The Amityville Horror*. That film has to be the scariest thing I've ever seen. It's about this family that moves into a house that has ghosts or spirits in it, and all these horrible things keep happening. The flies were the least of it, believe me! Scenes from the film flashed through my mind as Charlotte and I looked at the flies, but I gritted my teeth, took Charlotte's hand, and kept walking around the house. We'd gone almost all the way round it by now anyway. I wasn't going to let some silly old spooky house get the better of me.

"Oooooohhhhhhh. . ."

What was *that*? I looked at Charlotte. Had she moaned? She looked back at me. We kept walking.

"Ooooooooooohhhhhhhh. . ." I heard it again, and this time I knew it hadn't come from Charlotte. It had come from the house. I tightened my grip on her hand,

and we took off. That spooky old house had got the better of me. We were history.

We made it back to my house in record time. Charlotte was looking a bit shaky. I was feeling a little shaky myself. But once we were away from the house I felt better. It was as if there was a bad feeling coming from that place. I didn't plan to go back there in the near future.

"What do you think made that noise, Stacey? That was scary," said Charlotte.

I couldn't really come up with an answer, and I just wanted to forget all about the house for now, so I dodged the question. "I don't know, Charlotte. But guess what? I have a Babysitters Club meeting at five-thirty, and you get to come with me!"

I'd checked with the other members to see if it would be okay to bring Charlotte. With my mum at a job interview, I didn't know what else to do with her. But even Kristy had said it would be fine to bring her.

Charlotte got all excited. She knew it was an honour to be invited to a club meeting. Not too many "outsiders" had attended meetings. She decided she wanted to change back into her school clothes. This was an important occasion for her.

"Does this mean I'm an honorary member, Stacey?" she asked. "I've always wanted to be in a club, and the Babysitters Club is the greatest. Should I bring my pocket money so that I can pay subs?"

I explained that paying subs really wouldn't be necessary, and she looked a little disappointed. To cheer her up, I asked her to help me organize my Kid-Kit. By the time we'd finished that job, it was 5:15. Time to set off for Claudia's. Charlotte begged to be allowed to carry the Kid-Kit, and even though we don't usually bring them to meetings, I said she could.

When we walked into Claud's room, I could feel Charlotte getting shy again. Everybody else was already there, and I suppose she felt a bit overwhelmed at seeing all the babysitters in one place. But then Dawn patted the bed and invited Charlotte to sit next to her.

"Crisp, Charlotte?" Claudia offered the bag to her. Charlotte just stared at Claud's earrings. They were pretty wild. One was shaped like a little record, and the other looked like a stereo. I nudged Charlotte.

"Oh! Yes . . . I mean, thanks, Claudia. I love these."

"I like your blouse, Charlotte," said Mary Anne. That was nice of her. Charlotte's blouse wasn't that special. But Mary Anne is sensitive, and she knew her comment would help put Charlotte at ease.

Kristy took off her visor, leaned over from her spot in the director's chair, and stuck it on Charlotte's head. Charlotte grinned.

"Wait till we tell you all what happened this afternoon," I said. "Remember that old house they're tearing down? Well, we went over to have a look at it, and—"

"We heard the scariest noises!" finished Charlotte.

"And you wouldn't believe what I saw," I said.

"Stacey, Charlotte – we want to hear all about it, but it's time to start the meeting," said Kristy. She brought the meeting to order, and we dealt with business for a while. The phone rang a few times and we assigned jobs. Then there was a lull in the action.

"Claud, remember that film we saw, *The Amityville Horror*? Well, this afternoon was just like a scene out of that film, I swear," I said. "Remember those flies?"

Claudia shrieked. "Ugh! I'll never forget them. They were totally disgusting."

"Well, we saw a whole swarm of them over at that house. And I saw a face at one of the windows, too."

Charlotte looked at me. I hadn't told her about that. I'd decided she was scared enough as it was.

"It was probably just one of the workmen," said Dawn.

"Yeah," said Jessi. "He was probably surprised to see you, too."

"No, that was the really weird thing," I said. "There were no workmen. They had all gone – long gone, it looked like. And it was only about four when we got there, too."

Charlotte looked really scared all over again. In fact, she looked as if she might start crying. Kristy must have noticed, too, because just then the phone rang and she said, "Charlotte, want to answer that?"

Charlotte looked over at Kristy. "Me?" she asked.

"Yeah, you!" said Kristy.

Charlotte beamed. Then she realized she'd better grab the phone. It'd been ringing for a while by then.

"Babysitters Club," she said. "No job too small!"

The room was quiet for a second as we all looked at each other. Mallory was the first to crack up, and soon we were all hysterical. Charlotte was a natural!

6th CHAPTER

Saturday

You lot would not believe the sitting experience I had on Friday. Mum and Watson had tickets to something or other, Nannie had taken off in the Pink Clinker for League Night at the bowling alley, and Sam and Charlie naturally had plans, so it was just me and the Wild Bunch: Karen and Andrew, David Michael, and of course Emily Michelle. Maybe if we hadn't had a storm that night Karen wouldn't have got started on the Ben Brewer stories, and the whole evening would have gone differently... maybe, but somehow I doubt it. First she started in on the Morbidda Destiny stories, though...

"And if she ever catches Boo-Boo again, she's going to put a spell on him. He'll still *look* like Boo-Boo, and he'll still come when we call him, but something about him will be different. He won't purr any more, and his tongue will be as cold as ice, not warm like it is now." Karen was really getting carried away.

Andrew was sitting on Kristy's lap, and David Michael was huddled on the floor near her feet. Emily Michelle was rooting through the toy basket, looking for her "baby". She was the only one in the room who wasn't spellbound by Karen's tale.

Kristy usually has no patience with Karen's silly ghost stories, but after hearing what Charlotte and I had been through that afternoon, she was feeling a bit spooked.

It wasn't that late yet, but the sky was completely dark. Thunder rumbled in the distance, and lightning flickered. The storm was on its way.

Andrew looked up at Kristy. "She won't really do that, will she? I like Boo-Boo the way he is."

Kristy shook herself. Andrew really looked scared. She had to break the mood before things got out of hand. "Of course not, Andrew. Karen's just telling stories again. Listen, everyone. How about if I make a big bowl of popcorn and we play a game or two of Snakes and Ladders?"

"Popcorn! Yea!" said David Michael.

"Can we play the Name Game while you make it?"

Kristy sighed. The Name Game soon gets pretty boring, but the kids love it. "Okay. Who's first?"

"Me!"

"I am!"

"No, me!"

They all yelled at once. Kristy should have known better. She stalled for time, opening and closing cupboards and setting up the popping pan. "Okay, let's do Emily first. Then *she* can decide who's next. Ready? Here goes." And Kristy started to sing:

> *"Emily Emily bo bemily*
> *Bananafana fo femily*
> *Me mi mo memily*
> *Emily!"*

Karen joined in, and so did David Michael. Andrew got some of the words right, but he got stuck on the "bananafana" part and just kept doing it over and over again.

"Who's next, Emily?" Kristy asked. Emily pointed to Karen, who's a favourite of hers. They all sang, Karen loudest of all.

> *"Karen Karen bo baren*
> *Bananafana fo faren*
> *Me mi mo maren*
> *Karen!"*

The Name Game continued as Kristy made the popcorn. Running out of names didn't stop them: they just went round the kitchen, singing about everything they saw:

> "*Toaster toaster bo boaster*
> *Bananafana fo foaster*
> *Me mi mo moaster*
> *Toaster!*"

Things got pretty silly for a while. When the popcorn was ready they trooped into the living room to play Snakes and Ladders. The game wasn't over when Karen started up again.

"I heard Ben Brewer walking around last night. His footsteps went up and down, up and down. He was pacing. He was restless. Finally he stopped and sat down. I heard the bed creak. Then he took off his boots. The first one dropped. *Boom*. Then the second."

And just as she said "second", there was a huge clap of thunder. Everybody jumped, and Karen shrieked and leapt into Kristy's lap. She'd even scared *herself* that time. Her Ben Brewer stories are about the ghost who supposedly lives on the third floor. (Proof? Boo-Boo won't go above the second floor. Animals are sensitive to ghostly presences, according to Karen.) Karen's stories are mostly old hat by now. But the storm's timing had certainly contributed to the drama of this one.

Thunder was really booming then, and the garden outside was lit up by lightning. It was pouring. Kristy had all four kids piled into her lap, and they just sat and hugged each other and watched the storm. Finally the thunder and lightning moved on, though the wind and rain didn't seem to let up much.

"Okay, time for bed, everyone," Kristy said. "David Michael, Andrew, and Karen, brush your teeth and get your pyjamas on. I'll put Emily Michelle down and then come and read to all of you."

Kristy knew that the kids were a little spooked, but it had got late while they waited for the storm to pass, so she thought they'd be sleepy.

No such luck. She read five chapters of *Ozma of Oz* (they were going through all the Oz books, since they'd just seen the film), and everyone was still wide awake. Then she sang some lullabies with them. "All the Pretty Little Ponies" was Karen's favourite. The Ghostbusters song, "Who Ya Gonna Call" was David Michael's. Finally Kristy tucked them all in, sleepy or not, and told them it was bedtime. She went downstairs and sat on the sofa to read.

"Kristee-e-e-e, I need a drink of wa-a-a-a-ter." That was David Michael. He was in a whiny mood. Kristy brought the water, and he made her stay while he drank it. She waited, then closed the door to his room almost all the way and went back downstairs.

"Kristy?"

Karen was standing at the door of the living room. "I can hear Ben again," she said. "He's walking around."

"It's just the wind," said Kristy. "Go back to bed, Karen."

Then Emily called out, and of course Andrew wanted a drink, too. Kristy thought they'd never go to sleep. But finally the house was quiet. Quiet, that is, except for the wind rattling the shutters outside.

Kristy found that she couldn't concentrate on her book. In fact, she couldn't stop thinking about the old house and the experiences Charlotte and I had had there.

She wandered into the kitchen and ate the last handful of popcorn. She washed out the bowl. She opened the fridge door, looked inside, and closed it without having any idea of what she'd seen in there. Then she tiptoed upstairs to check on her brothers and sisters. Everybody was fast asleep. Kristy thought that that was a good thing, except that all of a sudden she felt a bit lonely. (I think she was at what my mum would call "a loose end".)

Finally, Kristy ended up downstairs in the library. (That's right. Watson's mansion is so big that there's a whole room just for his books.) The library at Watson's is a cosy place, with big red leather armchairs, lamps that look as if they're made out of stained glass, and, of course, hundreds – maybe thousands – of books.

Kristy looked round and spotted a big box in the corner. She remembered Watson telling her that he'd just bought some old books at a book fair. She also remembered him saying that some of the books were about the history of Stoneybrook. She was hoping that maybe she could find something out about that old house!

She pulled a couple of books out of the box and had a look at them. They were pretty dusty, and smelt as if they'd been in someone's basement for a while. The covers were cracked and the edges of the pages were yellowed. She opened one of them. Straight away she spotted the name Brewer. Wow! Watson's family really *had* lived in Stoneybrook for a long time.

She kept reading, just standing there by the cardboard box. There were other names she recognized, and places, too. Of course, there was no record of her old neighbourhood: that whole area had just been woods and farmland at one time. But she found a chapter on the building of the library, and one on what the great blizzard of '88 had done to Stoneybrook. (That actually sounded fun – people could walk out onto the snow from their second-storey windows!)

Kristy took an armful of books over to one of the armchairs. She switched on a lamp, made herself comfortable, and settled down to read. The storm still blew outside, making the doors shake. Rain splattered against the windows. But Kristy was lost in "Olde Stoneybrooke".

She couldn't find a thing about the old house, though. She skimmed through each of the books, looking for information on the turreted mansion. Then she went back and leafed through each one again. There was absolutely nothing.

She was about to give up when a crumbly piece of paper fell out of the book she was holding. She unfolded it carefully, but even so, it ripped a little along the crease. It was very, very old. It was a map.

It looked hand-drawn, and the locations were all hand-lettered. She turned it this way and that, trying to work out how it related to the town she knew. It was a very early map of Stoneybrook. Only a scattering of houses were shown, along with a bank and a church. The church was still there, and so was . . . the house itself. Kristy had finally located "our" old house. At first she couldn't quite make out the writing in the area in and around the house. What did it say?

"Oh, my lord," said Kristy out loud. (That's one of Claud's favourite expressions, and we've all picked it up.)

From what she could see on this incredibly old map, Kristy worked out that the entire town of Stoneybrook had been built over ancient burial grounds. And "our" house was built on – oh, my lord – the most sacred spot of all!

Kristy noticed that the map was shaking. Then she realized that it was her hands that were shaking. She let go of the map and it drifted to the floor. Kristy thought again about all the things that Charlotte and I had told her that day. She was scared out of her wits.

She decided not to read another word in those books. She decided to put the map away and never look at it again. She decided she wished that her mum and Watson would come home SOON.

Kristy got up and turned off the lamp she'd been using. She picked up all the books and brought them over to the box in the corner. As she packed them away, she suddenly got the strangest feeling that she was being watched (she told me this later). There was a definite presence in the room. She didn't want to turn round, so she just kept packing the books into the box, very carefully. The presence was still there. Finally, she knew she had to turn and look. She spun round quickly and saw Sam and Charlie just standing there in the doorway, grinning and making horrible faces at her. She screamed and fell into the nearest chair. Sam and Charlie didn't stop laughing for at least half an hour.

7th CHAPTER

I was walking down Fifth Avenue, past Rockefeller Center. Gary Rockman was running after me, calling my name over and over again.

"Stacey," he called. "Stacey, please come to me!"

I woke up with a start, back in my ordinary old bed in Stoneybrook. It was morning. Gary Rockman was nowhere in sight, but someone was calling my name. It was Charlotte, and she didn't sound too good.

I went into the guest room. Charlotte was in bed, the covers tangled around her legs. She looked flushed and hot. I put my hand on her forehead. She was burning up!

"Stacey, my throat hurts. I feel awful." Charlotte *looked* awful. A couple of tears ran down her cheeks. "I miss my mummy," she said.

"I know, Charlotte, but don't worry. We'll take good care of you." I ran to get the thermometer, and while Charlotte held it in her mouth, I went to find my mum. She came upstairs with me and we took a look at the thermometer. A hundred and two degrees. Charlotte was definitely ill. Mum and I glanced at each other. I knew she was feeling as bad as I was about the way we'd played down Charlotte's earlier symptoms. I'd been so sure it was just that Charlotte was nervous and homesick.

Charlotte's parents had left a list of emergency numbers. I checked it to see which doctor we should call, and it said she went to Dr Dellenkamp. Mum went downstairs to phone for an appointment. I helped Charlotte get up, wash her face, and get dressed. She moved slowly. Finally we all piled into the car and drove to the doctor's surgery.

When we walked into the waiting room, we could see straight away that it was going to be a while before we saw the doctor. There was a woman with a crying baby, another mother trying to convince her toddler to sit and play quietly with some blocks, and a girl of about my age who was sitting there alone, sort of hunched over. She looked as if she had a stomach ache. Mum decided that she might as well get the grocery shopping done, since I was there to wait with Charlotte, so she left.

Charlotte and I sat down on the couch. It was quite an ugly couch, made of that fake leather stuff that sticks to your legs when you try to get up. Why do waiting rooms always have such ugly furniture? Charlotte put her head in my lap and closed her eyes. I stroked her hair. It's the worst feeling when you're ill and you have to be anywhere but home in bed.

Charlotte seemed comfortable, so I looked at the table by the couch to see what magazines they had. Oh, boy. I had a choice between a July 1979 *Reader's Digest* and this month's *Highlights for Children*. I picked up *Highlights*, just to see if it had changed at all since I used to look at it in my paediatrician's office. Nope. There were good old Goofus and Gallant, same as ever. Even as a kid I'd thought that Gallant was a bit of a goody-goody.

I was still flicking through the magazine when the outer door opened and the most gorgeous guy walked in, holding the hand of a little boy who must have been his brother. I stared. Blond curly hair, blue eyes . . . he reminded me of Scott, a lifeguard I'd had a crush on once in Sea City, New Jersey. He looked back at me, and then I saw his gaze fall to the magazine I was holding. I dropped it like a hot brick. He smiled at me, as if to say he understood.

I was totally humiliated. Luckily, the receptionist called Charlotte then, and I went with her into the examining room, still blushing.

The examination didn't take long. Dr Dellenkamp knew what it was straight away.

"Tonsillitis *again*?" Charlotte wailed.

"That's right, Charlotte. Back on the old penicillin," the doctor said. "We may have to do something about those tonsils at some point," she said to me quietly as Charlotte hopped off the table. "But for now, since her parents are away, we'll just hit the germs again with this." She wrote out a prescription.

"Charlotte has trouble taking pills, so we usually give her liquid penicillin. She should take a teaspoon of it four times a day. She'll feel better pretty quickly – in a day or so, I'd say."

The doctor put her arm around Charlotte as we walked out. "I know you must miss your parents, but you be a good patient for Stacey. She'll take good care of you," she said. She winked at me as we said goodbye.

My mum was waiting for us. Fortunately, the gorgeous guy was busy keeping his little brother's hands out of the aquarium, so I was able to dash out of the waiting room without meeting his eyes again.

We stopped at the chemist to pick up Charlotte's prescription. As soon as she saw the bottle she started to . . . well, she started to whine. There's no nicer way to put it.

193

"I *hate* that stuff," she moaned. "It tastes so awful that I want to throw up when I take it. Do I have to take it? Oh, I want my mummy. It's not fair!"

I knew how she felt, but really. Her whining was a little hard to take, especially since she didn't let up the whole way home.

When we got to our house, I went into the kitchen for a spoon. Charlotte stayed in the living room, where she'd thrown herself on the couch. When I walked in, she turned over so that her face was buried in the cushions.

"I *won't* take it," she said. "I'd rather be sick."

I rolled my eyes. "Charlotte, look. It says 'New Cherry Flavour' on the bottle. Maybe it'll taste better than last time." I opened the bottle and sniffed the liquid inside. Oh, yuck! It *did* smell vile. There's nothing worse than that fake "cherry" flavour, unless it's fake banana. Ugh!

"It smells okay, Charlotte," I lied. "Come on, all you have to take is a teaspoon. If you hold your nose, you'll hardly taste it. And I'll make you a chocolate milk shake. You can drink that to take away the bad taste." I was bribing her, and I knew it. This wasn't the right way to go about getting the medicine down her throat.

"No," she said flatly. Oh, well. My bribe hadn't worked anyway. She burrowed deeper into the couch cushions. This was really getting frustrating. I tried not to feel angry with Charlotte. She wasn't feeling well, she missed her parents, she was worried about her grandpa, and she was stuck in a strange house. I suppose I might have felt grumpy and uncooperative, too, if I'd been her.

If I were her. . . Suddenly I had a brainwave. Maybe taking just a teaspoon full of nasty medicine wouldn't seem all that terrible if she could see what I had to go through every day, just to stay healthy. It might just work.

"Charlotte, you know I have diabetes, right?" I knew she knew, because I've discussed my diabetes with Dr Johanssen, in front of Charlotte.

Charlotte sort of grunted, but she didn't budge from her "nest" on the couch.

"Want me to show you the medicine I have to take?" I asked. "We'll forget about yours for now."

That got her moving. She followed me upstairs and I opened the desk drawer where I keep all my equipment. I tried to explain a little bit about diabetes and why it makes me ill and how insulin helps to control it. I'm not sure how much she understood. She'd probably never heard of a "pancreas" before.

"I never *used* to have to do this," I said. "But since I haven't been feeling too well lately, I now have to check my glucose level a few times a day. All I do is prick my finger, like this—"

Charlotte gasped as I pricked my finger and squeezed out a tiny drop of blood. I wiped it onto something called a test strip and put the strip into a little machine. In a minute the number came up. 110. That was about normal for me at this time of day. Charlotte was fascinated.

"Knowing what my number is helps me make sure I take the right amount of insulin. When I'm ready to take my insulin, I fill up this syringe and give myself a jab." I wasn't going to show her how I did that. It might really scare her.

The injections don't hurt me any more – I'm so used to them by now. But to someone else, especially someone of Charlotte's age, it might be frightening.

I told her a bit more about what it meant to be a diabetic. That this was something I'd have to deal with every day for the rest of my life. And how I had to be extremely careful about what I ate, and why. Charlotte's eyes got rounder and rounder. She'd had no idea of what I went through just to control my illness.

"Injections every single day? Oh, Stacey, you're so brave," she said when I'd finished explaining everything.

"Not really, Charlotte. That's just how things are for me. I don't have any choice in the matter," I said. "Anyway, it feels good to take care of myself."

Well, after all that, it was no trouble at all to get Charlotte to take her medicine. She barely made a face as she swallowed it down.

"Good girl," I said. "Now, let's get you into bed."

She changed into her pyjamas while I put a clean pillowcase on her pillow. I always think it feels good to have a fresh pillowcase to rest your head on when you're ill. I also prepared her room for the day. I brought in our little portable TV and stocked the shelves with more games, drawing paper and crayons, and books.

While Charlotte got settled into bed, I went down to the kitchen to make her a snack. I set out a tray with that milk shake I'd promised her. When I'm not well my mum always puts a flower in a little vase on my dinner tray, so I did that, too. Charlotte deserved to be spoiled a little; just think, she'd been getting ill all that time and nobody had paid attention to her complaints. I got myself a glass of iced water and took the tray upstairs.

Charlotte and I spent the whole day in her room, playing every game I had. Yes, that does include Snap, if you're wondering. We also watched TV and I read to her for a bit before she dropped off for a nap. While she slept, I just stayed in the room and read to myself. It was a peaceful afternoon.

That night, Charlotte phoned her parents. She wanted to let them know that she was ill but getting better. She also wanted to ask about her grandfather. She talked to her mum for just a few minutes, and by the end of the call she was beaming. Her grandpa's operation had gone very well and he was feeling much better. The Johanssens would be back home on Thursday, just as they'd planned. Charlotte was definitely on the road to recovery.

8th CHAPTER

By Sunday morning, Charlotte was feeling much better. Penicillin does work fast. It hadn't been easy getting her to take her medicine regularly – she still hated it – but at least she'd taken most of it.

Charlotte came downstairs for breakfast, and Mum made special sugar-free blueberry pancakes. Yum. I love them because they're so good on their own that I don't even miss being able to have maple syrup. Charlotte ate a big stack of them. She was definitely better.

But Dr Dellenkamp had said that even if she was feeling all right, Charlotte should take it easy on Sunday and Monday. She wasn't supposed to go to school until Tuesday.

Tuesday seemed a long way off. I was sick of playing Snap, sick of being Professor Plum in Cluedo. and very sick of TV. I was even sick of reading *Charlotte's Web*.

What were we going to do all day? I think Charlotte was just as tired as I was of being cooped up, especially now that she was feeling more normal.

Then I remembered that Kristy had phoned on Saturday to tell me about some map she'd found on Friday night. Maybe she could come over and bring the map, along with some of those old books of Watson's. Kristy had said she really hadn't found much in the books, but maybe if we went through them all, we'd come up with something. It would be fun to play detectives, anyway. I phoned Kristy up.

"Kristy, it's Stace. What're you doing today?"

"I've got no plans," she said. "I don't even have to look after the kids, since Mum and Watson have taken them into town to buy shoes."

"How about bringing over that old map and the books?" I said. "Charlotte's at home ill, here, and we'd love to look at them."

"Great," said Kristy. "Hold on, let me see if Nannie can drive me over."

The arrangements were made. While we waited for Kristy, Charlotte and I washed up the breakfast dishes. Then she took her medicine without too much fussing. Finally we settled down on the front steps (Charlotte had felt good enough to get dressed that morning) and waited for

Kristy to turn up. While we waited, we talked about the old house.

"I'm glad we were together when we heard those noises, Stacey," said Charlotte. "That was scary. But you know, I feel as if there's something interesting about that house. I hope we can find out more about it."

I told her a little about the map Kristy had found, but not too much. I thought that the idea of burial grounds might be scary for Charlotte, but she was fascinated.

By the time Kristy got out of the Pink Clinker (Nannie's old car) in front of our house, Charlotte's excitement was at an all-time high.

"Where are the books, Kristy?" she asked, without even saying hello. She would have dived into the back seat and hauled out the box if I hadn't stopped her.

"Easy, Charlotte. You're still not well, remember?" I said. "I know you love mysteries, but let's take our time. We've got all day."

Charlotte does love mysteries, and I have to say that she's a pretty good sleuth. She played a big part in solving the mystery of an old diary that Mallory had found in a trunk in our attic. That mystery had led us to find the portrait of a beautiful woman, which now hung over our fireplace. At that time we thought my house might be haunted, but that was nothing compared to what we were facing now.

We brought the box of books inside and spread ourselves out in the living room. We each took a book and began to read. After a while we swapped books and read some more. Kristy had been right. There wasn't much in them. They were interesting, but we couldn't find any clues to the mystery of the old house.

"Where's that map, Kristy?" I asked. "Let's have a look at it."

Kristy took it out and opened it carefully.

"Wow, that's really old, isn't it?" asked Charlotte. "The writing on it is so weird. What does it say?"

I couldn't make it out too well, either, but it did seem to show that house. As far as the burial-ground business, I couldn't be sure. The map wasn't like any I'd ever seen. It had strange signs and symbols on it, and markings in a faded red colour. I wondered if it was the real McCoy or just something someone had made up for fun.

"How do we know that this map is really as old as it looks?" I asked.

Kristy and Charlotte both just gave me a look. They wanted to believe in the map and in the mystery of the old house. They had no doubts about the map being genuine.

"I wonder who owns that house," I said.

I was really starting to get interested in that "silly old house", in spite of myself. Laine would never believe it. If she ever got involved in a mystery back in New York, it would probably be something like, "Who stole the countess's jewels from the hotel safe?" or "Does the ghost of Elvis haunt the Hard Rock Cafe?"

"I don't know who owns it. Nobody's lived there for years," Kristy said. "But I don't remember there ever being a 'For Sale' sign in front of that house."

"Do you think the owner is even still alive?" asked Charlotte. She gulped. "Maybe that was his ghost we heard."

"No, he must be alive somewhere. How else could that developer ever have bought the house in order to knock it down?" Kristy looked thoughtful. "I wonder if we could find him."

"You keep saying 'he'," I said. "The owner *could* be a woman, you know. Anyway, can we find out who the owner is? Do you think *she* still lives in the area?"

"We could find out everything we need to know about the house if only we could track him – or her – down," said Kristy. "Maybe Mary Anne would have some good ideas. Her family has lived around here for ages."

I went to the phone and dialled Mary Anne's number. Luckily, she was at home.

"Mary Anne, did you hear about the map that Kristy found?" I asked, after we'd said hello, how are you, and all that. She hadn't, so I told her about it.

"It sounds like a mystery, all right," she

said. "But where do we go from here?" I didn't know what to tell her.

Kristy motioned for me to give her the phone. "Mary Anne," she said. "Keep on the look-out for clues. You never know where you might find one. Maybe there are some old books or documents somewhere in that old house of yours."

Since Mary Anne lived with Dawn now, they really might find some clues in their house. It's one of the oldest houses around here, and it has some mysteries of its own. That secret passage has been the site of all kinds of strange happenings.

"Dawn's sitting for the Rodowskys, but as soon as she gets back I'll ask her if she's got any ideas," said Mary Anne. "Isn't it fun solving another mystery."

Next we called Claudia. She got all excited about the books and the map, and she wanted to come straight over and look at them and hear more about what Kristy had found out. She was stuck at home, though, doing homework. (Claud's really bright – even if she isn't an actual genius like her sister, Janine – but her grades don't show it. If she doesn't keep her grades up she might have to give up the Babysitters Club. No way did we want that to happen.)

"Stay put and do your homework, Claud," I said. "But keep your eyes and ears open over the next few days. You can never tell where or when a clue might turn up."

We tried to phone Mallory, since she loves mysteries, too, but Mrs Pike said that Mal had taken Margo and Claire (two of her little sisters) on a special Teddy Bears' Picnic. Mal's such a terrific big sister. I remembered now that she'd been planning this for a while. She was going to make little sandwiches and "tea", and help the girls dress up their teddy bears in special outfits. It sounded like fun. I asked Mrs Pike to tell Mallory to phone me when she got home.

We didn't even try to call Jessi, since we knew she was away for the weekend. So that was everyone. If we all kept on the alert for clues, maybe we could crack this case.

To be honest, I didn't even really know for sure if we had a mystery on our hands. This burial-ground story was hard to prove, and that old map was so hard to read. I wasn't positive that Kristy had got it right. Maybe all that stuff we'd seen and heard at the house was just our imaginations. Maybe we were making something out of nothing.

But there was Charlotte, sitting on the couch with one of Watson's old books. She was flipping through it one more time, combing for clues. I could see that, for a while anyway, she'd forgotten that she was ill. She'd forgotten that she was stuck inside for another day and a half. And she'd forgotten that her parents were a plane ride away. Mystery or not, the old house was keeping us both busy. I was thankful for that.

9th CHAPTER

monday

I know you lot dont think of the wordes 'libary' and 'Claud' as belonging in the same sentense, but boy, they do now. I never knewe just how much you coud find out just by looking in a few reference books. Maybe when I'm older I'll will be a libarian like my mum oh yeah, P.S. Gabie and Miryiah had a grate time at the libary to.

On Monday, Claud had a job looking after the Perkins girls, Gabbie and Myriah. Gabbie's almost three, and Myriah's almost six. We all like them a lot. They also have a baby sister called Laura. Mrs Perkins was taking Laura to Dr Dellenkamp to have her cough looked at.

When Claudia arrived, Chewy – the Perkinses' big black Labrador retriever – was running around in circles. Myriah was holding his favourite toy, a disgusting, ancient well-chewed tennis ball. She wouldn't throw it for him, and it was driving him mad. He barked as he ran, begging her to throw it.

"Claudee Kishi!" yelled Gabbie. "Hi, Claudee Kishi! Toshe me up!" Gabbie always calls us by our full names, and "toshe me up" is an expression she invented and uses all the time. Basically, it means, "Pick me up and give me a big hug." Claud was glad to oblige, since Gabbie is extremely huggable.

"I've got a great idea!" said Claud. "How about if we go to the library for Story Hour? Today they're going to read a couple of your favourite books. Guess which ones. *Mike Milligan and His Steam Shovel* and *The Little House*. And then, after they've read the books, everybody gets to help make a mural of the town in *The Little House*."

Claud had found out about Story Hour from her mum. Mrs Kishi is the head librarian, so she knows about all the things that go on there. Claud had thought she'd check out Story Hour to see if it was a good way to spend some time with the kids we were sitting for.

"Yea!" yelled Gabbie. "What's a mural?"

"It's a big, giant picture, Gabbers," said Myriah. "Can Chewy come, Claudia? Oh, boy, I can't wait!"

They do love those two books. Have you ever read *The Little House*? It's about this house that was once in the country, and then slowly a big city gets built up around it. I won't spoil the ending, but trust me, it's a great book.

Claud had another motive for going to the library. She couldn't stop thinking about the old house being on the site of a burial ground. Maybe, she thought, she could find out more by browsing through the local history section. She must have been *obsessed* with that house: it's not like her to do much voluntary reading (apart from Nancy Drew, of course).

Claudia, Gabbie and Myriah – she'd vetoed the idea of Chewy coming along – set off for the library. The girls were pretty excited about going, as the library is one of their favourite places. They go every week to borrow books and this would be a bonus visit for them.

"Can we take out a book today, Claudee Kishi?" asked Gabbie.

"I want to take out *five* books," said Myriah. "This many," she added, holding up all five fingers on her right hand. "Because I'm five years old. Five and a half, really. Right, Claudia?"

"That's right, Myriah. And you can both take out as many books as you like today," said Claudia. "Did you know that my mummy is the boss of the whole library?" she added.

"Does she *live* there?" asked Myriah. "I always wanted to sleep overnight at the library. I bet she gets to whenever she wants."

Claudia's mum had told us once that kids really do think she lives at the library. After all, she's always there! When they see her somewhere else in town, like at the supermarket, sometimes they just stop and stare at her. They can't believe she's just an ordinary person. She's the "liberrian".

Claud cleared up Myriah's confusion, and the girls sang as they walked.

"*The sun'll come out tomorrow*," sang Gabbie.

"*Bet your bottom dollar there'll be sun*," chimed in Myriah.

Claudia smiled. Gabbie and Myriah seem to know all the words to a million songs, and they love to sing them all the way through. After they'd finished "Tomorrow", they ran through "You're Never Fully Dressed Without a Smile".

They must have seen *Annie* a couple of hundred times.

"*I know you, I danced with you once upon a dream,*" sang Myriah. They'd started to act out their favourite scenes from Sleeping Beauty. Myriah was playing the part of the prince.

"Oh! I have to go now!" said Gabbie, dramatically. She was Sleeping Beauty. She was very convincing in the role.

When they got to the library, Claud stopped off at the office to see her mum. The girls followed her quietly. They know how to behave in the library, especially when the big boss is looking right at them.

Claudia then settled the girls in the children's room. Story Hour was just about to start. They were right on time. Then she headed back into the main room. She'd forgotten where the local history books were kept, even though we've looked at them before. But there was no way she was going to ask her mum. It was embarrassing to be the head librarian's daughter and not even know her way around the library. Fortunately this guy we know, Bruce Schermerhorn, is working there, shelving the books that people return. Claud asked him where the books were, and he helped her find the ones she wanted.

She took them to a chair where she could be comfortable and also keep an eye on Gabbie and Myriah. They seemed to be having a good time listening to the stories.

The first two volumes Claudia looked at were hard to get through. They were the kind of dry historical books that are absolutely no fun to read. But Claud did her best. It wasn't easy for her, trying to plough through that material. Still, she stuck at it. Finally she realized that she wasn't getting anywhere.

She picked up one of the other books and took a look at it. It seemed to be full of old records of the town of Stoneybrook. There were birth records and death records and property-tax records and even a map. This stuff looked even more boring than what she'd looked at before. Claud gritted her teeth and kept looking. She was determined to get *something* out of this visit to the library.

She picked up a second book of old town records and worked her way through it until she came across a couple of paragraphs that looked as though they had something to do with "our" house. From what she'd read so far, it *did* seem as though the town was built on ancient burial grounds. And the house *was*, she thought, on a sacred spot. The people who had written down the records didn't seem to be too concerned about it, but Claud was getting chills up and down her spine. How could anyone think that such a thing didn't matter? What about the spirits of the dead who had been buried there? How could they ever be at rest with houses and banks and Burger Kings on top of them?

Claud got a grip on herself. Before she got too carried away, she knew she should keep looking to see if she could find out who owned the house. Property tax records should be just the ticket, she thought. She kept poring over the musty old book. And then she found it! The owner's name. Ronald Hennessey. It was right there in black and white.

Claud felt like cheering. This was a major discovery. But what good did a name do unless she could find out more about who Ronald Hennessey was? Was he still alive? Where did he live now? He certainly didn't live in the house he owned, and he hadn't for years.

Claud sat for a moment and thought. Where could she look next? She glanced into the children's room. All the Story Hour kids were working on a big messy mural full of blocks of flats and streets. There seemed to be dinosaurs roaming the streets, too. The Little House stood forlornly in the middle of the picture. Story Hour was almost over.

Finally, Claud went over to her mum's desk. "Mum, where would you look to see if someone who used to live in Stoneybrook still *does* live in Stoneybrook?"

Mrs Kishi looked up at Claudia, surprised. She must have wondered what Claud was up to, but she didn't ask. She just smiled a little and said, "Well, I suppose I'd try the phone book."

Claudia told me later that she wished there'd been a trapdoor she could fall into just then. How stupid she'd been! She'd got so wrapped up in her complicated historical research that she'd never even thought of using an ordinary old phone book.

She went to the reference desk, where they keep all the phone books for the whole country. She found the local one and opened it right at the exact page that Ronald Hennessey was on. Guess what? He was in there. It was as easy as that.

Claud looked at the address listed. Stoneybrook Manor. That was a nursing home. Of course, Mr Hennessey must be pretty old by now, she realized. She copied down the address and went off to collect Gabbie and Myriah.

Story Hour was just ending, but Claud had to hang around for a while as the girls chose some books to take home. Gabbie just sort of grabbed randomly, but Myriah seemed to have definite ideas about which ones she liked and which ones were "ucky". While she waited, Claud strolled over to look at the finished mural. There was a lot going on in that picture, a lot that the illustrator of *The Little House*

213

wouldn't recognize. Besides the dinosaurs, there were soldiers with amazing weaponry, witches holding brooms, ballerinas, and a Fantasy Land-like area where lollipops grew. It was a great mural.

Finally, the girls had all the books they wanted. They went to the desk to get them checked out.

"What's your name?" asked the lady at the desk.

"Gabbie," said Gabbie. "What's yours?"

Claudia laughed and went over to help. "These are the Perkins girls," she said. "Gabbie and Myriah." The librarian must have been new, or else she'd have recognized them. She looked up their cards and checked out the books. It had turned out to be a pretty big stack, so Claud helped carry them home.

The girls journeyed home with their books and spent the time telling each other and Claudia the story of Mike Mulligan. They decided that Mike should have lived *in* The Little House.

Claud got them home just as Mrs Perkins returned from the doctor's office. Dr Dellenkamp had given her a prescription for Laura and said that she'd be fine in no time.

By then it was almost time for the Babysitters Club meeting, so Claud ran home as soon as she'd said her goodbyes to the girls and to Mrs Perkins. She was excited about what she'd found out and proud of herself for sticking with the research. She was dying to tell us all about Mr Ronald Hennessey.

10th CHAPTER

While Claudia was doing her research at the library, Charlotte and I were doing some research of our own.

It was Monday afternoon. I'd arrived home from school to find Charlotte feeling "all well", as she had put it. My mum, who had spent the day with Charlotte, went out to do some errands.

"There's a snack for you on the table, darling," she said. Sometimes she still treats me like a fourth-grader, which isn't such a terrible thing. It's nice to feel taken care of.

I sat down with Charlotte and ate my fruit and crackers while she told me about her day. Since she'd been at home all day, her story wasn't that exciting: she'd watched TV, read, and taught my mum how to play Snap! But it was nice to come home to find my "little sister" waiting for me. I'd really been enjoying Charlotte's company, probably even more than if she really *were* my little sister. Real sisters do things like argue and tease each other, and we never do that. We just have a good time together.

After I'd eaten, Charlotte followed me upstairs. I wanted to change out of my school clothes, since I'd worn a new outfit that day and I wanted to keep it nice. I'd got this pink polka-dotted short skirt with braces and had worn it with an oversized white T-shirt. I had on my pink high-top sneakers, folded down to show their striped lining. I'd also worn some great earrings Claud had given me for my last birthday. They had all these little pink plastic hearts dangling down from one bigger heart. In case you haven't noticed, I do like the colour pink!

By the time I'd finished changing, Charlotte and I had decided to go for a walk. Charlotte was feeling great – she'd definitely be able to go to school the next day – and she wanted to get outside. Guess where we went? That's right. There was something about that old house. We just couldn't stay away from it.

When we got there, the workmen were packing up their tools and getting ready to leave. It was early again, not even four o'clock yet, but they seemed to be in a hurry. Charlotte and I stayed out of their way until they had driven off.

We decided to walk round the house

again, just as we had the last time we were there. It didn't look all that different. The workmen must have still been taking things out from the inside. A couple of windows had been pulled from the walls and they were leaning against the house. The bushes around the sides looked a little beaten down where the workers had been walking. And the railing on the back porch had come loose and was hanging at a weird angle.

"You know, Charlotte," I said, "I think all those noises we heard last time were just in our imaginations."

She looked at me. Maybe she could tell by my tone of voice that I was really just trying to convince myself – and her – that there was nothing to be scared of. "But what about the things we *saw*, Stacey?" she asked. "What about the flies, and that face at the window?"

"I'm sure there's an explanation for everything," I said. "Maybe those flies were actually termites." The face I wasn't so sure about. Maybe I'd just imagined that. After all, I'd been the only one to see it. That must be it. My imagination had just run away with me last Friday.

"Fire! Fire!" yelled Charlotte all of a sudden. She sounded terrified.

She was pointing towards a window on the ground floor. Sure enough, flames were shooting out of it. Uh-oh. This was *not* my imagination. This was serious.

I looked around frantically. How could I put out the blaze? What if the whole house started burning? There was no hose, and even if there had been one, I didn't see any taps on the outside of the house. Finally I saw a wheelbarrow off to the side, almost hidden in the weeds. It was full of rainwater! I ran to grab it and started to push it towards the house. Water sloshed around and spilled all over my legs, but I kept on pushing.

Charlotte had been shrieking all this time, but suddenly she stopped. I'd got the wheelbarrow almost up to the house. Now I looked at the window and saw that the flames had disappeared. I felt as if I was going mad. What was happening here?

My heart was pounding like mad, and I could hardly catch my breath. I put the wheelbarrow down and walked towards the window. Charlotte hung back. I looked at the empty frame. The wood wasn't charred, and the paint wasn't blistered. I couldn't smell smoke. I reached up gingerly and touched the sill. It wasn't even warm. I couldn't see inside the window, but I could tell that where there once had been fire there was no fire now. The house stood silent and cold.

I turned to look at Charlotte. Her face was white and she was hugging herself as if to keep warm. "Our imaginations again?" she asked in a small voice.

I just shook my head, bewildered. Why

had we ever come back to this place? Something very weird was happening here. This house was not at rest. I grabbed Charlotte's hand and walked home quickly, without looking back.

At the Babysitters Club meeting that afternoon, we told everybody what we'd seen, and Claud filled us in on her research. That was one meeting where not much business got done.

I tried to shut the house out of my thoughts completely for the rest of the evening, and I think Charlotte did, too. We were both pretty quiet at dinner that night, but luckily my mum didn't ask any questions. I didn't want to have to try to explain anything.

At bedtime I read to Charlotte for a while, and then we talked. We talked about her going back to school the next day. We talked about her parents and how they'd be home in just a few days. We talked about her grandpa. We did *not* talk about the house.

When I went to bed I was still feeling pretty keyed up. I didn't think I'd ever get to sleep, but finally I drifted off. . .

I was standing outside the old house. This time the flames shot out of every window and up through the roof. It was really burning this time. I tried to yell "Fire!" but my mouth wouldn't form the word. Then I tried to run for help, but my feet were stuck to the ground. I looked helplessly at the house and saw, to my horror, a figure at one of the windows. The person, whoever it was, clearly needed help. Again, I tried to move, but I was frozen in position. I could only watch as the person gestured to me, pleading to be rescued.

I sat bolt upright in bed. What a nightmare! My heart was beating wildly. I tried to calm myself. The dream had seemed so real. I still felt the terror of seeing that helpless person trapped in the incredible blaze. If only I could have saved him. I lay back down, but my eyes were wide open. I didn't really want to go to sleep. What if the nightmare came back?

I almost wished I were a little kid again, so I could tiptoe into my parents' room and wake up Mum. I would tell her all about my nightmare and she'd tell me it was just a bad dream and that she'd take care of me. Then I'd snuggle up in the big warm bed and go back to sleep, feeling safe. But I wasn't a little girl any more. I was an eighth-grader who should be able to sleep alone without being scared.

I tried to think of other things, nice things. I thought of lying on a beach, the warm sun soaking into my skin. I thought of the waves crashing against the shore with a steady beat.

Bang! My door slammed open and Charlotte flew across the room. She leapt into my bed and buried herself beneath the covers. She was shaking.

"Charlotte, what is it?" I asked. "What's the matter?"

She wouldn't – or couldn't – talk at first, but slowly it began to come out. Charlotte had also had a nightmare. And hers was also about the house.

"There was a storm coming," she said, still breathing hard. "I could hear the thunder, and lightning was flashing in the sky. Then all of a sudden the ground where I was standing – right there by the house – started to shake!" She shivered. She was really frightened.

"It's okay, Charlotte," I said. "What happened then?" I knew she would feel better if she finished telling me her dream. I hugged her close and smoothed her hair.

"The ground was rumbling. It was like an earthquake or something. I thought it was going to open up and swallow me!" I don't know how she knew what an earthquake was like. Maybe she'd seen one of those nature specials on TV.

"The sky was all dark, a kind of greenish colour. I was so scared, Stacey, but I couldn't move. I wanted to run, or scream, or do *something*, but all I could do was stand there and stare at the house."

I knew *that* feeling.

"Then the worst part happened. I was looking at the front of the house, and all of a sudden I saw something at the front door, or at the hole where the front door used to be. It was a pair of hands, two old, old hands. They were all skinny and bony, and they were waving at me. It was as if they were saying, 'Come in, Charlotte. Come in.' Oh, Stacey! It was so awful!" She started crying.

I shuddered. It sounded terrifying. I just couldn't believe it. We'd both had nightmares at the same time, and both of them had been about that creepy old house.

What kind of power did that house have? What was it that drew us there at the same time that it scared us away? Had anyone else seen what we'd seen, heard what we'd heard? I suddenly realized why it was that the workmen packed up and left so early every day. It must have been the house. It had them in its power, too. Those workmen were probably just as scared as we were.

I almost had to laugh at the thought of those big men being as scared as two girls. But it wasn't really funny. I pulled the covers around Charlotte and let her snuggle up next to me. I'm sure she thought she was being allowed to stay with me because she'd been scared by her dream. She didn't realize that she was as much of a comfort to me as I was to her.

11th CHAPTER

I suppose Charlotte and I both managed to get back to sleep. When we woke up the next morning it was a little late, and we really had to rush to get ready for school. Charlotte couldn't wait to get back to her classes – she was tired of being at home.

She took her medicine (she still had to finish the bottle even though she felt fine) without too much fuss, for once. When we had raced through breakfast, my mum drove us to school so we wouldn't be late.

I don't know about Charlotte, but my day at school was not brilliant. I was sleepy from being awake in the middle of the night, but that wasn't really the problem. The problem was that I still felt totally frightened by the nightmare I'd had, and by the fact that Charlotte had had one, too. That old house was all I could think about.

I was having a hard time concentrating on

my classes. In Maths, while I was supposed to be working out what "X" equalled, I was really thinking about flames and bony hands and swarms of flies. I don't even remember what we talked about in English, because I wasn't listening. I was remembering that face at the window. And forget about gym class. The volleyball bounced right off my head as I stood there trying to recall exactly how that moaning had sounded.

I was a mess.

By the time lunchtime came around, I was dying to see my friends. I could talk to them about this. They would understand. They were all obsessed with the house, too.

I met up with Dawn in the lunch queue. She and I were both picking and choosing very carefully from what was available. Dawn usually brings some kind of wholegrain stone-ground organic stuff, but she must have been running late that morning, too. We both avoided the "chicken chow mein" (gluey looking grey stuff on noodles) and reached for fruit, milk, and plain cheese sandwiches.

"Are you okay, Stace?" she asked, as we walked over to our usual table. "You don't look too good."

"I'm fine. I'm just a little tired, I suppose," I said. "I had a terrible nightmare last night."

By that time we'd arrived at our table, and everyone else was already there. They all wanted to hear about my nightmare, so I described it in all its gruesome glory. Then I told them that Charlotte had also had a nightmare, and I repeated her scary details.

I think they could tell that I was really frightened, because they took it seriously.

"We've got to get to the bottom of this," said Kristy. "Is there really something going on at that house? It sounds as if it might be very dangerous. There are a lot of kids living in that neighbourhood. What if something happened to one of them? I hereby call an emergency meeting of the Babysitters Club!"

Wow. We rarely have emergency meetings, and when we do, they're usually about babysitting or club problems.

"I'll be there," said Claud. "Today's art class was cancelled. I can't think about anything else, anyway."

"Me, neither," said Mary Anne. "That house really gives me the creeps. And if the whole town of Stoneybrook is really built over a burial ground, just think of all the terrible things that could start happening." I knew she'd seen that Stephen King film *Pet Sematary*. She'd let Dawn talk her into going, but afterwards they were both sorry. They were probably thinking about the film a lot these days.

Everybody agreed that an emergency meeting was a great idea. As it turned out,

Jessi was the only one who wouldn't be able to make it. She had a ballet class.

I felt better knowing that we were all in this together. I was able to pay a little more attention to my afternoon classes, but even so, the day seemed to drag on forever.

When school finally ended, I ran home to meet Charlotte. She'd had a rough day, too. She was thrilled to hear that an emergency club meeting had been called and that she'd been invited again.

"I'm almost like a real member now," she said.

I knew it would be a few years before Charlotte would be a sitter, but I also knew that being invited to the meeting meant a lot to her. "That's right, Char," I said. "Maybe one day you'll be chairman of your own babysitters club. You could wear a visor to every meeting, just like Kristy."

We set off for Claudia's early, since we were both so eager for the meeting to start. I suppose everybody felt the same way, because by four-thirty they were all there. Except for Jessi, of course.

Kristy called the meeting to order and announced a special agenda. "This is an emergency meeting to address the mystery of Stoneybrook, and especially to work out what's going on at that old house. Let's go over what we know so far," she said.

"We know that there are some very weird things happening there," I said, "and that the house has – or the spirits of the people buried beneath it have – some kind of power."

"That's right," said Claud. "The power to drive us mad!" She was sitting on her bed, chewing bubble gum and blowing pink bubbles, which matched her tie-dyed T-shirt dress. "I mean, really. None of us can think about anything else."

"I hear you had a nightmare last night, Charlotte," said Mary Anne. "That sounded scary."

"It was!" said Charlotte. "Those bony old hands . . . I'll never forget them."

"Tell us again about everything you saw and heard at the house," said Dawn.

Charlotte and I told the whole story once more, from faces to flies to flames. Then Kristy told us again about what she'd found in Watson's old books, and Claud repeated the stuff she'd learned at the library.

"There's something else, too," she said. "I wasn't going to tell you all, because it sounds so weird. I thought you'd think I was crazy. But I went past the old house today, just before I came here."

We all leaned forward. She looked scared, almost as if she didn't want to think about what had happened.

"I was standing there looking at the house. I wasn't even very close to it. All of a sudden, I felt a hand on my arm, but when I looked, nobody was there. It was as if an invisible person was standing next to me, and he – or she – wanted my attention." Claud was being very serious. She wasn't kidding about this.

My mouth was hanging open. So was Charlotte's. I was glad that had never happened to me! That would really have been the last straw. Maybe we should just forget all about this house, I thought. This was getting too scary. I looked around the room. Everybody looked as scared as I felt, but they all looked fascinated, too. I knew we'd never give up now.

"What did you *do*, Claud?" asked Mary Anne.

"I ran!" said Claudia. "I wasn't about to hang around and find out what it was they wanted from me. They probably wanted to steal my soul!"

"More likely they wanted to steal your marshmallows," I said. "Even spirits like junk food."

We all laughed. I think everybody was feeling a little tense, and we just needed an excuse to giggle for a while.

But the laughter stopped when Mallory spoke up. "You know," she said, "I've just remembered something that happened to me a long time ago. It must have been last year some time. It was spring, and Vanessa and I had gone hunting for flowers together. We wanted to make a Mother's Day bouquet for our mum. We walked over to that house because I had remembered that old overgrown garden there. Sure enough, there were some really pretty flowers hidden in the weeds."

I had noticed those old flower beds. They lay along the side of the house.

"We picked the flowers and went home. My mum loved her bouquet, but that night I had the strangest nightmare." Mallory's voice went a bit dreamy. "In it, I was back at the house, staring up at it. In every window and doorway there were people, looking at me and holding out their bony hands. They didn't say anything, but I got the distinct feeling that they were angry with me for stealing their flowers. They wanted them back." She shivered. "Of course, I couldn't give them back – they'd already been picked and given to my mum. What a scary dream. I just remembered it today!"

We all sat there quietly. We'd succeeded in scaring ourselves silly. Kristy tried to calm us down.

"Maybe we're letting this get to us too much. You know, I showed Watson that map I found, and he said it's just a part of Stoneybrook – the part where the cemetery is now."

"I found a map, too. Remember, Kristy?" said Claud. "And at first I thought that mine showed the same thing yours did. But you know how I am at reading maps and following directions."

Charlotte spoke up in a timid voice. "Does it really matter if the house – and the town – is built on a burial ground? Everybody's still having all these weird experiences."

As usual, Charlotte had got to the heart of the matter. She may be a kid, but she's sharp.

"You're right," said Kristy. "It doesn't matter at all. There are too many other strange things going on. That's why it's time to find Mr Ronald Hennessey and pay him a visit. Any volunteers?" She raised her own hand.

We all looked at each other. Slowly, Charlotte put up her hand, so I did, too. I had to stick with her. After all, I was her babysitter. Then Claud's hand crept up, too.

"That's enough," said Kristy. "We don't want to overwhelm him. He might be ill or something."

Dawn, Mary Anne, and Mallory all looked relieved. Charlotte, Kristy, and Claud looked terrified, and I'm sure I did, too.

12th CHAPTER

Wednesday
I suppose if anything could take my mind off that scary old house it would be sitting for the Pikes. Even with Mallory there to help, it was like being in the middle of a three-ring circus. Maybe a circus would even be easier. I'd almost rather put my head in a lion's mouth than go through another dinner hour at the Pikes'! (Only kidding, Mal.)

That's okay, Dawn. I know it's a madhouse. But we had fun, too. You're not cross because you had to play the Wicked Witch, are you?

No way! I love being the Wicked Witch. "I'll get you, my pretty... and your little dog, too!" Hee hee hee.

It was Tuesday night, after our emergency club meeting, and Mallory and Dawn were sitting at the Pikes'. I do really like being an only child, but sometimes when I hear about an evening at the Pikes' I get a bit jealous. It must be fun to have a built-in gang of friends around all the time. The Pikes are: Byron, Adam, and Jordan, the triplets, who are ten; nine-year-old Vanessa; eight-year-old Nicky; seven-year-old Margo; five-year-old Claire. And, of course, Mal, Dawn's co-babysitter.

Dawn arrived at six-twenty, just as Mr and Mrs Pike were about to leave. She'd known when she accepted the job that she and Mal would have to give the kids dinner, but she'd forgotten what dinner hour at the Pike house can be like.

Mr and Mrs Pike are very good at raising a big family. They know that some things just aren't worth making a fuss about, not with eight kids to deal with. For example, meal-times. Since some kids will eat anything while others are fussy eaters, and some will eat a ton while others just pick, the Pikes have decided not to try to make many rules about what the kids do and don't have to eat. Especially when they have a sitter. When Mal is in charge, she usually just opens up the fridge and stands back. The kids rummage around, and each one finds whatever they want to eat. They call it a 'smorgasbord".

That's exactly what happened on Tuesday night. Dawn did her best to help out, but she had a hard time dealing with some of the choices the kids made. Remember, Dawn is a true health-food fanatic. So how do you think she felt when Byron pulled out the bologna sausage and a jar of grape jam and began to make a sandwich?

"Are you sure that's what you want, Byron?" she asked faintly.

"Yeah! It's my favourite," he said, carefully spreading the right amount of jam on the bread.

When he'd finished, Dawn looked around. There was Nicky, holding a jar of peanut butter.

"Okay, Nicky. Peanut butter and jam, right?" Dawn asked. She was relieved. This was a little more normal. But "normal" was not what Nicky had in mind.

"Nope. Peanut butter and bologna," he said. Dawn made a face, but she also made the sandwich. If that's what he wanted. . .

Adam and Jordan both wanted Spaghetti Rings but they refused to let Mal heat them up. They wanted to eat them straight out of the can. She convinced them to at least put their servings on plates.

Margo just wanted bread and butter for dinner. She's going through a fussy phase, and there are very few foods she'll eat.

Dawn asked Vanessa what she was having.

"A fried egg will do the trick. Butter the pan, so it won't stick," said Vanessa.

Mal groaned. Was Vanessa, who longed to be a poet, going to drive them crazy by speaking in rhyme all night?

While Dawn fried the egg, Mal helped Claire get her dinner. She wanted cereal, but it had to be in a certain bowl (the one with Big Bird on it) with a certain spoon (the one with the red handle). The milk had to be poured precisely so that it came right up to the border painted inside the bowl, and no further. Finally the bowl of cereal was just right, and Claire carried it to the table.

"Thank you, Mallory-silly-billy-goo-goo!" she called over her shoulder.

"You're welcome, Claire," said Mal, rolling her eyes. It looked as if Claire was in her "silly" mood again.

Mal made herself a ham sandwich, while Dawn checked the fridge for anything resembling health food. Finally she found a couple of carrots, a container of yogurt, and some wheat germ left over from one of Alal's cooking experiments.

"This'll do just fine," she said. "Let's sit down."

There was a mad rush for the "good" seats. Claire had already claimed Mrs Pike's Usual spot, and Margo sat next to her. The triplets jostled each other, tripping and blocking as they competed for Mr Pike's seat. While they were occupied,

Nicky slipped into it. Vanessa drifted in and seated herself daintily in Adam's usual spot but was forced to move almost immediately when he sat in her lap, pretending not to see her.

Finally, everyone was seated. Dinner had begun.

"Want some Spaghetti Rings, Nicky?" Adam asked.

"Yeah!" he answered. His face lit up. His brothers usually only paid attention to him when they were teasing him.

"You *do*?" asked Jordan. "Don't you know they're made out of worms?"

Nicky's face fell and he went back to eating his sandwich. Byron quietly offered him a bite of his sandwich, but Nicky looked at it closely and shook his head. "Worms" had reminded him of something.

"*The worms crawl in, the worms crawl out, the worms play pinochle on your snout,*" he sang, looking very cheerful again.

"Ugh!" cried Claire. She dropped her spoon into her cereal. Milk flew in all directions.

"C'mon, Nicky. We're trying to eat," said Mallory. She reached over with her serviette and wiped up some milk.

"Okay, how about this one?" he asked. "*I'm Popeye the sailor man, I live in a garbage can,*" he started.

Adam reached around Nicky and tapped him on the shoulder. Nicky stopped singing and whipped his head around to see Jordan, looking innocent. When he turned back to check on Adam, Jordan reached around to tap him on the other shoulder. Nicky looked like a spectator at a tennis match as Adam and Jordan took turns.

Dawn tried to distract them. "What shall we do tonight?" she asked.

Everybody spoke up at once. Claire wanted to play Candy Land, the only game she's old enough for. Margo thought that sounded fine, too. The triplets voted for volleyball, except for Adam, who wanted to play dodgeball. Nicky thought it would be fun to build a tent out of blankets and play Indians.

It was Vanessa, though, who came up with an idea that everyone liked. "Let's put on a play!" she said.

"Yea!"

"Let's do *Batman*!" said Byron. He loves to be the Joker.

"No, *Snow White*!" said Claire.

Dawn thought quickly. What could they do that would please everyone? "How about *The Wizard of Oz*?" she said, remembering what Kristy had said about how much her brothers and sisters liked that film.

"Great choice, Dawn," said Mallory.

"I want to be the Scarecrow!" yelled Jordan.

"I want to be the Cowardly Lion!" yelled Adam.

"I want to be the Princess!" yelled Margo.

"Princess?" asked Nicky. "I don't remember any princess in that film."

"There's always a princess, right, Mallory?" Margo looked at Mal for support.

"Sorry, not in this story," said Mallory. "But you can be the Good Witch. That's the closest thing to a princess in this play. Anyway, let's clear the table and tidy up the kitchen before we get started. And anyone who's got homework has to do it first."

When everyone was ready, they had a quick meeting to assign the rest of the parts, and then everyone ran off to put together costumes.

The house was a bit quieter for a few minutes while the actors and actresses dressed up. Downstairs, Mal and Dawn looked at each other and smiled.

"Well, at least we got through dinner," Dawn said.

Just then, the triplets slid down the banister, one after the other. Adam, as the Cowardly Lion, wore a yellow fringed bedspread tied around his shoulders. Jordan had on old jeans and a flannel shirt. He looked pretty good as the Scarecrow. Byron was the Tin Man, and his was the hardest costume to put together. He'd found a funnel to wear as a hat, and he was carrying a toy hatchet.

The rest of the cast gathered, and Dawn and Mal were given parts, too. Dawn was the Wicked Witch, and Mal was the Wizard. By the time everyone was onstage, they realized that there were no people left over to be an audience, but by then it was too late.

Vanessa, as Dorothy, carried her schoolbook bag instead of a picnic basket. Nicky, who was playing Toto, trotted along beside her. Vanessa pretended to step out of a house. "Come on out, Toto, close the door. We're not in Kansas any more," she rhymed.

"Woof, woof," said Nicky.

Claire did a short rendition of the Munchkin song, with lots of added "silly-billy-goo-goos".

Then Byron stepped out. "Hi, Dorothy! We'll come with you. Don't cry. Here are my friends, the Scarecrow and the Cowardly Lion."

"Oh, good," said Vanessa, forgetting to rhyme for once. "But how will we get to the Emerald City?"

"I'll take you in my spaceship," said Margo, as the Good Witch.

"We're off to see the Lizard!" sang Jordan.

This was getting a little off the track, but Dawn and Mal hid their smiles and went along with it. Dawn made a truly scary Wicked Witch until Claire started to cry. Then Dawn used "magic" to turn herself into another good witch.

Halfway down the Yellow Brick Road, Nicky got bored with playing Toto. After all, he had no lines except for, "Woof, woof." "Want to hear me count to one thousand by twos?" he asked. Nobody answered – they were all busy just then – so he just started chanting. "Two, four, six. . ."

At the end of the play, Mal, as the Wizard, solved everyone's problems. She declared that it was bedtime in Oz. Nicky had got up to 782 by then, but he was winding down and didn't insist on finishing.

The cast members gave themselves a big round of applause, since there was no audience to do it for them. Then Dawn took Margo, Claire, and Nicky upstairs to get ready for bed. Mal and the older kids tidied up the living room, which looked as if that tornado really *had* been through it.

By the time Dawn got the younger Pikes to bed, Mr and Mrs Pike were home. Dawn and Mallory shook hands solemnly and congratulated each other on making it through the evening. Then Mr Pike walked Dawn home. She breathed a huge sigh of relief as she entered her quiet old house.

13th CHAPTER

Charlotte and I got home from school at about the same time on Wednesday afternoon. I could see straight away that she was as nervous as I was about going to see Mr Hennessey.

"Are you sure you want to go, Charlotte?" I asked. "You don't *have* to do this, you know." I wondered if this thing was completely out of hand. Was I so involved with this mystery that I was forgetting to be a responsible babysitter?

But Charlotte, although she *was* a little scared, was also very determined to do everything she could to help solve the mystery. There was no way she was going to give up now.

We headed over to Claud's, where we'd planned to meet Kristy, who arrived at the same time we did. Claudia opened the door before we even had a chance to knock. It seemed as if we were all eager to get going, so we set off for Stoneybrook Manor.

It took us a while to get there – it was a longer walk than I'd thought. We didn't talk much along the way. I suppose we were both busy with our own thoughts. Finally we stood on the pavement in front of the nursing home. It was a new-ish building, but it had a nice homely feeling about it. It was all on one storey, and there were lots of pretty plants and flowers along the front and bordering the path to the main entrance. A few elderly men sat in wheelchairs on a patio area to the left, playing chess.

After a few minutes passed with all of us just standing there, Kristy took the lead. "C'mon, let's go in," she said, and she walked up the path. The rest of us followed her. She stopped and waited for us at the front door. We walked in together, looking round the lobby. How were we supposed to find Mr Hennessey? Then a young man stood up from the desk where he'd been sitting. "How may I help you?" he asked.

That was when I noticed the sign that a trailing plant had hidden: RECEPTION DESK. None of us said anything for a moment. I thought the man might tell us to get lost when we told him what we wanted. After all, we were just a bunch of kids. Finally, Claud spoke up.

"We're here to see a Mr Ronald Hennessey. I understand that he is a resident here," she said. I think she was trying to sound like her heroine, Nancy Drew. The "girl detective" usually talks like that when she's on a case.

The man behind the desk gave us a big smile. "Why, how nice for Mr Hennessey to have some young visitors," he said. He turned to a woman who was working at the desk next to his. "Ruth, can you bring Mr Hennessey to the lounge?"

Well, this was easier than I'd thought. I looked at my fellow "detectives". Kristy seemed relieved, but Claud and Charlotte still looked nervous.

"Would you girls sign the guest register?" asked the receptionist. He gestured to a large book on a stand next to his desk. We signed in, each of us filling in our name, address, and phone number. Claud used her pink fluorescent pen that she loves. For some reason that made me want to giggle, but I held it in. Then we walked over to the lounge area and sat down to wait. We didn't talk much. Claud fiddled with her charm bracelet, Kristy twirled her hair around a finger, and Charlotte sat and stared at the other people in the lounge until I signalled to her to stop.

After about ten minutes, Ruth returned, pushing an old man in a wheelchair. And when I say old, I mean *old*. He was all shrivelled up – he looked about the size of a ten-year-old – and hunched over. He had a blanket over his legs, and he wore a heavy sweater, even though it didn't seem all that cool in the building. I saw hearing aids in both of his ears. His hands, the papery skin covered with brown spots, lay on his lap, picking at the blanket. But his eyes looked bright as he focused on each of us in turn. He cleared his throat and looked straight at me.

"What's your name, young lady? And what do you want with Ronald Hennessey?" His voice sounded rusty, as if he hadn't used it much lately.

"I . . . I'm . . . Stacey McGill." I finally got it out. "And these are my friends Claudia, Kristy, and Charlotte."

He nodded at each of them, but he didn't smile. He didn't seem all that delighted with his "young visitors". He looked back at me. I realized that I hadn't told him yet why we were there.

"Mr Hennessey, we came to ask you about the old house on Elm Street. Didn't you once own it?" I asked. I thought we might as well keep on going, as long as we were there.

"Own it? Yes, I owned it. Lived there all my life. Born in the east bedroom," he said shortly. "What about it?"

"Well, we've been noticing some strange things happening there lately," I said. "Ever since they started to tear the house down."

"Oh?" he said. He was still acting

grumpy, but I thought I could see a spark in his eyes all of a sudden. We'd got him interested. "Strange things? Like what?"

"We've heard odd noises," I said.

"And we've seen some scary things, too!" added Charlotte.

We started to tell him the story from the beginning, and I could see him perk up as he listened.

"And Charlotte and I both had awful nightmares about the house, on the same night," I told him, and then Claud chipped in with her story about feeling a hand on her arm.

"I have to tell you girls that none of this surprises me," said Mr Hennessey. "I lived in that house for almost eighty years, and I couldn't begin to tell you all the things that happened there. But I loved the house just the same. I'd never have sold it but for the fact that I know I'll never be able to live there again by myself. I'm just not able to get up and down those stairs any more."

Looking at him, we could see that it was more than just stairs that kept him from living alone. He didn't look capable of taking care of himself any longer. He was frail and tired and very, very old. But what kinds of things was he remembering about the house? I asked him to tell us more.

"Well," he said, "the very first thing I remember was when I was just a lad in short trousers. I was seven or eight years old, I suppose. I woke up in the middle of the night to the sound of very heavy footsteps. Someone was pacing in the corridor outside my room. I crept out of my bed and peeped through the door, which was open a crack. What a funny-looking man! He wore the strangest old-fashioned clothes, and his nose . . . well, his nose looked as if it was made of rubber! I stifled a giggle, and he turned and glared at me. I drew back. I was very afraid.

"Later I learned that this man was a ghost, a ghost who went by the name of Old Rubbernose. When he was living, a horse had bitten off his nose, and the town doctor had fashioned a new one out of rubber. Children laughed at Old Rubbernose, and women spurned him. He died a lonely, sad, and bitter man, and it was said that he would never rest until he found a mortal woman who would love him despite his disfigurement. He may be pacing still!"

We were all leaning forward to hear every word of his story. I was fascinated and terrified, all at the same time. Could he be telling the truth? Old Rubbernose? I looked at Claud. She raised her eyebrows. Mr Hennessey started another story.

"And then there was the time my Uncle James came to visit. One morning he told us about a beautiful woman with red hair who was wearing a green velvet dress. She came into his room with a lit candle and bade him follow her. He got out of bed, but as he followed her out of the door and down the hall, she became more and more transparent and finally disappeared. The rest of us never saw her, but every time Uncle James came to visit she would turn up. I suppose she'd taken a liking to him."

That story sounded as if it was out of one of those books Dawn likes to read all the time. One was called *Stories NOT to Be Read After Dark*. Was Mr Hennessey for real?

He told us a few other stories about the house, one involving a man who carried his own head around and another about an attic door that wouldn't stay shut until a spirit was put to rest. His eyes were really sparkling now. It was obvious that he was enjoying his "young visitors" after all. Kristy caught my eye and shrugged. I knew that the others were as doubtful as I was about some of these stories. But then Mr Hennessey said something that really grabbed our attention.

"I suppose that all of these events had a single cause," he said. "All those restless spirits . . . they were all justly unhappy because a town had been built over their graves. And if Old Rubbernose had ever killed us all in our beds, it would have been because he was angry with us for building a house right on top of his grave."

I gasped. We hadn't told Mr Hennessey about the maps Kristy and Claud had found. Could all his stories be true after all? None of us were able to say a word. I noticed that Claud was white as a sheet.

"I think we should respect those spirits. I don't blame them one bit for being upset about having their graves disturbed," Mr Hennessey went on. "All they want is to rest peacefully, with grass and sky over them. But then a house is built over them. And, if that wasn't enough, the house has to be torn apart and the earth around it defiled! It's no wonder they've been reacting as they have."

"Are – are you saying that my neighbourhood is *haunted*?" I asked.

"Well, missy, I can't say for sure," he answered. "But you'll know once the house is finally torn down."

That was supposed to happen the next day! What did he mean? What was going to happen?

"*How* will I know?" I whispered. I could hardly speak.

Mr Hennessey wouldn't answer. Kristy, Claud, and Charlotte just sat and gaped at him. I asked him again.

He shook his head. "Sometimes people are safer not knowing," he said. "I'd stay away from that house. I don't like the sound of what you've seen and heard there." He stopped with that and wouldn't say another word about the house.

I felt frustrated and more scared than

ever. But Mr Hennessey looked tired all of a sudden, so we decided it was time to leave. I thanked him, and he nodded wearily and raised his hand in a wave. "Just be careful," he said.

Once again, we didn't get much done at our club meeting later that day. Of course we answered the phone and arranged jobs and everything – nothing gets in the way of that – but that was about it. We spent the rest of the time talking about the house, and about Mr Hennessey's stories. Claud did a great rendition of the "Old Rubbernose" story – in fact, she really had us laughing for a few minutes. But by the time Charlotte and I walked home from the meeting, I wasn't laughing any more. Mr Hennessey's words echoed in my mind. "Just be careful." It was a warning.

14th CHAPTER

The next day was Thursday, the day the house was scheduled to come down. I didn't get much sleep at all on Wednesday night. Neither did Charlotte, judging by how bleary-eyed she looked at breakfast that morning. Once again I sleepwalked through all my classes that day. Maybe it was a good thing that the house was coming down at last. If this went on much longer, my grades might really suffer. Lately I just couldn't concentrate on anything but that house.

Charlotte and I had talked it over seriously and decided that we would pay attention to Mr Hennessey's warning. We would not go and watch as the house was torn down. Maybe Mr Hennessey was a bit mad – or senile – but it didn't matter to us. We didn't know *what* might happen when the house was knocked down, and we didn't plan to be there to find out. Our nightmares had been scary enough; we didn't need the real thing.

We were sitting on the front steps of my house, trying to talk about anything *but* the house, when we noticed that there seemed to be more traffic than usual on my street. Kids went by on bikes and skateboards. Mums pushed prams. Older kids cruised by in their cars. Everybody was heading in the same direction. I suppose the demolition of the old house was a big event in Stoneybrook. Everybody wanted to be there.

Including Charlotte. "Stacey, why can't we go if everybody else is going?" she asked. "Let's go. Please?"

Part of the reason I'd decided to stay at home was for Charlotte's sake. I'd been behaving less than responsibly towards her, exposing her to all these scary stories and everything. At least that's how I was beginning to feel. But if she really wanted to go, maybe we should, I thought. Anyway, what could happen with such a big crowd of people around?

"Okay, Charlotte. We might as well go," I said. I took her hand and we set off down the street to join the party.

As we got closer to the house, I started to see people I knew. I saw Suzi and Buddy Barrett standing on the corner together. They waved to us. All the Pike kids were there. They made a crowd all by themselves. The triplets were playing Tag with some other kids, and I heard Nicky teasing Claire by singing *his* version of "The Wheels on the Bus". He sang, "*The wheels on the bus go back and forth, back and forth . . .*" Then, "*The wipers on the bus go round and round, round and round. . .*" Mallory, who was keeping an eye on her brothers and sisters, made him stop when Claire started to cry.

Mary Anne was there with Jenny Prezzioso, whom she was sitting for that day. Jenny was dressed up for the occasion, which was nothing new. Jenny is always dressed up. She had on a white frilly dress with a pink pinafore over it. Her tights had rosebuds on them and she wore white party shoes with big pink bows on them. Charlotte stared at her while Mary Anne and I said hello. Jenny looked back at Charlotte and preened a little.

"Do you like my most beautiful new dress?" she asked coyly.

Charlotte seemed unsure of what to say, so I spoke up. "It's very nice, Jenny. I hope it won't get dirty, though, while you watch the house get torn down." Maybe one day Mrs Prezzioso will start dressing Jenny like a normal kid.

Charlotte was waving at someone. I looked in that direction and saw Claud, with Myriah and Gabbie in tow. They looked excited by the action. It *was* exciting. It was like a fair or something, with all these people milling around. Some adults were there, too. I saw a woman who works at the bank talking to our postman.

Then I heard someone calling my name and turned around just in time to see Kristy drive by with her brothers Charlie and Sam. They parked, and she came over to stand with me and Charlotte.

"This is the big day, right, Stacey?" she said. "I wonder if Mr Hennessey's stories were true. Soon we'll know for certain."

Just then the workmen came out of the house. I think they'd been making some last-minute preparations. One of them got into the operator's seat of a crane nearby and turned it towards the house. The big wrecking ball swung forward and crashed into the uppermost tower. This was it!

The ball kept swinging and the crowd hushed as we all watched the house start to crumble before our eyes. Charlotte held my hand tightly. The few windows that were left in the house shattered as the ball shook the building. The porch railing finally let go entirely and fell off into the weeds below. It wasn't long before the whole of the second storey was gone, and it was clear that the rest of the job would go quickly. I started to calm down. It looked as though nothing was going to happen after all.

Boy, was I wrong. Just then, I saw something *very* awful. The house – what was left of it – suddenly went up in flames. The fire crackled and roared as it engulfed the wreckage. I looked around, terrified. What should we do? But everybody was just standing there, looking slightly bored. Kristy had wandered off to talk to Sam. Charlotte was watching one of the workmen pack his tools away into his truck. Nobody else seemed to see the fire!

I turned back to check again. Maybe I'd been imagining things once more. But the flames were even higher by now. Smoke curled up as the fire moved quickly through the tumbledown structure. And then, just as in my dream, I saw a figure. It was calling for help. It looked like an old, old man. Was it – could it be – Mr Hennessey? I couldn't believe my eyes. Just as in my dream, my feet were rooted to the ground. I wanted to help, but what could I do? Then I felt Charlotte tugging at my hand.

"Let's go, Stacey," she said. "This is getting kind of boring. Nothing weird's happened at all. I suppose there wasn't really any mystery after all. Mr Hennessey probably *is* just a crazy old man."

I shook my head, trying to clear my thoughts. What was going on? When I looked at the house again, there was no fire. But I had a terrible feeling in the pit of my stomach, and it had to do with Mr Hennessey. I felt as if he needed help, and it was up to me to go to him. It was the weirdest feeling, let me tell you, but it was overwhelming and I couldn't ignore it.

I dragged Charlotte over to where Claud stood with Myriah and Gabbie. "Claud, can you watch Charlotte for a little while? I've got to go and see Mr Hennessey right now," I said breathlessly. She must have thought I was nuts, but she just nodded. I knelt down and gave Charlotte a hug. "Be good, Char. I'll be back soon," I said.

I took off for Stoneybrook Manor, running until I got a stitch in my side, then walking, then running some more. I still didn't understand exactly why I felt I had to go there, but the feeling was stronger than ever. It seemed to take ages to reach the home, but finally I stood on the pavement, just as I had yesterday, looking at Stoneybrook Manor. I took a deep breath, walked up the path, and pushed open the door. The man at the reception desk rose from his seat as I approached.

"How may I help you?" he asked, just as he had yesterday. I could see that he didn't remember me.

"I . . . I'm here to see Mr Ronald Hennessey, please," I said. I was still breathing hard from all that running.

The man's eyes lit up. He did remember me! But then a sad look came over his face. He walked round his desk and put his hand on my shoulder. He looked straight into my eyes and said, "I'm so sorry. Mr Hennessey passed away just last night."

15th CHAPTER

I was in shock. Mr Hennessey was dead! I just couldn't believe it.

And I couldn't say a word. I must have looked pretty silly. Finally, someone spoke. "Aren't you Stacey McGill?" It was the woman, Ruth, who had wheeled Mr Hennessey out to see us.

"Mr Hennessey couldn't stop talking about you after you left," she said. "He was very pleased to make your acquaintance. He left this note for you." She pulled a folded piece of paper out of her pocket and handed it to me.

I took the note and thanked her. Then I walked over to the lounge and sat down to read it. Sure enough, my name was on the outside of the paper. *"Miss Stacey McGill"* it said, in an old-fashioned-looking script. I opened it up.

"Dear Miss McGill," I read. *"I hope to be*

able to tell you this in person, but if for some reason I cannot, this letter will serve my purpose."

It was almost as if he'd known he was going to die! I read some more.

"I enjoyed our brief meeting. You and your friends brought a moment of interest and a spark of fun to a lonely old man's life. In fact, I'm afraid that I must confess to being a bit carried away with your 'mystery'."

What was he saying?

"I sincerely hope that my tall tales did not disturb you too greatly. And, to set the record straight, there was not one grain of truth in any of them! I know that children your age love a mystery, but please don't be too sad that this one is over. That old house was nothing but a lovely and comfortable home for my family and me."

The note went on for a few more lines, but that was his basic message. There was no mystery after all. I felt relieved, but I was a little sad that it was all over. And I definitely felt sad that Mr Hennessey was gone. He seemed to have known all about what we were going through, without our even having to tell him. Now we'd never know the whole truth about the house.

I walked slowly out of the lobby and up the path. The honking of a car horn made me look up. Kristy waved at me from the backseat of Charlie's car.

"We came to pick you up, Stace!" she

called. "Claudia told us you were here."

I was glad to see them, and not just because I wouldn't have to walk home now. I still felt shaky, and it was good to see familiar faces and have someone to talk to. I climbed into the backseat. Charlie started the car and we drove off.

I told Kristy about Mr Hennessey. Then I showed her the note. She read it and smiled. "I knew it," she said. "Oh, well, it was fun while it lasted."

"But Kristy, what about all the weird things that happened to me and Charlotte?" I asked. "And to Claud and Mal? We still don't know how to explain them."

"Listen to what Charlie and Sam have to say about that," she said.

It turned out that Sam and Charlie had spent some time talking with the workmen once the house was demolished. The workmen had explained the whole process they'd gone through in taking it down, and a lot of other things got explained along the way. Charlie and Sam had heard about our "mystery" from Kristy, so they were especially interested in clearing up some of the strange things we'd seen and heard.

"That moaning sound *was* the pipes, Stacey," said Charlie, looking at me in the rear-view mirror. "The plumbing was ancient, and it took those men ages to get it out intact. But the Historical Society insisted."

Sam turned to smile at me. "And you know that fire you and Charlotte saw? Well, there was one workman who stayed behind that day. He was using an acetylene torch to loosen the bathtub from its fittings. It must have been his face you saw at the window that first day, too."

Kristy was grinning. "And remember those yucky flies that reminded you of that film?" she said. "That was a swarm of bees whose hive had been disturbed by those men. You're lucky you didn't get stung!"

I listened to everything they said, and it was clearer and clearer that *all* the members of the Babysitters Club had let their imaginations work overtime. I suppose we sort of enjoyed being scared. But there was still one mystery left. Why had I seen the house go up in flames when it was being knocked down? I suppose I had just been imagining things again, remembering my nightmare. I decided to forget about that "fire". If I told Kristy now, she'd think I was mad!

Kristy and I decided not to tell the others all the details that Charlie and Sam had told us. The mystery was over, but we didn't have to spoil the fun for everyone else!

I asked Charlie to drop me off at the Perkinses' so I could pick up Charlotte. "Thanks for the ride," I called as I hopped out.

Claud was sitting on the front porch with Gabbie, Myriah, and Charlotte. She was reading to the girls from a book of fairy tales. They all looked up as I crossed the lawn. Then Charlotte hugged me.

"Hi, Char," I said. "Ready to go?" I looked over at Claud. She looked back at me curiously, but I just shook my head slightly, so she'd know that I didn't want to talk about anything just then. We've been best friends for so long now that it doesn't take much to get an idea across.

"Thanks, Claud," I said.

Charlotte started to ask about my trip to Stoneybrook Manor, but I gave her a vague answer and then got her off the track by reminding her of what was going to happen in just a little while. "Charlotte, let's go back to my house. Guess who'll be there really soon?"

"My parents!" she yelled, remembering. "They're coming to get me today! 'Bye, Gabbie! 'Bye, Myriah! 'Bye, Claudia!" She grabbed my arm, pulling me down the street.

Charlotte and I spent the rest of the afternoon packing up her belongings. Then we played a few games of Snap while we waited for her parents to arrive. A couple of times she brought up the house and the "mystery", but I steered the conversation away from those topics.

We'd just got started on our fourth game of Snap (after that week I hoped I'd never play it again) when we heard a car pull into the drive, honking. We ran to the window.

Sure enough, it was the Johanssens. Charlotte tore down the stairs, flung open the front door, and raced into their arms.

"Mummy! Daddy! Guess what? I got to go to the Babysitters Club meetings. And we had a mystery and it was really scary! And I was ill, very ill, but now I'm better, and Stacey took good care of me!" She was bubbling over with all her news. Charlotte was definitely proud of herself for having survived a whole week without her parents.

Dr Johanssen and I smiled at each other over Charlotte's head. Charlotte went on chattering about the old house and the mysterious noises we'd heard and the scary things we'd seen. I helped Mr Johanssen pack Charlotte's things into the already jammed backseat. As we juggled suitcases around to make everything fit, I quietly told him not to be concerned about Charlotte's "mystery of Stoneybrook" tales.

"We thought there was a big mystery, but there wasn't really much of one in the end," I said. "And it was scary at times, but it was *fun* scary, like a film. I think Charlotte liked having a mystery to solve. It took her mind off missing you."

He told me that he understood. Then he thanked me for taking such good care of Charlotte. I told him it had been my pleasure. It really had, too!

Charlotte came over to give me a big hug. It was time for her to go home. I reached into my pocket and handed her a tiny package. "This is for you, Char. But don't open it until you get home," I said. It was a couple of hairslides – glow-in-the-dark hairslides. Claud had got a pair for her last birthday, and we'd all thought they were so cool. I knew Charlotte would love them.

I hugged her one more time and then helped her into the backseat. Mr Johanssen started the car and backed down the drive. I stood and waved until they disappeared.

When I went back into the house, it seemed awfully quiet and still. I went to the guest room. It looked neat and tidy and empty. I missed my "little sister".

Mum and I had a quiet dinner that night. As I was finishing the dishes, the phone rang. It was Charlotte.

"I miss you," she said. "I wish you were here to read *Charlotte's Web* to me."

She sounded sad, but I knew she must be glad to be home with her parents, too. She told me that she loved the hairslides and that she planned to wear them to school the next day. She told me all about her grandpa and how much better he was feeling. We talked for a long time, and we didn't mention our "mystery" once. Finally, it was time to say goodbye.

"I have to go to bed now, Stacey," said Charlotte. "Good night, big sister!'

I felt sad, but I smiled and said, "Good night, little sister. Love ya!"

The Babysitters Club

JESSI'S BABYSITTER

This book is dedicated
to the memory of
Eugene Dougherty,
who taught me how to
make writing exciting.

1st CHAPTER

"*Plié* first pozeetion, *plié* second pozeetion – nice and slowly – *plié* sird pozeetion, *plié* fourse pozeetion – *veeerry* slowly – *plié* fifs pozeetion . . . and . . . stop. . . Non, non, non!" cried Madame Noelle. "Do not fall to zee floor. Come to a nice, graceful stop like zee lovely ballerinas you are. Now, once again."

We *pliéed* in all the pozeetions again and then came to a nice, graceful stop, even though I – and every other pupil in my class – just wanted to lie down and sleep for a week. We had been working hard.

I am Jessica Ramsey, otherwise known as Jessi. I am eleven years old. I'm in the sixth grade at Stoneybrook Middle School (SMS). In case you can't tell, I am also a dancer. (Or as Madame Noelle would say, a doncer.) I live in Stoneybrook, Connecticut, but I have ballet lessons at a special school in Stamford, another Connecticut town (actually, a city), which isn't too far from home.

Ballet is a very important part of my life. Maybe I'll go to a dance school in New York City. Maybe I'll even become a professional dancer.

Class ended that day when my friends and I didn't keel over after the last round of pliés. We changed out of our toe shoes (I am proud to say that I can dance *en pointe*), and slipped jeans or skirts over our leotards. Then we waited for our parents to pick us up.

Usually my mum comes to get me, but that day I waited and waited. Finally, fifteen minutes after everyone else had left, my dad drove up. He works in Stamford, but my lessons usually end long before he's ready to leave the office.

I ran to his car.

"Daddy!" I cried. "How come *you're* picking me up? Where's Mama? Has something happened to Becca or Squirt?"

Becca is my younger sister. She's eight. Squirt is my baby brother. His real name is John Philip Ramsey, Jr., but since he was the smallest baby in the hospital when he was born, the nurses started calling him Squirt. And the name stuck, even though now Squirt is the same size as most other toddlers his age.

Daddy smiled at me. "Don't worry," he

said, as I slid into the front seat of the car. "Everyone's fine. I decided to leave work early today, so I phoned your mother and told her I'd bring you home. It would be silly for her to make the trip when I'm already here."

"Why'd you leave early?" I wanted to know. And just then a smell (well, not a smell; a wonderful chocolaty aroma) drifted to me. I turned round and saw a white cake box on the back seat. "Hey, what's that?"

"You're certainly full of questions today," remarked Daddy. "Let's see. I left early because we have something to celebrate tonight, and the box on the back seat is part of the celebration."

"A celebration? Oh, goody!" I cried, reaching for the box.

"No peeking," said Daddy.

"But I want to see what's in there."

"The celebration is a surprise. You'll find out all about it after dinner."

I couldn't help guessing. "You've been promoted!" I exclaimed.

Daddy shook his head.

"You've got a pay rise."

"Nope."

"We're moving back to New Jersey?"

I wasn't quite as excited by that idea. The funny thing is, a few months ago, I would have jumped at the chance to leave Stoneybrook and return to Oakley, New Jersey, the town in which I grew up. My family and I had been happy there. We are black, and our neighbourhood, school, and even my ballet school in Oakley were all mixed up – black people and white people, living and working together. Also, my relatives lived nearby. One of my cousins, Keisha, was my best friend. When Daddy's company offered him a better job in Stamford, he jumped at the chance. But it meant we had to move. I didn't want to leave Oakley. But I wasn't prepared for what would greet us in Stoneybrook – prejudice, that's what. We moved to a town with only a few black residents. I am the only black pupil in the entire sixth grade. People teased my family. People said nasty things to us. People ignored us.

At first.

Slowly, though, a change came about. I made some friends. They became good friends. Becca and I each made a best friend. Now I can't imagine going back to Oakley. I'd have to leave too many memories behind – like my babysitting adventures. Or the time our whole school went on a trip to a ski lodge in Vermont. Or the time my friends and I went to summer camp.

But luckily Daddy said, "No, we're not moving."

Then it hit me. "You're having a baby, aren't you? You and Mama are having a *baby*! Oh, I hope it's another boy. Then our family would be even. Two girls, two boys."

Daddy chuckled. "It's not a new baby, either," he said. "And why don't you stop guessing? I'm afraid I'll give it away if you really do guess it."

"Okay," I said, but I continued guessing in my head. We'd won the lottery. We were going on a trip to Disney World – or maybe even Texas. I had always wanted to see Texas. Then I got another idea. I bet Mama and Daddy really were having a baby, but Daddy was too clever to let on.

All the way to Stoneybrook, I hugged the secret to myself. As soon as Daddy parked the car in the drive, I ran inside and straight up to Becca's room.

"Guess what! Guess what!" I cried.

Becca looked up from her third-grade homework. "What?"

"Daddy's brought a cake home and he says we're celebrating something tonight, but he won't say what. You know what I think, though? I think Mama and Daddy are going to have another baby!"

"You *do*?" Becca's eyes widened.

"Yup. I really do."

I was wrong. After dinner that evening, Daddy brought out the cake. When he had cut it and served it, he said, "We have something wonderful to celebrate."

I glanced at Becca. She glanced back, trying not to smile.

"Your mother—" Daddy began.

"I knew it! I knew it!" I cried.

"You knew that your mother's found a job?" Daddy asked me.

Mama's got a job?" I repeated.

Mama was grinning away at the end of the dining room table. "That's right," she said. It's time for me to go back to work. I was in advertising before you girls were born, and at last I can go back to that. I'm really looking forward to it. My job starts on Monday. Five days a week. Nine to five, probably longer days every now and then."

Becca and I knew how important this was to Mama, so we cheered, jumped up from our places at the table, and ran to hug her.

Then I said, settling down again, "Boy, I suppose you'll really need me to babysit now. I'll take care of Becca and Squirt every afternoon that I can. But who will look after Squirt while I'm at school? And who will babysit while I'm at my dance lessons? And, hey! Who will *drive* me to my ballet class?"

Mama and Daddy exchanged a look. I didn't like the look of it.

"What?" I asked. "What is it?"

"Well," Daddy began, and cleared his throat, "your mother will need more than just a sitter. She won't have time to shop or cook or do the housework. So . . . um . . . so your Aunt Cecelia is going to move in. In a couple of weeks."

"Aunt Cecelia!" cried Becca and I at the same time. "Nooo!"

Aunt Cecelia is absolutely awful. I can't tell you how many things are wrong with her. She may be Daddy's older sister, but she smells funny. Bad perfume, probably. And she's bossy and mean and thinks Mama and Daddy aren't bringing up Becca and Squirt and me properly. She thinks they let us run wild, which couldn't be further from the truth. What happened was that not long ago, Mama and Daddy went away on a three-day weekend. They left me in charge, since we had a mini-holiday from school. It was the first time I'd been allowed to babysit overnight. Unfortunately, Becca had been invited to go sailing on Saturday – and the boats got caught in a storm, and Becca and the others were stranded on an island off the coast of Connecticut for two days. No one knew where they were. Aunt Cecelia came to stay until the crisis was over, and she was appalled that Mama and Daddy had left me in charge of Becca and Squirt.

She thought something was seriously wrong with our family.

I think she also wanted a family to live with, since her husband had died recently, and she was all alone in the house she'd moved to in Queenstown, Connecticut. After that she found that she couldn't bear to stay in her home in Oakley. The house had too many memories.

This is my Aunt Cecelia: bossy, strict, mean.

Becca and I cannot stand her. And now she would be *living* with us. She would be caring for Squirt, cooking, and helping with the housework. She would also be . . . my babysitter. I'm far too old and responsible to need a babysitter. After all, I'm a sitter myself.

But Aunt Cecelia doesn't trust me. She thinks it was my fault that Becca got lost at sea, even though Mama and Daddy gave Becca permission to go on the sailing trip.

When the "celebration" was over, Becca and I huddled in my room.

"Can you *believe* this?" I asked her. "Aunt Cecelia coming here. Moving *in*. This is a nightmare."

"A triple nightmare," agreed Becca. "Maybe we could talk Mama and Daddy out of letting her come."

"I don't think so," I said. "But I bet we could fix it so that Aunt Cecelia wouldn't want to stay once she got here. You know, put shaving cream in her slippers, a fake spider on her pillow."

"Honey in her hairbrush!" cried Becca.

"Shh!" I hissed. "That's a great idea, but keep your voice down. We don't want Mama and Daddy to know what we're up to."

2nd CHAPTER

Becca and I plotted about a dozen ways to get Aunt Cecelia to leave. Most of them were very mean. We wrote them on a list, which I hid way back in my desk drawer.

Then Becca left.

I sat on my bed and felt depressed for a while. Then I did what I always do in a tough situation.

I called my best friend, Mallory Pike.

Ring, ring went the Pikes' phone.

"Hello?" said a voice. It was Nicky, Mal's brother. (Mal has *seven* younger brothers and sisters.)

"Hi, Nicky. It's Jessi. Is Mal home?"

"Yup."

"Well, can I speak to her, please?"

"Maybe."

"*Nicky.*"

"Okay, okay, okay. . . Oh, wait a second. I've just remembered. Mal isn't here after all. She went to the shops with Mum."

"Could you ask her to call me back, please?" I asked. "I really need to talk to her. This is a matter of life and death . . . sort of."

"Life and death?" repeated Nicky. "Gosh."

We got off the phone. I went back to my room. I closed the door. Then I opened my door again and hung a sign on it that I'd made. The sign read (in big bold letters):

KEEP OUT (please)
THIS MEANS YOU
PRIVACY NEEDED
(THANK YOU FOR YOUR COOPERATION)

Mallory thinks the sign is silly. She says that if you want people to stay out of your room, you should put up a sign that just says: STAY OUT OR ELSE.

I think one reason Mal is my best friend is because I like her family. The Pikes are very open and relaxed. There aren't too many rules in the Pike house, even though there are a lot of kids. Here's who's in Mal's family, besides Mal and her parents: Byron, Adam, and Jordan, who are *identical triplets* (they're ten years old); Vanessa, who's nine, very dreamy, and wants to be a poet; Nicky, who's eight, and gets pushed around by his big brothers; Margo, who's seven, and likes to tease; and Claire, who's five, the baby of the family, and seems to be stuck in a silly stage. She calls everybody "silly-billy-goo-goo".

At the Pikes', something is always going on. With eight kids, I suppose that's not surprising. Anyway, Mal's household certainly is different from mine. Even so, Mallory and I are alike in many ways. We're both the oldest in our families, but we feel that our parents won't let us grow up fast enough. We practically had to kick and scream in order to be allowed to get our ears pierced. Then Mal, who wears glasses, asked if she could have contact lenses, but her parents said no. They think she's too young. (Furthermore, Mal now has a brace, so she isn't feeling particularly pretty these days, despite her pierced ears.) As for me, well, talk about being treated like a baby. Now Aunt Cecelia was going to move in. I would have a *baby*sitter – and I'm a sitter myself!

Mal and I also have some good things in common. We both love reading. Our favourite books are horse stories, especially the ones by Marguerite Henry, such as *Misty of Chincoteague* and *Stormy, Misty's Foal*. Mal likes to write, too. She's kept a journal for years and recently talked me into keeping one as well.

However, we do have our differences. As

you know, I want to be a ballerina one day (I think), but Mal wants to be an author and illustrator of children's books. The other difference is pretty obvious, I suppose – our looks. Mal is white, with red hair and freckles, and she's about average height. I'm black, with long eyelashes (Mama is jealous of them) and long, *long* legs. I'm lucky to have those legs for dancing.

I'm also lucky to have found a best friend in Stoneybrook, especially after leaving Keisha behind in Oakley, but I feel even luckier to have made other friends as well. It's always nice to have a group of friends, I thought, as I settled down for a good daydream. And my group of friends are the members of the Babysitters Club.

I suppose I haven't mentioned the BSC yet, have I? Well, the BSC consists of seven girls who have a business doing babysitting in our neighbourhoods. We meet three times a week and get lots of sitting jobs. Mal and I are both members – junior officers. We feel honoured to be part of the club, because the other members are all thirteen-year-old eighth-graders.

Kristy Thomas is the club chairman. Her family is as big as the Pikes', but it's much more complicated. Let's see. How do I even begin to tell you about her family? I suppose I should start a year or so ago when Kristy was living in Bradford Court in the house she'd grown up in. She lived with her mum;

her older brothers, Sam and Charlie; and her little brother, David Michael. Her father walked out on her family not long after David Michael was born. Kristy rarely heard from him. (She still doesn't.) Anyway, the summer after the seventh grade, Kristy's mum married this man she'd been going out with. His name is Watson Brewer and he's a millionaire. Honestly. Watson moved Kristy's family into his mansion across town. That was when things began getting confusing. Watson has two children (Karen, who's seven, and Andrew, who's four) from his first marriage. Karen and Andrew live with their father every other weekend. Then, not long ago, the Brewers adopted Emily Michelle, a two-year-old Vietnamese girl. And *then*, Nannie, Kristy's grandmother, moved in to help take care of Emily Michelle. (Nannie is not a bit like Aunt Cecelia. She's nice.) The Brewers also have a dog and a cat.

Kristy is nice but bossy. She's a tomboy, and she coaches a team of little kids who like to play softball. She's *full* of ideas. (She started the Babysitters Club.) Kristy is also a bit immature compared to her friends. She's not very interested in clothes yet, she *never* wears make-up, and she doesn't like boys particularly. But she does like a boy in her neighbourhood! His name is Bart and he's very nice.

Kristy's best friend is Mary Anne Spier,

the secretary of the club. Kristy and Mary Anne are similar to Mal and me in that they're very alike in some ways and very different in others. For one thing, they look a little alike. They both have brown eyes and brown hair and are short. (Kristy is shorter.) And Mary Anne used to dress in a babyish way, but now she cares much more about clothes than she used to. I think the similarities end there. Mary Anne is quiet and shy – although she's the only one of us to have a steady boyfriend. Her boyfriend is Logan Bruno, and he's actually part of the BSC, but I'll explain how later. Mary Anne's family used to be as different from Kristy's as you could imagine, but now it has changed. Mary Anne's mum died when Mary Anne was really little, so Mary Anne grew up an only child living with her dad, who was quite strict. Then Mr Spier met an old high-school girlfriend of his (who was divorced by then), and after a pretty long time, they finally got married. Guess who the girlfriend was – the mother of Dawn Schafer, another club member, and Mary Anne's other best friend. Dawn, her brother, and her mum had moved back to Stoneybrook (they'd been living in California) after the Schafers' divorce. Dawn and Mary Anne became friends, then their parents began going out together, and now the best friends are stepsisters, too. They all live in Dawn's house, which is a colonial farmhouse.

Dawn is *so* cool. (Or, as Claudia Kishi, another BSC member, would say, she's *fresh*.) Dawn has long pale blonde hair that reaches halfway down her back. Her eyes are sparkling blue. She dresses in a casual style all her own. And, although she likes Stoneybrook and her new family, she longs for California – for a couple of reasons. In the first place, she was brought up there. She misses the house she grew up in, the warmer climate, and of course, her father. She also misses her brother. That's right. Jeff is back in California, living with Mr Schafer. He just never adjusted to Connecticut the way Dawn did. He had trouble at school and he wasn't happy. So he returned to California. At first Dawn felt terrible. She felt as if her family had been ripped in two. Now that she's got a stepfather and a stepsister (not to mention a kitten – Mary Anne's), she feels more complete. But she still visits her father and Jeff whenever she can.

Things at the Schafer/Spier home got off to a troubled start after the wedding. Dawn and Mary Anne were friends, but they weren't prepared to be stepsisters. And Dawn and her mum are as different from Mary Anne and her dad as night and day. They have varying ideas on everything from meals to housecleaning. But they're overcoming things. I think that deep down,

Dawn and Mary Anne are happy to be stepsisters.

Let's see. The two remaining BSC members are Claudia Kishi, club vice-chairman, and Stacey McGill, club treasurer. Claudia and Stacey are best friends and also have their similarities and differences. (I suppose all best friends do.) Both Claudia and Stacey are pretty *fresh* themselves. They are the most sophisticated of all us members. None of us really comes straight out and says that, but we all know it's true.

Claudia comes from a pretty normal family. It's like mine, I suppose. She lives with her parents and her older sister, Janine. Janine, however, is a genius in the true sense of the word (she has an amazingly high I.Q.), while Claudia, who's bright, is a terrible pupil. She just doesn't like school. (Oh, and she's an awful speller.) What she does like is art, and she's really talented. Claud can sculpt, paint, draw, you name it. She even makes wild jewellery to go with her wild clothes. Claud wears things my mother won't even let me *look* at in shops – short, short skirts and tight black trousers and off-the-shoulder sweat shirts. Also, she can think of a thousand ways to wear her hair, which is long, silky, and jet-black. Claud is Japanese-American and very exotic-looking. She's also good fun. She loves reading Nancy Drew mysteries and eating junk food, but her parents don't approve of either habit. Does that deter Claudia? No. She just hides the books and food all round her room. Once, I dropped a pencil on the floor and it rolled under an armchair. I reached down to pick it up, and my hand closed over a Yorkie Bar! Claud likes boys and goes out on dates and to school dances, but she doesn't have one special boyfriend yet. There's one sad thing about Claudia. Her grandmother, Mimi, used to live with her family. I think Claudia was closer to Mimi than to anyone else in the world. Then Mimi got ill and died. That was a hard time for all of us, but especially for Claud.

And now we come to Stacey. Stacey shares Claudia's sense of fashion and, if this is possible, she's even more sophisticated than Claud. Her mother lets her perm her hair, she has pierced ears (well, so do all of us, except for Kristy and Mary Anne), and her clothes are even more cool than Claudia's. I think. Actually, maybe they're about equal on the coolness scale.

But there's one thing about Stacey that none of us can top: she grew up in New York City. Big, thrilling, exciting New York City, the shopping capital of the world. How did Stacey end up in Stoneybrook? Well, the company Mr McGill works for transferred his job to Stamford, so Stacey and her parents settled in Stoneybrook.

(Stacey's an only child.) Then, after they'd been here about a year, Mr McGill was transferred *back* to New York. (When they left, they sold their house – to my family!) Anyway, that was when the trouble started. Mr and Mrs McGill began having problems. Finally, they separated. Mrs McGill wanted to move back here, while Mr McGill stayed in the city. It was a tough decision, but Stacey finally chose to live with her mum in Stoneybrook. (Boy, were we glad to have her back.) So Stacey's life might seem glamorous, but it hasn't been easy. Especially when you consider that on top of everything else, Stacey has a disease called diabetes. She has to stay on a strict no-sweets diet and give herself daily injections of something called insulin (Ugh!). All in all, though, Stacey copes pretty well, even when she isn't feeling too great. And she's a very good friend to all of us.

The phone rang then, and it jolted me out of my daydream. I jumped off my bed. I hadn't begun my homework. I hadn't practised at my *barre* in the basement, either. Even so, I hoped the phone call was from Mallory. Homework or not, practice or not, all I wanted to do was pour out the story of Aunt Cecelia to my best friend.

3rd CHAPTER

"'Bye, Mama!" I called. "I'm going to Claudia's for the meeting. I'll be back in time for dinner!"

"Have fun, darling," my mother replied.

I dashed into our garage, hopped onto my bike, and cycled towards Claud's house, hurrying. It's never a good idea to be late for a meeting. Kristy feels it is her duty as chairman to run the BSC meetings in as official a manner as possible. So I pedalled along quickly.

On the way I thought about how nice it was having Mama at home. I'd never thought about it before; I suppose because there was no reason to think of her *not* being there. Even when she began to job-hunt, I didn't think what it would be like to have two working parents. It didn't seem real enough.

But now that Mama would soon *not* be at

home, I spent a good deal of time appreciating having her around. It was nice to get in from school and find her in the study, paying bills; or on the phone, doing voluntary work; or best of all, in the kitchen, baking, with Squirt at her heels. Soon all that would be over. I'd come home to . . . Aunt Cecelia. (I always imagined scary music playing when I thought of her name.) And when I left for a club meeting, I would have to call goodbye to . . . Aunt Cecelia.

My own babysitter.

I pulled into Claud's drive and chained my bike to a lamppost. Then I let myself into the Kishis' house. There's no point in ringing the bell, because both Mr and Mrs Kishi work, and Janine isn't often at home, so all us club members just run upstairs instead of making Claudia come downstairs when we know perfectly well where to go.

"Hi!" I said, entering Claud's room.

Claudia, Kristy, and Dawn were there, in their usual places. I took *my* usual place.

"Hi, Jessi!" my friends replied.

Claud and Dawn were sitting on Claud's bed, leaning against the wall. Kristy was perched in the director's chair, which she has claimed as her own – the chairman's throne. She was wearing a visor, and a pencil was stuck over one ear.

I sat on the floor. We were waiting for Mallory, Stacey, and Mary Anne. While we waited, I only half listened to the others, who were talking loudly. I couldn't help thinking about Aunt Cecelia, about how Mama and Daddy had got me a *babysitter*. And then I began to think about our own sitting club.

This is how the BSC got started. It all began more than a year ago, when Kristy, Claudia, Mary Anne, and Stacey were new seventh-grade students at SMS. I still lived in New Jersey then, Dawn still lived in California, and Mal was a lowly fifth-grader at Stoneybrook Elementary. She wasn't even a sitter yet.

Anyway, back then, Kristy lived across the street from Claud, and Mary Anne lived next door to her. All three of them had grown up together and all liked to babysit, but they did their sitting on their own. Then one day Kristy's mum (who was just beginning to see Watson Brewer) needed a sitter for David Michael, who was only six. No one was available – not Kristy, not Sam or Charlie, not any of the sitters Mrs Thomas had phoned. It was while Kristy was watching her mother make all those telephone calls that she got what was probably the most brilliant idea of her life. Wouldn't it be easy if her mum could make just *one* phone call and reach a lot of sitters at once? Of course it would!

So she told Claudia and Mary Anne about her idea for a sitting business, and they formed the Babysitters Club. They asked Stacey to join, too. She and Claud were already getting to be friends, and the girls thought that four sitters would be better than three. That was the start of the BSC.

The club did well from the beginning, thanks partly to all the advertising the girls did and partly to the fact that they were (and still are) excellent sitters, so people asked them back after they'd done a good job. Soon the BSC business was booming, and when Dawn moved to Stoneybrook, they asked her to join. Everything went smoothly until Stacey had to move back to New York. By then, a year had gone by, the original club members were in the eighth grade, and Mal had joined them at SMS as a sixth-grader. She was old enough to sit (and she certainly had plenty of experience with young children), so they asked both Mal and me to replace Stacey. Then, of course, Stacey moved back here (I felt guilty that she couldn't move into her old house, since we were living in it), and she settled into the club routine again. We have seven members now, and Kristy says that's enough. I think she's right. Claud's bedroom is getting crowded.

How does the club run? Well, we meet three times a week, on Monday, Wednesday, and Friday afternoons from 5:30 until 6:00. People know that we meet then and they phone us to arrange sitters. They also know they must phone us at Claudia's, whose bedroom is BSC headquarters.

Kristy, as I mentioned, is our chairman. Her job is to conduct meetings, solve problems, get good ideas, and generally keep things running smoothly. These are two of Kristy's ideas: Kid-Kits, and the club notebook. Kid-Kits are terrific. Kristy suggested that we each get a cardboard box, decorate it, and fill it with things kids like to play with – our old books, games, and toys, plus stickers, colouring books, and art materials. We sometimes take the Kid-Kits with us when we babysit, and children *love* them. This is good for business, because when our charges are happy, then their parents are happy, and then the parents ask us to sit again.

The club notebook is a good idea, too, but not nearly as much fun. In it, each of us has to write up every single job we go on. I think that's a royal pain, but I have to admit it's helpful. Once a week we're supposed to read the notebook to see what happened while our friends were sitting, and often I find out how they solved difficult sitting situations, or learn about a problem a kid is having whom I'll be sitting for soon.

Claudia is the vice-chairman because we're always using (or eating) her things. Three times a week we take over her room. We use her phone and eat her junk food.

Claud's pretty good-natured about this. In fact, I think she likes having us around.

The job of the secretary, Mary Anne, is a big one. Mary Anne is in charge of the club *record* book (not the notebook), in which she keeps track of our clients, their addresses and phone numbers, and the rates they pay. More importantly, she schedules every single one of our sitting jobs. She has to keep track of all our other activities and appointments, such as my ballet lessons, Mal's orthodontist appointments, and Kristy's softball practices. I don't think Mary Anne has ever made a mistake.

Stacey is our treasurer. She's good with numbers. It's her job to keep a record of the money we earn (just for our interest), to collect subs from each of us every Monday, to preside over the treasury, and to dole out money when it's needed – to help Claudia pay for her phone bill, to replace items in the Kid-Kits that get used up, such as crayons, and to shell out for a club pizza party or pyjama party every now and then. The funny thing is, Stacey loves collecting money – *having* it – but hates parting with it, even though it isn't her own. Nothing pleases her more than the sight of a fat treasury envelope.

Dawn is our alternate officer. That means that if one of us has to miss a meeting, Dawn can take over that person's job. She's a bit like an understudy in a play. She has to know how to cope with the treasury, schedule appointments, etc.

Then there are Mal and me. As junior officers, we take on a lot of the afternoon sitting jobs. This is mostly because we aren't allowed to sit at night yet unless we're sitting for our own brothers and sisters. But it does mean that the other girls are free for evening jobs, so all in all we're important club members, too.

Believe it or not, there are a couple of other club members whom I haven't described yet. This is because they are associate members and don't come to meetings. They're our backups. They're responsible sitters we can rely on if a job comes up that none of us seven regular members can take, which does happen sometimes. Our associate members are Shannon Kilbourne, a friend of Kristy's, and . . . Logan Bruno, Mary Anne's boyfriend!

"Ahem," said Kristy loudly.

I looked up guiltily. I'd been daydreaming again. The rest of the BSC members had arrived and Kristy was starting the meeting. She called the meeting to order. Then Stacey collected our subs, gleefully exclaiming over the contents of the treasury and beaming when no one said they needed any money. After that, we waited for job calls to come in.

The first was from Mrs Rodowsky. She and her husband have three boys – Shea,

Jackie, and Archie. Jackie, the seven-year-old, is a walking disaster, completely accident-prone, but we love him.

I got the job.

When the phone didn't ring again for a while, we began talking.

"When's your aunt coming, Jessi?" Stacey wanted to know. (By then, practically the whole world knew my aunt was moving in.)

"I'm not sure," I said. "I mean, Aunt Cecelia isn't even sure. She still has to hire removal men, sell some of her furniture, things like that." I paused. Then, "Ohhh!" I moaned. "*Why* does she have to come? There must be some other solution to this problem. Perhaps my parents could hire a jailer."

Kristy giggled. But then she said, "Really, Jessi. How bad could having your aunt move in actually be? Nannie moved in with my family, and it's been great. We love having her around."

"And Mimi lived with us for as long as I can remember," added Claud. "You know how I felt about her. She was like another mother."

I knew. And I knew that Nannie was wonderful, too.

But Aunt Cecelia would not be wonderful, and my friends wouldn't understand that until they personally saw Aunt Cecelia in action.

4th CHAPTER

Wednesday

Well, here we go again. Another afternoon with Jackie Rodowsky, the walking disaster. Actually, I have to admit that this time he wasn't much of a klutz. Only a few little things happened. What was interesting is that Jackie decided to enter the science fair. And he wants to do a very interesting project. Have you ever seen those miniature erupting volcanoes? Jackie wants to build one. (Leave *it to Jackie to choose the messiest possible project!) What have I got myself into?*

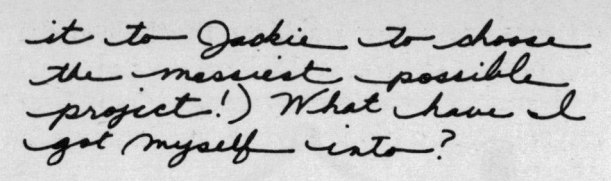

I raced directly to the Rodowskys' from school. Mrs Rodowsky needed me by three-thirty so that she could drive Shea to his music lesson and little Archie to his football practice. (Can you imagine a bunch of four-year-olds playing football? It must be quite a sight.)

As I pedalled along, I remembered telling Mama that morning that I would be going straight to a sitting job after school. I knew she wouldn't worry about me. But, I thought, would things be different when Aunt Cecelia was in charge? Would she let me go to places without checking with her after school? Would she remember my afternoon plans when I told them to her over breakfast in the morning?

Aunt Cecelia is an old prune.

I arrived at the Rodowskys' right on time, parked my bike, and rang their front doorbell.

I heard running footsteps inside, then a whoosh, a crash, and a cry of, "Oh, drat, drat. Oh . . . *bull*frogs!"

I giggled. I knew that was Jackie.

"Jackie!" I called. "It's me, Jessi. Are you okay?"

Jackie opened the door, looking sheepish.

"I was running to answer the bell and I slipped on the rug and fell on my bottom."

I smiled, shaking my head. Then I let myself in and helped Jackie straighten out the rug.

"Jessi?" called Mrs Rodowsky. "Is that you?"

"Yes!" I replied. (I hoped she didn't think *I* had slipped on the rug.)

Mrs Rodowsky was in a rush.

"Archie!" she exclaimed. "You're supposed to be in your football kit. And, Shea, where are your piano books?"

The house was in turmoil for about five minutes – Jackie added to it by somehow getting his foot stuck in one of his old wellington boots – but finally Mrs R. and the boys were backing hurriedly down the drive. I was left with Jackie and the boot.

"I know I can get this off your foot," I told him.

"But what if you can't?" whimpered Jackie.

"Jackie," I said, "have you ever heard of someone who got a boot stuck on his foot and *never* got it off?"

"No," replied Jackie, as I braced myself against a wall and pulled.

"I wonder," said Jackie, trying not to slide forward. "You know, wellington boots are sometimes called galoshes. Is *one* boot called a galosh?"

"I haven't the faintest – *Oof*! Well, there

you are, Jackie. The boot's off. You're free."

"Thanks," he said gratefully.

Jackie wandered round the playroom, looking bored.

"What do you want to do?" I asked him.

"I don't know."

"Do you have any homework?"

"Nope. Well, not really. We're just supposed to think about whether we want to enter the science fair at school."

"Do you?" I asked him.

"*Me*?" squeaked Jackie. "Are you kidding? I have such bad luck. I would never enter a contest. . . Even though I think it would be fun to make a volcano."

"Fun to do *what*?" I repeated.

"Make a volcano. I saw it on *The Brady Bunch* once. You can build a model of a volcano, but it really works. I mean, lava really comes pouring out. That would be great. Lava everywhere."

The thought of "lava everywhere" made me feel a bit queasy. Even so, I said, "Jackie, you ought to make a volcano for the science fair! It would be a great project. Everyone else would probably just have, you know, things like leaf collections, or insects in jars, but you would build a *volcano* that would *erupt*. You'd win for sure."

Jackie looked doubtful. "I don't know," he said. "I bet some kids would do really, really good projects. I'm not very good at science. Besides, as I said, I have bad luck. I can't show a project to judges and an audience. Things never go right for me. Something bad would happen."

"Jackie. That's no way to talk. You've got to have confidence in yourself. A volcano – a spewing, dripping, running volcano – is a really terrific project. The kids would love it. More important, so would the teachers and judges."

"I don't know," said Jackie slowly.

"Oh, come on," I said. "This'll be great. Let's go to the library right now and see what kind of information we can find on volcanoes and how to make them. I'll leave a note for your mum in case she comes home early."

I didn't give Jackie a chance to say no. I just handed him his jacket, wrote the note, put on my own jacket, and marched Jackie to the public library. He barely said a word as we walked along.

When we reached the library, the first person we saw was Mrs Kishi, Claudia's mother! She's the head librarian.

"Hello," she greeted us, as we entered the children's section. "What are you two doing here?"

I explained Jackie's project to Mrs Kishi.

"Hmm," she said, "let's look in the science section."

Claud's mum helped us find three books. One was about volcanoes, one was about earth sciences, and the third was a book of science experiments, including a chapter called "How to Make an Erupting Volcano".

"Gosh," said Jackie. "I didn't think we'd find this. It's exactly what I need. It has all the instructions."

"You never know what you'll find in a library," said Mrs Kishi, smiling. Then she left Jackie and me sitting at a table with our books.

Jackie began to read about the exploding volcano experiment. "You know," he said, "this doesn't look so easy. It says you have to make a frame out of wood and glass to put your volcano in. They didn't do that on *The Brady Bunch*."

"Well, *we're* going to," I informed him. "We're going to make the best project in your whole school."

"But there are words here I don't understand. The books says you have to get different coloured day to make ig – iggy—"

"Igneous," I supplied.

"Okay. Igneous rocks. And . . . and metal—"

"Metamorphic rocks."

"And . . . oh, boy."

"Sedimentary rocks."

"Whoa," whispered Jackie. "And then you have to get stuff called, um—"

Even I had to pause for that one. "I'm not sure what this is," I said at last.

"So where are we going to get it?" asked Jackie worriedly.

"It says you can buy it at a chemist."

Jackie was quiet. He seemed stumped.

"What's wrong?" I asked him.

"On *The Brady Bunch* they just made a mound of papier-mâché or something and put this goo in and – *whoosh*! Why do I need to know about rocks? And why do I have to make a glass box? That sounds hard. And expensive. I've just spent all my pocket money."

"First of all," I replied, "as I said, we're going to make the best project in the school. I bet the volcano on *The Brady Bunch* didn't win a prize, did it?"

"No," answered Jackie triumphantly. "It was just for fun."

"Oh," I said. "Well, ours will be special. Also, I'm sure your parents will help you buy the materials for your project. Now, come on. Sit next to me. I have to learn all about volcanoes first. If you want to win at the science fair, you can't just make your volcano erupt. You have to tell the judges about volcanoes."

Jackie sat next to me while I learnt about lava and fire and fountains and ash and gas and some pretty disgusting things. He looked at the volcano experiment with a frown.

After about twenty minutes, I stood up. "Well," I said, "I think I've got volcanoes sussed out now."

"Good," replied Jackie, "because I haven't."

"We'll take these books out and go home."

"Oh," said Jackie, brightening. "I haven't got my library tickets."

"Never mind. I've got mine," I told him.

So we took out the books and walked back to Jackie's house. When Mrs Rodowsky returned with Shea and Archie, she found Jackie and me still looking through the books. Well, Jackie was looking (sort of). I was making a list of materials he would need.

"Jackie's entering the science fair?" said Mrs Rodowsky, after I told her what we were doing. She looked both pleased and surprised.

"Yes," I said happily.

"But, Mum, we need clay and glass and some things from the chemist. It might be expensive," said Jackie.

"I don't think it'll be *too* expensive," said Mrs R. "Jackie, I'm so proud of you for wanting to work on a project. And, Jessi, thank you for inspiring him. I'm impressed that you convinced him to enter. Listen, would you mind helping Jackie with his project? The two of you seem to know what you're doing. Maybe you could arrange with the members of the Babysitters Club to be our only sitter between now and the science fair. That way you and Jackie will have plenty of time together."

"I think that's possible," I said. "I'll have to check with my friends, but I'm sure they'll understand."

"Great!" said Mrs R.

I left the Rodowskys' with a smile on my face. I knew I could help Jackie all the way to a prize.

5th CHAPTER

Saturday

Today, Dawn and I sat for my younger brothers and sisters. It was a fun afternoon, wasn't it?

Definitely, Mal. Your family is really something. With eight kids, you lot can come up with pretty good projects. I think the most ambitious thing Jeff and I ever did was set up a table in front of our house in California. We sold bunches of flowers that grew wild everywhere. Nobody bought any, of course. Oops, I'm off the subject.

That's okay. Well, to get back to our job, two things were going on. One, Margo *decided to enter the Stoneybrook Elementary science fair. Two, the other kids needed something to do so they... opened a true and actual lending library!*

It was a peaceful Saturday at Mal's house. Dawn had arrived to help her babysit, Mr and Mrs Pike had just left, all of Mal's brothers and sisters were at home, and nobody was arguing. Not even Nicky and the triplets. Dawn had brought over her Kid-Kit (Mallory's is no good at her own house, since it's mostly full of the Pikes' things), and Claire, Margo, and Vanessa were looking through it. The boys were playing their endless imaginary game about the Wandering Frog People. That has been going on for about two years now, which is one year and 364 days longer than Mal had hoped it would last. At any rate, the triplets were occupied.

"Look!" said Claire, peering eagerly into Dawn's Kid-Kit. "It's the new Sindy doll. Cool! She's got sleepover stuff with her."

"Here's a jigsaw puzzle," said Vanessa. "Ooh, this looks hard."

"It is," Dawn told her, "but I think you'll like it. When you put it together it's a poem. It's the one by Robert Frost about walking through woods on a snowy evening. And all around the poem are snowflakes."

"I'm going to try it," said Vanessa,

immediately dumping the pieces out on the floor. Vanessa loves to read and write poetry.

Margo looked half-heartedly through the box. She didn't seem to want to play with anything.

"Something wrong, Margo?" Mallory asked her. Margo has the world's weakest stomach. Mallory sincerely hoped it wasn't upset.

Margo shook her head. "I'm just thinking," she replied.

"About what?" asked Dawn.

"Well, our school is having a science fair and anyone can enter."

"Do you want to enter?" asked Mal. "I entered three times when I was at Stoneybrook Elementary. I'm not great at science, but the fair was a lot of fun anyway."

"It was?" said Margo. "Maybe I'll enter then. Our teacher said we'll get extra marks just for entering. Will you help me, Mallory?"

"Of course," replied Mal. "I mean, I'll *help* you, but I won't do your project *for* you. Deal?"

"Deal," said Margo. She grinned.

"Do you have any idea what you want to do your project on?" asked Dawn.

Margo thought for a while. "No," she said at last.

"Well, let's go upstairs and look at the books in our rooms," suggested Mallory. "We have some science books."

"Maybe we'll find the Wandering Frog People while we're at it," said Dawn, with a little smile.

Mallory looked up. The boys were gone. That wasn't much of a surprise, since Wandering Frog People is a very quiet game.

What was a surprise, though, was finding Nicky and the triplets in their room, poring over a set of encyclopaedias.

"What are you doing?" Mal asked her brothers as she and Margo stopped in the doorway.

"Looking up frog stuff," replied Jordan. "Adam says there's such a thing as an African tree toad, but I don't believe him."

"Don't we have a book on reptiles somewhere?" asked Mal.

"And I need to find a book about . . . about the sky," said Margo, suddenly inspired. "I want my project to be about constellations or maybe the planets."

"What we need is a library," said Mallory.

"Hey!" exclaimed Byron. "We could make a library right here in our rooms. Altogether, we have science books; mysteries; your horse stories, Mal; Claire's picture books; the Hardy Boys and Nancy Drew books" (Adam made a face at the mention of Nancy Drew); "Vanessa's poetry books; Nicky's dog stories; and all those other books." (The Pike kids get a lot of books on their birthdays and on holidays. They love reading.)

305

"Yeah. . ." said Nicky slowly. "A real library. Great."

"We could organize it like the public library," said Jordan, getting excited, too. "And we could really let kids around here borrow our books."

"We need a librarian," said Adam.

"Vanessa!" cried the others immediately. "Vanessa would be a great librarian. She's always reading or writing."

"But I have to work out my science-fair project," said Margo. "How can I do that while you're all having fun making a library?" Margo looked (and sounded) miffed.

"Easy," said the ever-practical Byron. "You help us with the library. Then, when it's all ready, you can go to the science section to work on your project. You can be our first customer."

"All *right*!" cried Margo.

"Margo, go and tell Dawn and Claire and Vanessa to come up here," said Jordan. "We'll need everyone to help us."

Margo turned and faced the stairs. "DAWN! CLAIRE! VANESSA!" she yelled. "COME HERE!"

"Margo," said Mallory, giggling, "Jordan could have done *that* himself."

It wasn't long before preparations for the library were underway. Mallory and Dawn were amazed at how organized the kids, especially the older ones, were about their project.

"First," said Byron, "we have to group the same kinds of books together. We've all got science books in our rooms. They should go on the same bookshelf. Margo, you've got your Secret Seven books; Vanessa, you've got Nancy Drews; and Nicky and I both have Hardy Boys. We should put those mystery series in another bookcase."

"I think all the animal stories should go together, too," said Nicky.

Well, for a while, the upstairs of the Pike house was a pretty big mess, with the kids carrying books back and forth, in and out of rooms.

"What are your parents going to say when they get home?" Dawn asked Mal, looking worried.

"Nothing! They'll love this!"

When the books had been organized, the kids divided themselves into four groups. Well, not exactly *groups*, since one of the groups consisted of just one person. Anyway, Vanessa, the chosen librarian, set up her desk as the checkout counter, and Claire helped her. Byron made signs that read ANIMAL STORIES, MYSTERIES, etc. Jordan and Margo made a huge stack of pockets to tape inside the covers of the books, and Adam and Nicky took index cards, wrote the title of one book on each card, and stuck it in the pocket that Jordan and Margo had just made. It was a real assembly line and took quite a bit of work, but by late that afternoon, the library was ready. The Pike kids looked satisfied.

Vanessa manned her desk. The others stood in the bedrooms, as library assistants, Mallory guessed. And Margo announced, "Here I am! Your first customer. I need to see the science section, please."

"Right over here," said Adam, pulling his sister into the boys' room. "What are you looking for?"

"I'm not sure," replied Margo. "I suppose books about space."

Adam handed Margo several books, she sat down at a desk, began reading, and. . .

"Now what?" asked Nicky. "Where are our other customers."

"Um, nobody else knows about your library," Dawn pointed out gently.

The Pike kids looked wounded, but just for a minute.

"We'll advertise!" said Vanessa

"Yeah, we'll make a big sign that says 'Pike Library' and put it in the front garden!" exclaimed Jordan.

So the triplets made the sign, and then they, Nicky, and Claire went from house to house in the neighbourhood, telling all their friends about the *very* local public library. They returned with Matt and Haley Braddock.

"We're bored," said Haley, who's nine. "We need some new books to read."

Actually, Haley didn't just speak. She

spoke and used sign language at the same time, since Matt, who's seven, is profoundly deaf and can't speak or hear.

"Yeah," signed Matt. "I want a book about baseball."

Beaming, Nicky helped the Braddocks find their books. While they were looking, the doorbell rang. Buddy and Suzi Barrett were on the front step, also wanting books.

"This is great!" cried Nicky. "Our library is working!"

Vanessa was busy at her desk. Whenever a customer found a book, she removed the card from the pocket, wrote on it the name of the person who was taking out the book, and also the day's date. Then she put the card aside and stuck a Post-It on the book pocket with the due date written on it.

"Overdue books cost you ten cents a day," she told each customer, "so bring them back on time."

Meanwhile, Margo had decided on her science project. "I am going to make a space house," she said. "It will show what life would be like if the moon was our home planet."

"Great!" said Mal.

When Mr and Mrs Pike returned, they were pleased with the Pike Library, but not pleased when Buddy Barrett returned his book during dinner that night. Byron had to add something to the sign in the front garden:

Open weekdays from 3:30 - 6:00 p.m.
Open weekends from 10:00 a.m. - 5:00 p.m.
Not open during meals!

6th CHAPTER

Dum da-dum dum.

The dreaded day had arrived.

Aunt Cecelia was moving in.

It was the Saturday after the one when the Pike Library had opened. And it began early. Daddy and Mama were up at the crack of dawn. So was I. I was in the basement, practising at the *barre* Daddy had built for me, and scrutinizing my leg movements in the big mirror. But when I smelt coffee brewing in the kitchen, I went upstairs to see just how the awful day was going to start.

"She's hired a trailer," Daddy was telling Mama as I reached the kitchen. He was scrambling eggs while Mama cut up fruit.

"A trailer!" exclaimed Mama.

"Well, just a small one," said Daddy. "She's sold some of her things, put a lot of other things in storage, and the rest is moving here with her."

"Where's she going to put it all?" I asked.

"Good morning, Jessi," was Mama and Daddy's reply.

"'Morning," I answered. I didn't say *good* morning, because it wasn't.

"She's going to put it in the guest room. That will be her room. You know that," Mama told me.

"A whole trailer's worth of furniture?" I pressed.

Daddy gave me a look that plainly said, "Don't push it."

So I didn't.

At eight o'clock, Daddy left for Aunt Cecelia's. He would have to attach the trailer to our estate car and drive it back here while Aunt Cecelia drove her own car. I was pretty glad she had a car. That meant she wouldn't be stuck at our house day in and day out. As Kristy's big brother says, "A set of wheels is a necessity."

Daddy was gone a long time.

"He has to supervise the removal men," Mama explained to Becca and me as we ate lunch (our last meal without Aunt Cecelia). "And hooking the trailer to our car may take a little while."

Daddy and Aunt Cecelia arrived at our house at about two-thirty. Mama, Becca, Squirt, and I were sitting on the front step. We were sitting under a banner that read:

WELCOME, AUNT CECILIA. Mama had insisted that Becca and I make the banner, so we'd purposely spelt our aunt's name wrong. (Mama hadn't noticed.)

When the cars and the U-Haul pulled into our drive, Becca and I just looked at each other. We didn't even stand up until Mama nudged us and said, "What's happened to your manners?"

So we walked to the drive, trailing behind Mama.

Aunt Cecelia got out of her car, kissed us all, and then said, "Rebecca, don't slouch," and, "Jessica, *please* tidy up your hair."

What could we say? Becca stands like any normal eight-year-old, and I'd been practising all morning. Of course my hair was a mess.

"Well," said Daddy, sounding a little too cheerful, "let's all get Aunt Cecelia's things inside." We looked inside the trailer. It was *packed*!

I almost cried, "Where are we going to put all that stuff?" but I knew better. I just picked up a box and lugged it inside. Becca did the same.

After about half an hour, the guest room was overflowing, and there were still two chairs, this stupid bird cage on a stand (no bird in it), a little table, some lamps, a tea tray and even a small rug in the van. Not to mention more boxes.

"Mama," I said urgently, "those things

are *not* going to fit in Aunt Cecelia's room. You can barely walk around in there now."

"I know," Mama replied. "We'll find places for them."

"That's right." Aunt Cecelia had come up behind us. "A place for everything and everything in its place," she said primly.

I hadn't expected those places to be all over our house. We crammed a lot of things, including the bird cage, into the living room. The small rug was placed over a larger rug in the study. It looked terrible. One of the tables ended up in my room.

"Mama, *why* did she bring so much stuff?" Becca whispered when Aunt Cecelia was busy in the guest room. I mean, *her* room.

"Because it belongs to her. It's part of her past," Mama replied gently. "It reminds her of her life with her husband, and she misses your Uncle Steven very much."

For a moment, I felt sorry for Aunt Cecelia. But just for a moment. The next thing I knew, she was handing me two china eggs and asking me to put them in my room because there wasn't room in hers.

When she'd gone, I looked round my room. It was different. It didn't say "Jessi" any more. It said "Jessi and some old lady." Our house didn't feel like our house any more, either. Signs of Aunt Cecelia were everywhere.

Squirt was confused, and I didn't blame him one bit.

But Aunt Cecelia, looking at the not-yet-organized house said, "I'll have things in order in no time."

"I hope so," Mama replied. "I start my job on Monday."

Aunt Cecelia kept her word. By that evening, our house was tidy (but crowded), Aunt Cecelia had unpacked and put away all her stuff in her bedroom, and she'd folded the boxes, stacked them, and tied them up with string for the dustbin men to take away on Tuesday.

"She's efficient," Daddy remarked.

"She's a drill sergeant," I whispered to Becca.

"Girls, are you ready for bed?" Aunt Cecelia called upstairs.

Ready for bed? It was too early to go to bed. And why was Aunt Cecelia calling us, anyway?

"Not yet," I replied.

"Well, please put on your nightdresses."

Becca and I looked at each other, mystified. Then we put on our nightdresses, but we went downstairs afterwards to find out what Mama and Daddy were doing. Guess what? They were just sitting in the study, reading. Why weren't they stopping Aunt Cecelia?

"Mama," I whispered, "Aunt Cecelia

told me to get ready for bed, and it's only eight thirty."

"You don't have to go to bed yet," said Mama absently, but she was much more interested in her book than in the injustices Aunt Cecelia was carrying out against Becca and me.

My sister and I left the study.

"They weren't any help," said Becca.

"They're tired," I told her. "And Mama's probably enjoying this last weekend before she begins work. We should let them relax."

That was a bad move on our part.

The next morning, our family had just got up when Daddy said brightly, "I've got a great idea. Why don't we go out for brunch this morning? We'll celebrate your mother's new job and having my sister here with us."

"Oh, why don't you two go out alone?" Aunt Cecelia said to Daddy and Mama. "Now that I'm here, you can have a private brunch. Wouldn't that be nice? No children's menu to look at. No high chair to worry about. I'll stay here and babysit for Jessi and Becca and Squirt. After all, that's one reason I moved in."

Mama and Daddy were thrilled with the idea, but all I could think was, *She'll* stay here and babysit for *us*? On a Sunday morning? I could do that. I *have* done that.

But I kept my mouth shut.

So Mama and Daddy left, and Aunt Cecelia babysat for my sister and brother and me. And I *mean*, she babysat. She did everything for us. That's okay where Squirt's concerned, but Becca is too old to be reminded to use her serviette (she knows when to do that), and I'm *much* too old to be told to finish everything on my plate. Sometimes I can't. Besides, I have to watch my weight. I can't be a fat ballerina.

When our breakfast was finally over, I lifted Squirt out of his high chair and began to clean him up as I always do.

"I'll do that," said Aunt Cecelia. "You girls get dressed."

As Becca and I dragged ourselves upstairs, I said to my sister, "I've got a new name for Aunt Cecelia."

"What?" asked Becca.

"Aunt Dictator."

While Mama and Daddy were out, Aunt Cecelia left Squirt in his high chair (when I babysit, I play with him; it's much more stimulating for him) and prepared a salad for lunch, and also began preparing dinner. Aunt Cecelia was so busy cooking that she hadn't got round to cleaning up Squirt yet.

"Aunt Di – I mean, Aunt Cecelia," I said, entering the kitchen, "Becca and I are going to take Squirt for a walk." (After I wash his face and hands, I thought.)

I was dressed. And my hair was tidy.

Aunt Cecelia wouldn't be able to find anything to complain about.

"Where are you going to take him?" she asked.

"Just up and down the street like we usually do." I paused, then added, "I put him in his buggy and strap him in, and I never let him lean over and touch the wheels because he might get hurt."

Aunt Dictator looked outside. "Too cloudy," she announced.

I nearly exploded, but instead I said, "Okay. Then I'm going over to Mallory Pike's house."

"Who's Mallory?" my aunt asked.

"You met her once," I told her. "She's my best friend."

"Where does she live?"

"Nearby. I can ride my bike to her house."

"I don't think so." Aunt Dictator shook her head slowly. "No, I don't think so. I'm in charge now, and it looks like rain. The roads will get too slippery for bicycles."

That did it. I turned round and stomped out of the kitchen.

"Walk like a lady!" Aunt Cecelia called after me.

I didn't answer her. (But I did stop stomping.) Who did Aunt Cecelia think she was? Oh, yeah. My babysitter.

I ran upstairs to Becca's room. My poor sister had followed me to the kitchen before, but when she saw how unreasonable Aunt Cecelia was being, she had escaped back to her room. Becca is a little shy and very sensitive to criticism, so she wasn't about to face Aunt Cecelia until she thought the arguing was over.

"Becca," I said, "you can stop hiding now. I've got an idea. It's time to start our Aunt Cecelia project."

I whispered into Becca's ear, and she began to giggle. By the time Mama and Daddy returned, my sister and I had been hard at work. We'd turned Aunt Dictator's bed into an apple-pie bed. We'd filled one of her slippers with Daddy's shaving cream. We'd put a realistic rubber spider on her pillow and covered it with the bedspread.

Her room looked normal, but we knew better. Mama and Daddy couldn't see what we'd done, but when Aunt Dictator put on her slippers or got into bed, what would happen?

Would Mama and Daddy see how unfair our new sitter was? Would they give Aunt Cecelia a talking-to? Or would Becca and I just be in an awful lot of trouble?

Surprisingly, none of the above happened. At eleven o'clock that night, Aunt Cecelia was reading in bed. Mama stuck her head into the room to thank her for making her life so much easier. And all Aunt Cecelia said was, "You're welcome," even though she must have found the shaving cream and the spider. And she must have had to make her bed up again. I didn't know what to think of that.

7th CHAPTER

"Goodbye, Mama! Good luck!" I called.

"Have fun at work!" Becca added.

It was the next morning, and Mama and Daddy were leaving for their jobs together. I felt as though I was sending Mama off to her first day at nursery school.

My parents' cars rolled down the drive. It was time for Becca and me to get a move on or we'd be late for school.

"Take care of Squirt," Becca said seriously to Aunt Dictator, strapping her rucksack on and picking up her lunch box.

"Yeah," I said. "Remember, he's allowed to watch *Sesame Street*, and he always needs an afternoon nap and usually a morning nap, too. And he likes to take a bottle of water to bed with him. Oh, and—"

Suddenly I stopped talking. Whoa. If looks could kill.

"Jessica," said my aunt crisply. "I've raised children of my own."

You didn't raise Squirt, I thought.

I was not in a good mood by the time I left for school.

But when I came home that afternoon, I was in a much better frame of mind. I'd got an A in a maths test, I'd scored three goals during netball, my English teacher had said he was impressed with the story I was working on, and I had a full (and Aunt Cecelia-free) afternoon ahead of me. I was supposed to babysit at the Rodowskys' and then go to the Monday BSC meeting.

I bounced through our front door. "Hello!" I called.

"SHHH!" was Aunt Cecelia's reply. "Your brother's asleep."

"*Now?*" I said. "He's usually awake by this time."

"Well, he isn't today."

Auntie Dictator, Auntie Dictator, Auntie Dictator, I sang to myself.

I put away my rucksack hastily, changed my clothes, and dashed into the kitchen for a quick snack. I had to be at the Rodowskys' soon.

Aunt Cecelia was standing at the cooker when I came in. I opened the fridge and surveyed the snack possibilities.

"Snack's on the table," said Aunt Cecelia, without turning round to look at me. (I think some adults actually *do* have eyes behind their heads. The eyes are just hidden by their hair, that's all.)

I looked at the table.

Milk and biscuits. Kids' stuff.

"I usually have a sandwich," I said, opening the fridge again.

"Not this close to dinner, you don't. You'll spoil your appetite."

"But I *do* get to eat a sandwich. Mama lets me. We eat lunch really early. Before it's even twelve o'clock."

"Two biscuits," said Aunt Cecelia.

"I'll pass," I told her. "I'll eat at Jackie's house."

"Jackie? Who's Jackie? Not a boy, I hope."

"As a matter of fact, Jackie *is* a boy."

"Well, you're certainly not spending the afternoon with a *boy*."

"Aunt Cecelia, he's seven years old. I babysit for him."

My aunt was about to protest when Becca came home, as starving as I was. She also requested a sandwich and got two measly biscuits instead. Since she ate hers, I ate mine after all. (Oh, I think I forgot to mention that the biscuits weren't anything yummy, like chocolate chip. They were oatbran bars.)

"Okay," I said, jumping up from the table. "Gotta go! I'll be at the Rodowskys' until just after five. Then I'll be at Claudia Kishi's for our Babysitters Club meeting."

"Wait a minute," said Aunt Cecelia. "Where are you going?"

"To the Rodowskys' and then to Claudia's."

"I don't know those people."

"But I do."

"But I can't let you go running off to strange places."

"They *aren't strange!*"

"They are to me."

"Aunt Cecelia, you don't understand. This sitting job is my responsibility. I babysit all the time. You have to let me go."

"I don't *have* to let you do anything," said Aunt Dictator. "Besides, *you* are *my* responsibility now. I'm in charge while your parents are out. If anything happens to you, I'm—"

"I know. You're responsible," I said. "But I have a commitment. I told the Rodowskys a week ago that I would babysit this afternoon. They're counting on me. And a good babysitter never lets her clients down. Unless there's an emergency," I added.

Aunt Cecelia looked thoughtful.

"You can call Mama or Daddy at work and tell them what my plans are. They'll say I can go. This is my schedule. And these are *my* responsibilities."

"All right," said Aunt Cecelia at last. "What time will you be home?"

"Ten past six. Babysitters Club meetings

always end at six o'clock. Then I cycle home."

Aunt Cecelia nodded. "Very well, then."

I made a dash for the door – for two reasons. 1. I was about to be late. 2. I didn't want Aunt Dictator to change her mind.

I had to *speed* to the Rodowskys'. I was glad Aunt Cecelia couldn't see me. I didn't break any laws, but I nearly broke my head riding over a kerb. I arrived at Jackie's house in one piece, though.

"Hi," I greeted Mrs Rodowsky, breathlessly. I glanced at my watch. "Boy, I've just made it. I'm sorry I was almost late." (A good babysitter tries to get to any job, even the most routine one, a few minutes early in case the parents have special instructions, or there's a problem, such as a child who's going to cry a lot when Mummy leaves.)

"Don't worry, Jessi," said Mrs R. as she let me inside. "I know I can count on you."

I wish Aunt Cecelia would count on me, I thought.

A few minutes later, Mrs R. left with Shea. Archie was supposed to have gone with her – to be dropped off at football practice – but he had stayed at home that day, recovering from an ear infection.

"He's on the mend, though," his mother had told me. "He'll be back at school tomorrow. He doesn't need to stay in bed, and don't worry about medicine. I'll give him his next dose at suppertime."

So I was left with Jackie and Archie.

"Okay," I said enthusiastically to Jackie. "Let's get to work on your volcano. Did your mum and dad buy the things you need?"

"Yup," replied Jackie.

He and Archie and I were in the Rodowskys' playroom. Archie looked at his big brother and me with interest. "Can I help?" he asked.

"This is Jackie's project," I told Archie.

"Oh. Can I watch, then?"

"Of course," I replied. I turned to Jackie. "Now the first thing we need to do is build that box, the glass one with the wooden frame that we'll put our volcano in," I said.

"*Our* volcano?" asked Jackie.

"I mean yours. Now let's see. Where are the instructions?"

"You don't have to worry about that," said Jackie. "My dad and I made a box over the weekend. It doesn't look exactly like the one in the picture, but it's glass, and it's big enough for the volcano."

"Oh, good," I said. I felt relieved. Building the box had sounded difficult, even harder than making a working volcano. "Then we can get started on the next step," I told Jackie.

"Yea! Papier-mâché!" he cried. (Just the *idea* of something messy appeals to Jackie.)

"Nope," I said, referring to the instructions. "First we have to build up the layers of igneous, metamorphic, and sedimentary rock. We'll use the Plasticine for that. Did you buy three different colours of Plasticine?"

"What's Plasticine?" asked Archie, who was beginning to look bored.

"Modelling clay," I told him. "Did you get some, Jackie?"

"Yup. We got red, yellow, and brown. But, Jessi, *clay* doesn't look like rocks." Jackie sounded worried.

"It doesn't matter," I told him. "It's supposed to *represent* rocks."

"Can't we just build a volcano?" he asked.

"Not if you want to win a prize in the fair. You have to do a really terrific project. Now where's the clay? And the box?"

Jackie laid out the materials on an old table in the playroom. He watched while I built up the layers of rock that lie under volcanoes. It didn't take me too long.

"Goody!" he exclaimed as soon as I'd finished. "Papier-mâché time!"

Before I knew it, Jackie was mixing flour and water, and Archie was tearing strips of newspaper. Apparently, they had made papier-mâché before.

"Goop, goop, goop," sang Jackie, as he slurped his hands in and out of the pasty bowl. "Hey, this is a good batch, Archie," he said. Jackie was up to his elbows in goo. He grinned happily.

"Okay," I instructed, "take the papier-mâché and build a mountain on top of the clay, and around this tin can. Don't fill the can in. That's where we'll put the chemicals to make the lava."

"Mmmm," said Jackie. He held up his hands and let the goop drip back into the bowl. Then he got an itch and wiped his cheek, leaving papier-mâché smeared across it.

I tried to ignore that. I read up on igneous, metamorphic, and sedimentary rocks. But in the background, I was aware of cries of, "Got you! I'm the slime monster!" and, "Hey, Archie, look. If you wrap the papier-mâché around your arm you can make a cast," and, "Cool. Wrap me *all* up, Jackie. Make me a mummy!"

I glanced at the boys. They were having the time of their lives. Papier-mâché was everywhere – except surrounding the can in the glass box. Jackie hadn't started his mountain yet.

"This is good fun!" he exclaimed, just as I was about to tell him to get to work. "I can't wait to see lava, lava everywhere!"

I looked at my watch. "Time to clear up, you two," I said. "Your mum and Shea will be home soon."

"You know what, Jessi?" Jackie replied. "This was the best afternoon of my life!"

8th CHAPTER

Thursday

Another afternoon with David Michael and Emily Michelle. Nanny was practising with her bowling team. I'm glad she gets out in the afternoons, because her mornings are spent entirely with Emily. Anyway, it was a pretty quiet afternoon, but even so, something interesting happened:

Jackie and Margo now have one more competitor in the science fair. I'd never have guessed it, but David Michael wants to enter, so I tried to help him choose a project and work with Emily on naming the parts of her body at the same time. It was a challenging and fun afternoon. I'm still thinking of becoming a teacher some day.

Uh-oh. I should have known.

Competition.

When Kristy gets involved in something, the competition heats up right away. (I bet if you opened a dictionary and looked up "competition", you'd find a picture of Kristy's face.)

Kristy now saw the science fair as a competition between Mallory, herself, and me, as well as between all the kids at the fair. It would be as if . . . well, if David Michael won, Kristy would have won. In other words, she would have beaten me. At least that's what I thought at first. Things turned out quite differently.

Anyway, Kristy was babysitting that afternoon. Nannie had just driven off in her car, the Pink Clinker, and Kristy was trying to think of something fun to do with her little brother and sister. Usually, David Michael wants to play outside, but that afternoon he curled himself up in an armchair with his second-grade science book and began poring over it.

"What are you doing?" asked Kristy. (David Michael practically has to be bolted to his desk to do the small amount of homework he sometimes gets. He's bright but he doesn't like school much, and he *really* doesn't like homework, particularly during the softball season.)

"Well," said David Michael, "there's

going to be this science fair at school. Do you know what that is?"

Kristy hid a smile. Of course she knew what it was. She'd gone to Stoneybrook Elementary herself and had entered several of the fairs. But all she said was, "Yes."

"So *I* might enter it," said David Michael casually.

"Oh, yeah?" Kristy replied, just as casually.

"Yeah. There are prizes."

David Michael continued to flip through the book, while Kristy kept an eye on Emily, who was stacking blocks nearby.

"But," David Michael went on, "I'm not too good at science."

"You could enter anyway," Kristy told him. "Science isn't my best subject, either, but it's fun to enter the fair. Is there anything about science that you like?"

"Space," said David Michael immediately. "Aliens. Flying saucers."

"Some people say that's science *fiction*," Kristy told him. "You know. Made-up science."

"Well, I still like to think about Mars and Pluto and all the planets. I like Saturn best, because of its rings."

"Well, do a project on the solar system," said Kristy.

"Make a list of all our planets?" suggested David Michael.

"No. Something a little more ambitious.

Go out there and show what you can *really* do. Like when you're up to bat in a softball game. Think, 'I can do something big'."

"I'll make a huge Saturn!" cried David Michael, inspired. "I'll use a beach ball, and I'll put hoops round it for rings.'"

"That's the spirit," said Kristy, "but it isn't science-y enough. You're going to be competing against some kids who are playing hardball."

"Huh?"

"Kids who really know about science. Kids who will do great experiments. You've got to do something better than them if you want to win."

"Help me, Kristy," said her brother, plaintively.

Kristy paused. "I'll *help* you," she said at last, "but I won't do the project for you. Just like I can give you pointers on how to pitch a ball, but when you're on the pitcher's mound during a game, *you've* got to throw the ball, not me. Okay?"

"Okay." David Michael turned back to his desk.

"Hey, Emily," Kristy said, "what are you building?"

Emily looked up from a messy tower she was working on. "Building," she repeated, smiling.

"You're building a building?"

Emily looked frustrated. "No!"

"*What* are you building?" Kristy repeated patiently.

"Bwocks."

Kristy sighed. Emily Michelle is what the paediatrician calls "language delayed". And it's no wonder. The first part of her short life was spent in an orphanage in Vietnam, where she was spoken to in a foreign language (Vietnamese, of course), when she was spoken to at all. Then she was uprooted at the age of two and flown to a completely new country where she didn't understand a word anyone said to her. Believe it or not, *Claudia* has been working with Emily some afternoons, teaching her vocabulary and concepts and other things that most two-year-olds already know.

Emily looked frustrated with her block-building, so Kristy decided to give her something new to do.

"Hey, Emily," she said. She led her away from the blocks. "Show me your *nose*. Where is your *nose*?"

"Nose," said Emily, pointing to it proudly.

"Good girl!" cried Kristy. (Claudia said that Emily learned fastest when she was praised for her good work.)

Then, without being asked, Emily pointed to her eye, and said triumphantly, "Eye!"

"Great!" exclaimed Kristy. "Where's your ear?"

Emily pointed. "Ear."

"Oh! I've just thought of a great song for you, Miss Emily," said Kristy suddenly. "Come over here. We need space."

Kristy led Emily to the middle of the study away from furniture. "Watch this," she said, and sang a song she'd learned at nursery school.

Head, shoulders, knees and toes, knees and toes.
Head, shoulders, knees and toes, knees and toes.
Eyes and ears and nose and mouth and chin.
Head, shoulders, knees and toes!

Kristy pointed to each body part as she sang the word. The song is fun, especially when you get going fast. (I can't wait until Squirt's old enough for it.)

Emily had smiled while she watched Kristy. Now Kristy took her sister's hands and placed them on her head and shoulders and so forth as she sang the song again. Emily laughed.

Kristy and Emily were going through the song for the fourth time when David Michael cried, "I've got it!"

"What?" asked Kristy.

"I'll draw a picture of each planet in our solar system. I'll colour them in really carefully and I'll write their names by them."

"We-ell," said Kristy. "Are you putting your heart into this?"

"Suppose not," replied David Michael. "Hey! How about if I get all my space monsters and all my astronauts and show them having a big, big, fight . . . on Venus?"

Kristy hesitated.

"I know, I know. Not good enough," said David Michael.

An hour went by. David Michael suggested several more ideas to Kristy, who kept encouraging him to go one step further. Kristy and Emily sang their new song together.

It was just before Kristy's mum and Watson came home from work that David Michael jumped up from his chair and announced, "This time I really *do* have a great idea!"

"What?" asked Kristy, who was losing hope.

"I'll build a mobile and it will show all the planets. I mean, I'll hang them in the right order: Mercury, Venus, Earth, Mars. You know. And I'll put the sun in the centre. Maybe I'll even make moons. At least, I'll make *our* moon."

"Now *that*," said Kristy, "sounds like a good idea. You'd really be showing something. Maybe you could even fix up the mobile so the planets could turn around each other."

"Maybe. . ." said David Michael uncertainly. But Kristy said he was pretty excited when his mum and Watson came home.

He told them all about the science fair and his solar system mobile.

Then Emily had to show off, too. "Eyes and ears and nose and mouf and shin," she sang happily. Kristy couldn't get her to sing the rest of the song, but it didn't matter. David Michael was already clamouring for Kristy's help with his project.

Kristy and David Michael were now official competition in the science fair.

9th CHAPTER

Friday

I've always heard of playing music to plants, but I've never seen it done — until today. I was babysitting for Charlotte Johanssen, and she was working on her project for the Stoneybrook Elementary science fair. Okay, you lot, I know that some of you are helping kids get ready for the fair. Well, now I am, too. And I don't want to brag or anything, but you know how bright Charlotte is. She's a year ahead of herself in school. Anyway, I gave her a couple of suggestions for her experiment (she is conducting an actual experiment) and she caught on right away. Her work was interrupted when Becca Ramsey came over, though. Poor Becca. I feel sorry for her. You too, Jessi.

When Stacey arrived at the Johanssens' on Friday afternoon, Charlotte didn't run for the door as she usually does when she knows Stacey's going to be her sitter. Instead, Dr Johanssen answered the bell.

"Hi, Stacey," she said. "How are you feeling?" (Dr Johanssen knows about Stacey's diabetes and has been a help sometimes, even though she isn't Stacey's doctor.)

"Still a bit funny these days," Stacey admitted. "I'll probably see my doctor in New York soon."

"Well, that's good. Remember, you can always call me if you or your mum have any questions."

"Thanks," replied Stacey gratefully.

Dr Johanssen led Stacey into the kitchen. "Charlotte's as busy as a bee in here," she said. "I'll let Char tell you what she's doing, but I've got to get to the clinic now. You know where the emergency numbers are. Mr Johanssen will be home early today – around five o'clock or five-fifteen. You'll have plenty of time to get to your club meeting this afternoon."

"Okay," said Stacey. "Thanks. See you!"

"See you," Charlotte echoed absently, not looking up from her work.

Dr Johanssen smiled, shook her head, and left.

"What are you doing, Char?" asked Stacey. "What's your project?"

"It's not a project. It's an experiment."

Charlotte is only eight years old, but she's very bright. She's an excellent reader and does extremely well in school.

"An actual experiment?" said Stacey. "You mean you're going to discover something?"

"I hope so."

"Tell me what you're doing."

"Okay," said Charlotte eagerly.

In front of her were three jam jars. They had been cleaned thoroughly. In the bottom of each jar was some damp, white stuff.

"Well," said Charlotte, "my experiment will show if music helps plants grow better, or if some *kinds* of music help plants grow better."

"What's that white stuff?" asked Stacey, pointing to the bottoms of the jars.

"Wet cotton wool balls," Charlotte told her. "Can you believe it? If you bury seeds in damp cotton wool, they'll start growing faster than if you put them in ordinary soil. So I put three broad bean seeds in each jar. The seeds are just beginning to sprout. I keep the jars on this windowsill here in the kitchen. They all get sunlight part of the day. And I water them the same amount each day. *But*, here's the difference. Every afternoon, I take this jar, Jar Number One, upstairs to my room and play classical music to it for half an hour. I close the door so the other plants can't hear the music. Then, I bring Jar Number One downstairs, and take Jar Number Two upstairs. I play rock-and-roll music to those beans. I play it at exactly the same volume as I played the classical music."

"What about Jar Number Three?" asked Stacey, already impressed with what Charlotte was doing.

"Oh, I don't play any music to that one. Because maybe music *isn't* good for plants. After all, plants that grow wild don't hear music."

"And I suppose you're keeping track of how the plants grow and things like that," said Stacey.

"What?"

"Well, you're charting them or something, aren't you?"

"No. I mean, look at them. You can see for yourself. The sprouts in Jar Number One are bigger than in the other two jars. Those are the sprouts that hear classical music. I bet they're going to be tallest."

"But what if they were tallest, but the plants that heard the rock-and-roll music grew thicker than the others? Or their leaves were brighter or something?"

Stacey was going to keep on talking, but Charlotte got the message straight away. "Oh, wow!" she exclaimed. "I've got to keep all kinds of records and things, haven't I? I should make charts and graphs.

I should measure the plants every day." She giggled. "I could keep a growth chart for them just like Mummy and Daddy kept for me when I was little. And I could make a chart showing their colouring and – and what else did you say, Stacey?"

"The thickness of the plants."

"Oh, yeah. Boy, I've got a lot of work to do."

Charlotte assembled crayons, a pencil, a ruler, graph paper, and plain white paper on the kitchen table. Stacey sat down next to her to watch her work. But before Charlotte began, she jumped up, exclaiming, "Oops! I forgot! I've got to take Jar Number One upstairs. It needs its music."

Charlotte carried the jar up the stairs, and soon Stacey could hear a few strains of what she thought was some music by Vivaldi. (Mrs McGill loves Vivaldi.) Then Charlotte must have closed her door, because the music dissolved into silence.

For a while after that, Stacey and Charlotte sat at the kitchen table. Char worked hard, occasionally asking Stacey for suggestions for help. Then, after a while, Charlotte glanced up, looking like the timid child she used to be.

"Stacey?"

"Yeah, Char?"

"Do you think that maybe – I mean, if you have time – you could come to the science fair? Only if you want to. It's just a kids' thing. I know that. And you're thirteen, but—"

"Charlotte, you know I'll be there. If you want me there, I'll come. Even if you hadn't invited me, I probably would have come, anyway. You're like my sister. I'm interested in everything you do."

"Thank you, Stacey!" exclaimed Charlotte, jumping up to give her a hug.

Charlotte settled down to work again, and Stacey admitted to me later that she couldn't help thinking that Char's project for the science fair was the best one she'd heard of so far. It was a real experiment. Although if Jackie's volcano really did erupt, that *would* be pretty exciting.

A few moments later, the doorbell rang.

"Do you want me to get it?" asked Stacey.

"Please," said Charlotte. "Half an hour's up, and I've got to swap jars and music now."

So Stacey answered the door. Guess who was standing on the front step? Becca – my own sister and Charlotte's best friend.

"Come on in," said Stacey.

Becca stepped inside, looking glum.

"What's wrong?" Stacey asked.

"Everything," mumbled Becca. "Where's Charlotte?"

"Upstairs. She'll be right down, though. She's working on her project for the science fair.

"Oh, yeah. The plants."

Charlotte trotted downstairs then. "Hi," she said. "Well, Jar Number Two is listening to Duran Duran." She paused. "Becca? What's the matter?"

"Oh, it's Aunt Dictator," said Becca, flopping into a chair in the living room.

Char and Stacey couldn't help giggling. "*Aunt Dictator?*"

"Yeah. That's what Jessi calls Aunt Cecelia."

"What's your aunt doing?" asked Charlotte.

"What *isn't* she doing!" Becca countered. "You know, Aunt Cecelia is supposed to be a babysitter, but she could do with some lessons. She isn't like you lot at all," she said to Stacey. (Stacey guessed that "you lot" meant the members of the BSC.) "She never listens to Jessi and me; she just orders us around. And she doesn't believe us. She doesn't trust us, either. It was like when I got stranded on the island with Dawn and everyone the weekend Mama and Daddy left Jessi in charge. When Jessi called Aunt Cecelia to tell her about the emergency, Aunt Cecelia raced to Stoneybrook and took charge as if Jessi didn't even exist.

"And," Becca went on, "she *thinks* she's so great with Squirt, but she isn't. She leaves him in his playpen when he should be walking around exploring things, or playing with me.

"You know what else is weird? Jessi and I have been playing all these practical jokes on Aunt Dictator, and she hasn't said a *word* about them."

"What kinds of jokes?" Charlotte wanted to know.

Becca explained, and Charlotte giggled helplessly.

"We think," said Becca, "that if we do enough awful things, Aunt Cecelia will get fed up and leave."

Stacey let the girls go ahead and plot Aunt Cecelia's demise. She didn't think Becca would carry out any of their ideas, and maybe taking imaginary action would make Becca feel better.

The girls discussed: tying Aunt Cecelia to a chair and telling the Ramseys that robbers had done it; hiding Aunt Cecelia's hair combs, so that she couldn't look perfect one morning; dressing up as Avon ladies and selling Aunt Cecelia jars full of water; colouring Squirt's beautiful curls with wash-out green dye; and other things bound to drive poor Aunt Cecelia up the wall.

Stacey laughed along with the girls, but she was worried. There are serious problems in the Ramsey household, she thought.

10th CHAPTER

"I wonder what the world record for a paper chain is," said Mal thoughtfully as she and I worked dutifully at ours.

"I don't know," I replied. "Maybe we could look it up in the *Guinness Book of Records* under 'Paper Chain, Longest'."

It was Wednesday afternoon. Mal and I were in Claudia's room, waiting for a BSC meeting to begin.

"Claud?" I asked. "Do you have the *Guinness Book of Records* here?"

"Yes, but I don't know where it is," she replied. She was separating the contents of a packet of Lovehearts, pushing all the violet-coloured ones aside. Claud doesn't like purple Lovehearts.

"Oh," said Mal. "Well, I'll look it up at home. You know, if by some chance our paper chain beats the record, then I think we should try to weave the world's longest friendship bracelet next."

"But what would be the point?" I asked. "No one could wear it."

"So what? No one can eat a five hundred-pound pancake, but people are always making things like that, trying to set records."

"I know," I replied, "but five hundred people could each eat a *piece* of the pancake," I pointed out.

"Would you want to eat something that four hundred and ninety-nine other people were touching? And that had probably been buttered by an army of people skating across it with slabs of butter strapped to the bottoms of their shoes?"

"You two! Stop it!" exclaimed Mary Anne, looking absolutely green as she entered club headquarters and heard that last comment.

"Yeah, Mal. What's got into you?" I asked. "You'd think Aunt Dictator lived at *your* house."

"Nothing. I'm just pointing out to you lot that—"

"Order! Order! It's now five-thirty," Kristy interrupted.

I looked round. All seven of us were assembled in our usual places. Since it was a Wednesday, Stacey didn't have to collect subs.

"Any club business?" asked Kristy, as she always does.

"Logan babysat for the Arnold twins and Marilyn accidentally locked herself in the basement," said Mary Anne. "Logan had to rescue her through the outside cellar door."

We giggled.

"I know it sounds funny," Mary Anne continued, "but we should remember how that basement door works."

"Right," agreed Kristy. "Everybody, make a mental note of that."

(Claudia pretended to write something across her forehead.)

The phone rang then and Dawn answered it. "Hi, Mrs Perkins. . . A week from Saturday? I'll ask Mary Anne to check, and I'll phone you straight back."

Dawn hung up the phone. "The Perkinses have a big party to go to. They need someone to babysit a week from Saturday," she told Mary Anne. "It'll be a late night."

Mary Anne was already looking through the record book. "Hmmm," she said. "Believe it or not, we're all busy. We'll have to phone Logan or Shannon. I'll take care of it."

In the end, Kristy's friend Shannon ended up with the job for the Perkinses. Then the BSC members waited for the phone to ring again. It didn't. So we began talking.

"You lot should see Margo's entry for the science fair," said Mal. "I want her to win, and I'm helping her when she asks for help, but mostly she's working on her own. I don't know what kind of research she's doing, but she seems to have decided that Barbie, Ken, and Skipper inhabit the moon, and that they dress in pink and silver sparkly outfits, a bit like the ones that the Jetsons used to wear. You know, on that old cartoon show?"

"Yes," said several of us, laughing.

"So then I asked Margo what people on the moon would eat, and she said, "Well, I suppose they couldn't grow any food in moon dust. They'd have to bring food with them like the astronauts did. So she put little plastic pastries and eggs and things from her doll's house into the space ship. To be honest," Mal finished up, "the space ship looks like a Barbie scene with a picture of the earth in the background."

"Why don't you correct her?" I asked. "Help her start again. Give her some books to read. Make her do it right."

"Nope. That's not what I'm there for," said Mal. "As her sister *or* her babysitter. This is her project. She's got to learn for herself."

"Well, she won't win," spoke up Kristy. She paused. "But then, David Michael isn't going to win, either. He's making a model of the planets in the solar system, remember? I told you all about that."

We nodded.

"He happened to choose a very tough

project. It's difficult to set up the planets so that they're at different distances from the sun. Right now, he's got them all going around the sun in one big circle – Mercury followed by Venus followed by Earth, and so on. I tried to show him a way to get the distance right, but he doesn't understand what I mean and he won't let me do it for him. I don't blame him. I'm the most competitive person here – I think—" (Claudia snorted), "but I'm not going to do his project for him. That's his job and we both know it. This is like the Little Miss Stoneybrook Pageant, in a way." (The pageant Kristy was referring to had been held in Stoneybrook a while back. A whole load of the kids we sit for wanted to enter. We could train them and coach them and rehearse them all we wanted, but when it got down to the big day, the kids were on their own.) "David Michael has to work his project out himself."

"How come?" I asked. "We rehearsed the girls for the pageant."

"That was different," said Mal. "We *rehearsed* them, but we couldn't get up on stage for them."

That was when I began to see that my friends and I weren't going to be as competitive as I'd first thought.

"Stacey," I said, after we'd taken a couple of job calls, "aren't you giving Charlotte a lot of help with *her* project?"

"Not really. I suggested that she needed some – what do you call it? – some data, to show the results of her experiment. I didn't say much more than that and Charlotte was off and running, making graphs, keeping charts."

Hmm, I thought.

"How's Jackie's volcano coming along?" Dawn asked me.

"Terrific!" I said. "I hate to say this, but I think Jackie's project is going to be the best one at the fair." (I couldn't help bragging.) "I think it'll win first prize. His volcano isn't just going to explode, it's going to show the structure of a volcano. You know, the kinds of rocks a volcano sits on, all that stuff."

"And Jackie did this research by himself?" asked Mal incredulously.

"Well, no. I found the books for him. And I told him about igneous, metamorphic, and sedimentary rocks. And I'm helping him build the volcano around a tin can."

There was a silence in club headquarters.

Finally, Mary Anne said, "Jessi, it sounds like you're doing Jackie's project for him. . . Not being rude or anything."

"No, I'm not!" I exclaimed. "I'm not doing it for him. He's right there when I read about volcanoes or when I work on his project. He knows what's going on." I Stopped talking. I listened to what I'd just said. *Was* I doing Jackie's project for him? Nah. I just wanted to give him a lot of help so he could win for once in his life.

"You're sure you're not taking over?" asked Mal. "Maybe by accident?"

"No way! Of course not. But I'll tell you who is taking over. Aunt Cecelia. She won't let Becca or me do *any*thing on our own. It's rules, rules, rules. She lays out our clothes for us each night. She practically cuts our meat up for us. Becca and I know she doesn't trust us. I mean, not like she thinks we'd steal or anything. It's just that she doesn't believe we're capable of doing things that an eleven-year-old and an eight-year-old *are* capable of.

"If Aunt Cecelia were a good babysitter, she'd trust us. Our *parents* trust us. I mean, they set limits, but they do trust us. They let me use the oven and cook. They let us choose our own clothes. Not necessarily in shops, but once we have the clothes they let us decide what to wear to school or to a restaurant or wherever we're going. Aunt Cecelia doesn't trust us to do anything, right."

"Jessi, have you and Becca spoken to your parents about Aunt Cecelia?" asked Mary Anne. "Do they know how you feel?"

I sighed. "No. I mean, no, we haven't spoken to them, and no, they don't know how we feel."

"Why not?" asked Kristy sensibly.

"Because Mama and Daddy are so pleased to have Aunt Cecelia here. It solves all sorts of problems for them now that Mama's working. Also, they think they're making Aunt Cecelia happy. She's been so lonely since her husband died."

"But, Jessi," said Stacey, "Becca told me what you and she are doing to your aunt. Don't you think that talking to your parents would be a bit nicer than playing tricks on her?"

I could feel my face flush, especially as I explained to the other club members about the tricks. Then I added, "And that's another thing. Becca and I feel like we can't talk to Mama and Daddy *because* of the tricks. For some reason Aunt Dictator hasn't mentioned the tricks to our parents. It's as if they never happened. Becca and I are afraid that if we confront Mama and Daddy, Aunt Cecelia will tell on us. I'm completely stuck. I don't know what to do. And I *want* to talk to my parents, particularly because Aunt Cecelia really isn't a very good babysitter. She doesn't play with Squirt. She does things for him that he should be learning to do for himself, and, I don't know, it's a big mess."

I felt miserable. I know I looked miserable. This was because Dawn said, "You look *so* miserable, Jessi."

"Boy, I replied. "If I have kids of my own I'm *never* going to treat them the way

Aunt Dictator treats Becca and Squirt and me."

"Famous last words," said Kristy, laughing.

There was a pause, then we took some phone calls, and then, out of the blue, Mal said, "You know the five hundred-pound pancake? I wonder how they ever mixed the batter for it. In a cement-mixer?"

We left the meeting laughing.

11th CHAPTER

"Phoo! Phoo! Phee-*ew*! Jessi, when this volcano erupts, it is going to be the biggest mess." Jackie looked thrilled at the prospect.

There were just two days left until the science fair. The volcano had been built. The can inside it was filled with the chemicals, which we had been able to find, although Jackie and his mum had had to go to four different places before they found them.

"Jessi?" asked Jackie. I was sitting for him on another afternoon.

"Yeah?"

"Shouldn't we try the volcano just once? I mean, what if it doesn't work when the judges come around at the science fair?"

Although Jackie had a point, I had to tell him, "No. We can only let the volcano erupt once. Otherwise, you'll take a messy, gooey project to the fair. It won't be as impressive as if it erupts for the first time. Maybe we *should* test the chemicals, though. We could put them in another can, light them – *I* have to light the match, by the way – and make sure they really form the ash that's supposed to pour out of the crater. We'll test it in your drive and then wash the mess away with the garden hose."

"All *right*!" cried Jackie. "Oh, boy. A mess!"

Jackie and I carried the chemicals, an empty coffee can, and a packet of matches out to the drive. We followed the instructions for putting the chemicals in the can.

Then I said, "Okay, I'm going to toss a match in the can. By the way, Jackie, an adult will have to do that for you at the science fair, too. Me, your mum or dad, or one of the judges. Okay?"

"Okay."

"Now get ready. Stand back!"

Jackie ran to the edge of the drive. I lit a match, tossed it in the can, and ran. I turned around just in time to see ash spewing from the can and running down the sides. It was very realistic.

"Awesome!" exclaimed Jackie.

"It worked!" I cried.

Jackie ran to the can, but I stopped him. "Don't touch anything! The chemicals might burn your hands."

We turned on the hose, cleaned out the

can, and sprayed the ash down the drive and down a drain.

"Now," I said to Jackie, it's time to begin the final preparation of your project."

"Final preparation?" squeaked Jackie. "I thought we'd finished."

"Oh, no," I told him as we walked back into the house. "We have to work out how you're going to present your project. It needs a name. And you have to be able to tell the judges about it, not just have someone toss the match in and let the volcano erupt. How are you going to demonstrate your project?"

"Well," said Jackie, sounding sort of mixed up, "I'm not sure."

"All right. First, let's make a sign to label your volcano. What do you want to call your project?"

"I want to call it 'My Volcano'," said Jackie.

I shook my head.

"*The* volcano? *A* volcano?"

"No, no, no. It has to be much catchier," I told him.

We stood over the volcano in its glass box. "How about 'Welcome to the World of Volcanic Activity'?" I suggested proudly.

"Okay," agreed Jackie.

"You make the sign to hang in front of the volcano," I said. I handed Jackie a piece of paper and a Magic Marker.

Jackie worked laboriously for fifteen

minutes. Then he proudly held up a sign that looked like this:

> Wellcom to the Wurld of
> Vulcanice Acitivtie

"Jackie! No!" I exclaimed. "You've at least got to spell things right. You can't hang up a sign like that."

"But these are hard words. You have to help me."

"After all the studying we've done, you should know how to spell 'volcanic' and 'activity'," I said. "Here, *I'll* make the sign."

Jackie stared at the ground. And I thought, Boy, I have to do *all* the work. I even have to make the sign.

This is what I made:

> Welcome to the World of
> Volcanic Activity

"There. Now *that's* a sign," I told Jackie. I put it near his project. "What do you think of it?"

"Nice," he mumbled.

"Now, on to the next thing," I said enthusiastically.

"What next thing?" cried Jackie.

"We're heading over to Stoneybrook

Elementary to see where the science fair will be held. We've got to stake out the best spot for your project. Mal told me the judges walk around the main hall in a circle, starting at the front. I think your project should be one of the last they see. That way, they'll remember it when they're judging. Also, they'll be really impressed after all the goofy things they've looked at, like Barbie dolls on the moon."

Jackie didn't even ask what I was talking about. He just put on the sweater I handed him and followed me out of the back door and along the streets to the school.

"I hope the teachers are getting the hall ready for the fair," I said as we neared Stoneybrook Elementary.

"They are," said Jackie. "The hall was closed today."

"Good," I replied.

Jackie led me round to the back of the school, and we peeped through the windows of the main hall.

"There's Mr Peterson and Miss Handy. They're the caretakers," said Jackie. "It looks like they're putting desks in a big circle."

"I can see a banner," I pointed out. "Look, over the stage. Pretty good, huh?"

Stretched from one end of the hall to the other was a long paper banner that read: STONEYBROOK ELEMENTARY SCHOOL SCIENCE FAIR.

Jackie began to look excited. "And they're putting up pictures of dinosaurs and planets and birds and – and *everything* on the walls!"

"Yeah!" I agreed. "Now let's see. What would be the best desk for you?" I looked and looked and finally decided on one. "That desk. Over there," I said, pointing. "It must be at the end of the judges' rounds. We've got to get here early, Jackie, so you can set up your project on that desk."

Jackie nodded distractedly, still looking in awe at the decorations. "The fair's important, isn't it?" he said. "I've never been to it before."

"It certainly is important. Think how you'll feel when you win. I wonder what your prize will be?"

"I don't care," said Jackie. "I just want to have the best project here. Then I can show Ian and John and Danny and all the boys in my class that I can do something really good. I bet *they've* never built a volcano."

"Probably not," I agreed.

We began to walk home. "Okay," I said "Last thing. You've got two days to memorize what you're going to tell the judges about your project."

Jackie straightened his shoulders. "I'm going to say, 'This is my volcano. I built it myself. You light the chemicals and the ash goes *phoo*, *phoo*, *PHEW* out of the can!'"

"Oh, no, you're not. Jackie, this is a

science fair. You've got to explain how a volcano works. Remember the kinds of rocks we built our volcano on? Remember their names?"

"Iggus, morphus, and sedentary?"

I sighed. "Almost. Igneous, metamorphic, and sedimentary."

Jackie repeated the words fairly well.

"Okay, now what you want to say is that igneous rocks are born from fire, the molten that lies several miles below the surface of our earth. Above them are metamorphic rocks that have been changed by the heat. . ."

I finished my speech before we reached the Rodowskys'. I made Jackie start to memorize it. He wasn't bad. He stumbled on words a few times but he learned quickly.

When we'd been home for about twenty minutes, Jackie could spout off, "Igneous rocks are born from fire, the molten rock that lies several miles below the surface of the earth."

A while later, the speech was memorized.

"All right, hand signals."

"*Hand* signals?!"

"Yes."

"You mean as if I'm on my bike and I'm turning left and I stick out my left hand?"

"No. I suppose I meant to say 'hand *gestures*'."

"To impress the judges?"

Like I said, Jackie is a fast learner. "You've got it," I told him. "See, I think you should even have a pointer. When you say, 'igneous rocks', point to the bottom layer of Plasticine. When you say, 'metamorphic rocks', point to the next layer, and so forth. Also, just as the chemicals are about to be lit – throw your hands in the air and say, 'the miracle of a volcano comes to life before our very eyes.' *Then* give your speech."

Jackie was grinning. He was going to get to put on a show.

"This'll be fun," he said, showing almost as much enthusiasm as when we'd set off the volcano in the drive.

When Mrs Rodowsky, Archie, and Shea came home, Jackie gleefully demonstrated his entire project – pointers, hand gestures, and all. I was late leaving for home, but I didn't mind. I was glad to see Jackie so happy.

12th CHAPTER

I might not have minded that I left the Rodowskys' a little late, but Aunt Dictator certainly did. She met me at our front door. I mean, she was just standing there waiting for me, arms crossed, mouth grim.

"You're late," she said.

(I was ten minutes late.) "I know, I'm sorry. Jackie was so excited about his volcano that I wanted—"

"When I'm in charge," Aunt Cecelia interrupted me (When isn't she in charge? I wondered), "you follow my rules. You are answerable to me. You must phone me if you're going to be late. Is that understood? *You must be responsible.* And part of being responsible is letting people know where you are."

Honestly, I thought. If I'd known I was going to be half an *hour* late, of course I would have phoned. But *ten minutes*?

Mama and Daddy don't worry if I'm ten minutes late. They don't stand at doors with mental stopwatches going.

Aunt Cecelia had closed the door behind me and we were facing each other in the hall.

"Take off your coat," said Aunt Cecelia.

Obediently, I took it off.

"Aunt . . . Aunt Cecelia," I said. ("Aunt Dictator" had almost slipped out. I wondered if that would ever *really* happen.) "Mama and Daddy are strict with Becca and me. Squirt, too. But they're not . . . um. . ." (I almost said "not unreasonable") "I mean, they only get worried when they really need to. They wouldn't worry about ten minutes."

"Jessica, *I* am in charge. Late is late, whether it's two minutes, two hours, or two days." (That was a mean thing to say. She was referring to Becca getting stranded on the island, which she still claimed was my fault.)

"But honestly, Aunt Cecelia, Mama and Daddy really don't care about ten minutes. If I knew I was going to be much later, I would have phoned. I always do. Once I phoned home, and Mama said, 'Oh, Jessi. Thank you for letting us know – but we weren't even worried yet!' See, the rules here are that if—"

"I don't know how many times I have to tell you about the rules here, young lady.

They are mine when I'm in charge. End of story."

"Okay, okay, okay."

"Jessica! No answering back."

"That wasn't answering back!"

"It sounded like it."

"Well, it wasn't." I looked at my watch. "Uh-oh!" I grabbed my jacket back out of the cupboard. "I've got to go. I'm going to be late for the BSC meeting."

"*Oh*, no," said Aunt Cecelia. "You're not going to any meeting. Not today. Not after what you did."

"Because I was ten minutes late?!" I exclaimed. I couldn't believe it.

"Yes. Because you were late and you didn't phone me. You were irresponsible."

"Aunt Cecelia, don't you trust me? I'm not irresponsible. I can do things for myself. And I do the *right* things. If I were irresponsible I wouldn't have gone to Jackie's to babysit today. And missing a club meeting is very irresponsible. The other girls rely on me. We all rely on each other. We don't miss meetings unless we're ill or there's an emergency or something like a dance rehearsal comes up. When that happens, I let my friends know in advance. I can't just not go."

"Yes, you can. You're being punished. And if you carry on arguing, you won't be able to go to Friday's meeting, either."

My mouth hung open. I just stood there,

gazing at my aunt's angry face. Slowly the rest of the room came into focus – the clock on the chest, the open cupboard door, the boots on the floor of the cupboard, the striped wallpaper, and, standing in the doorway to the kitchen, Becca and Squirt. They were taking the scene in, and both looked frightened. Squirt was clinging to Becca's hand.

I think it was the sight of their scared faces that prompted me to do what I did next – defy Aunt Cecelia.

"You're not *really* in charge," I told her. "Maybe you're the sitter, but Mama and Daddy are in charge of our house, and I'm going to call them. If they say I can go to the meeting, then I can go. . . And you can't stop me from calling," I added, dashing into the kitchen.

I reached the phone before Aunt Dictator could even open her mouth. First I phoned Daddy.

"Mr Ramsey's office," said his secretary.

"Oh, hi, Ed," I said, trying not to sound shaky or upset. "This is Jessi. Can I speak to my dad, please?"

"He's out of the office, Jess," Ed replied. (Ed is one of the few people who calls me Jess. I quite like it.) "Is this an emergency?"

I hesitated. "No," I said at last. Emergencies are fires and accidents and injuries. I wanted to talk to Daddy badly, but this was not an emergency and I didn't want to do anything *irresponsible*.

"Do you want me to tell your father you called?" asked Ed.

"That's okay. I'll see him at home tonight," I replied.

"Okay."

Ed and I hung up.

I glanced over my shoulder at Aunt Cecelia, who was watching me carefully. I turned around, picked up the phone again, and started to dial Mama's new work number. But halfway through, I stopped. Mama had said that, until she'd settled in to her job, Becca and I shouldn't call her at the office – unless there was an emergency and we couldn't get hold of Daddy.

Okay. No emergency, no call to Mama.

I hung up, defeated. Have you ever heard the saying, "Someone's got you over a barrel"? Well, Aunt Cecelia had me over a barrel. It meant that she'd put me in a situation I couldn't get out of. I had no options. In this case, I couldn't go to the BSC meeting. Not unless I just rode off, completely disobeying her. And that would make Mama and Daddy (not to mention Aunt Cecelia) very angry. I knew I couldn't go without talking to my parents first.

"Can I at least phone Kristy to tell her I won't be coming to the meeting?" I asked Aunt Dictator. "That *is* the responsible thing to do."

My aunt let me make the call.

"Hi, Kristy," I said. "Guess what? I'm really sorry, but Aunt Cecelia won't allow me to come to the meeting today. I was ten minutes late getting back from the Rodowskys' and she blew a fuse."

"Over ten minutes?"

"Yes. Can you believe it?"

"No. That's so unfair!"

"Listen, Kristy. Can you do something for me?" I lowered my voice even though I didn't need to. Aunt Dictator had taken Becca and Squirt into another room. "Can you phone me a lot during the meeting? It'll make it look as if you can't get along without me."

"Good idea!" replied Kristy. I knew she was smiling. That kind of thing appeals to her. "Your aunt'll think *you're* the BSC chairman!"

"Oh, thank you!" I told her.

Boy, did my friends live up to their promises. Our phone rang *fourteen* times between five-thirty and six o'clock.

By the third call, which was from Stacey, I whispered, "Aren't you lot tying up the club phone? I don't want to make you do that."

"No. We're using the Kishis' phone We're taking turns going down to the kitchen and using the phone there," Stacey told me.

"Oh, okay." Then I raised my voice for

Aunt Cecelia's benefit. "No, tell Mrs Hobart I won't be able to sit then. I have a dance class that afternoon."

By 6:00, Aunt Cecelia had had it up to *here*. (Picture me holding my hand to my chin.) She couldn't believe all the phone calls, but there wasn't much she could do about them — except forbid me to attend another meeting, and she wouldn't do that again. Aunt Cecelia might be an old prune, but she's no fool.

After dinner that night, I just *casually* mentioned to Mama and Daddy that Aunt Cecelia and I were having some trouble, but I didn't make it sound like a big deal, so my parents didn't seem upset. They didn't even talk to Aunt Cecelia (at least, I don't think they did).

Aunt Cecelia and I were locked into an awful game now. I'd do something, she'd do something back, neither of us was happy — and Mama and Daddy hardly had any idea what was going on. They were too busy with their jobs and their grown-up lives.

That night, Aunt Dictator came into my room and announced, "We have *got* to do something about your hair." I suppose she was still annoyed about the fourteen phone calls.

Overbearing pig, I thought. I wanted to say those words to her face, but instead I said, "You can do whatever you want as long as Madame Noelle will approve."

Aunt Cecelia paused. For some reason, Mme Noelle is practically a goddess to my aunt. I suppose because I have come so far with my ballet – dancing lead roles and stuff.

Even so, Aunt Dictator was only slightly daunted. She got out a jar of cream, a brush, and some other things, and gave me the most awful hairdo possible. Fortunately, it was severe, so it was great for ballet. My hair would *never* be in my eyes. It couldn't escape the trap Aunt Cecelia had put it in.

"There," said my aunt. "Now you're someone I can be proud of."

Because of my *hair*?

I ran downstairs to complain to Mama and Daddy, but they were talking seriously about a problem Mama was having at work. They looked dead tired, too.

When they glanced up at me, standing in the doorway to the living room, all they said was, "Have you done something to your hair, Jessi?"

I left them alone. I didn't tell them what was really going on – that Aunt Cecelia was running our lives, and *ruining* mine.

13th CHAPTER

It was the evening of the science fair. I was so excited, you'd think *I'd* entered a project in it. (Well, in a way I had.) Anyway, the kids who were entering had to arrive at Stoneybrook Elementary by six-thirty in order to set up. The fair itself began at seven-thirty.

So at six-thirty, there were Stacey and Charlotte, Mal and Margo, Kristy and David Michael, Jackie and me, and a whole lot of kids and their parents or brothers or sisters or grandparents. Actually, Jackie and I had arrived at 6:20 to make sure we got our table sorted out.

Now, at nearly seven o'clock, the main hall was noisy and busy. All around Jackie and me were sighs of relief (when things went right) and groans (when things went wrong). Kids walked by carrying everything from huge pumpkins to complicated electrical things. I could hear the sounds of gears turning, tools tinkering, and video equipment. The main hall was a pretty exciting place to be in.

"How do you feel, Jackie?" I asked him

His volcano was loaded up and ready to explode. The "Welcome to the World of Volcanic Activity" sign was hung on the front of his desk. His pointer was in his hand.

"Fine," he replied, but he sounded nervous. "Listen to this: Igneous rocks are born from fire, the molting—"

"Molten," I corrected him.

"The molten rock that lies several feet—"

"Miles."

"Okay. Several miles below the surface of our wonderful earth."

"Just *our earth*, Jackie. Don't go over the top."

Jackie nodded miserably.

Seven-thirty. The main hall had really filled up. Teachers and parents and families and friends were pouring in.

"Look!" cried Jackie. "There are Mum and Dad and Archie and Shea!"

Boy, did Jackie seem relieved.

The Rodowskys made a beeline for The World of Volcanic Activity.

"Your project looks great, son," exclaimed Jackie's father.

"Yeah, it really does," Shea managed to admit.

"You know what?" I said. "I think I'm going to look around at the other projects before the judging begins. Jackie, you stay here and answer questions – but don't set the volcano off, okay?"

Jackie laughed. "Okay." He was beginning to feel pleased with himself. Even Shea hadn't seen the volcano explode. Jackie couldn't wait for the big moment. He wanted to prove something to Shea who, as his big brother, was always several steps ahead of him.

I walked slowly round the room, looking at the displays and experiments. I saw a model of a human heart made from PlayDoh (I think). I saw a small-scale "dinosaur war". I saw an impressive project about the Ice Age. I saw Charlotte's plants with her charts and graphs. One plant was considerably more healthy-looking than the other two, which were sort of scraggly.

"Which plant is that?" I asked, pointing to the full, green one.

"Guess," she said.

"The one that listened to classical music."

"Wrong." Charlotte grinned. "It's the Duran Duran plant. I'm not sure why. Maybe they were just really *fresh* seeds."

I laughed, and continued my walk through the exhibits. When I got back to Jackie's display, I found his family preparing to take a look around, so I said I'd stay with Jackie.

The volcano attracted a lot of attention.

"Hey! What's that?" asked a curly headed boy.

"A volcano," said Jackie proudly. "It can *erupt*. It makes ash and lava go everywhere. It's really messy."

"Can I see?" asked the boy.

Jackie's face fell. "Sorry. I can only make it explode once. I have to wait until the judges are here. You can see it then."

"Okay," said the boy, looking disappointed.

A few seconds later two girls walked past.

"A volcano!" exclaimed one. "Hey, I've always wondered. What *does* make a volcano?"

Jackie was prepared. "Igneous rocks are born from fire. . ." He said the entire speech without one mistake. I gave him the thumbs-up sign.

The girl frowned. "But *why*," she went on, "do igneous rocks do that? I mean, why does heat make a volcano erupt?"

Jackie was stumped. That wasn't part of his speech. And he couldn't demonstrate the volcano to the girls, either.

Just when I was beginning to feel guilty, my own family arrived. Well, Mama and Daddy and Becca did. Squirt was at home with Aunt Dictator. Becca had come because she wanted to see Charlotte's experiment, and my parents were there because of the volcano they'd been hearing about.

I began to feel better.

At eight o'clock, an announcement came over the PA system.

"Attention, please. May I have your attention? The judging will now begin. All participants in the science fair prepare to demonstrate and explain your projects to the judges. Visitors, please stand at the back of the room during the judging."

"That was our head teacher," Jackie informed me. (You'd have thought the President of the United States had just spoken.)

"Good luck, Jackie," I said. "I know you'll do fine. When it's time to make the volcano erupt, tell the judges you have to call me to light the match because you're not allowed to do that yourself."

Jackie swallowed and nodded. I joined my family at the back of the room.

The judging began.

Two women and a man walked solemnly from table to table. They looked each project over. They requested demonstrations. They asked questions.

Asked questions? Oh, no! Jackie couldn't talk about anything that wasn't in his speech. I hoped fervently that the judges would be so impressed with his demonstration that they wouldn't ask him any questions.

Tick, tick, tick. It was almost eight-thirty.

At last the judges reached The World of Volcanic Activity. I saw Jackie whisper something to one of the women. Then he saw me in the crowd and motioned for me to come forward. I did so, matches in hand.

"This," said Jackie as I reached his table, "is Jessi. She's my helper. She has to light the match for me."

(The judges smiled.)

I lit the match, told everyone to stand back, and tossed the match in the volcano. Jackie threw his hands in the air and cried, "The miracle of a volcano comes to life before our very eyes!"

PHOO! Lava was everywhere! It almost spattered the judges. Then it settled into a nice gooey flow down the sides of the volcano. The judges looked extremely impressed.

I stood at the side as Jackie made his speech, using the pointer.

The judges nodded and smiled.

And then the questions began.

"How," asked the man, "is the crater of a volcano created?"

"Um," said Jackie. He looked at me, but I couldn't help him. "Um," he said again. "I don't know." At least he didn't admit that I'd practically done the project for him.

"Well . . . what happens to the lava when it has flowed out of the crater?" asked one of the women.

"It – it's very hot. . ." Jackie said lamely.

I looked at the ground. This was my fault. I felt terrible as I watched the judges make notes on their pads of paper. They walked on to the last project of the fair without even telling Jackie, "Good work," or anything.

I went back to my parents and waited guiltily and nervously for the results of the fair to be announced.

"Jackie's project was great!" Dad said to me. "I've never seen such a thing. You really helped him."

A little too much, I thought.

Several minutes later, another announcement crackled over the loudspeaker. "The judges," said the principal, "have reached their decisions." (The judges were standing in the centre of the room.) "They have chosen first-, second-, and third-place winners. When the winners are announced, will they please receive their ribbons from the judges? Thank you." There was a pause. Then the principal continued. "Third prize goes to Charlotte Johanssen for her project entitled 'The Power of Music'."

Applause broke out. Charlotte, looking shy but pleased, edged over to the judges, received her yellow ribbon, and scurried back to her table, where she proudly attached the ribbon to the sign she'd made for her project.

The next two winners were announced. They went to kids I didn't know. I sought out Kristy, Mal, and my other friends in the crowd. Except for Stacey, they looked as disappointed as I felt.

But nobody looked more disappointed than Jackie, even though an Honourable Mention ribbon was already being fastened to his desk. (Every kid except the three winners was given an Honourable Mention.) The Rodowskys and I crowded around The World of Volcanic Activity.

"Don't be too upset, honey," Mrs Rodowsky told Jackie.

I had to speak up. "He has a right to be upset," I said.

Mr and Mrs Rodowsky turned to me. "Why?" they asked at the same time.

"Because – because I gave him so much help with his project that he really didn't do much of it himself."

"Yeah," said Jackie, giving me the evil eye.

"I'm really sorry," I went on. "I just wanted him to win. He's always saying he's no good at anything, or that he has bad luck. I wanted him to see that he *can* be a winner. I suppose I went about it all wrong, though."

Mr and Mrs Rodowsky were really nice. They understood what had happened. I got the feeling that they might have done things like this for Jackie in the past. Mr Rodowsky even admitted to building the glass and wood box for the volcano himself. (Well, with a *teeny* bit of help from Jackie.)

But Jackie, who's usually so easygoing and sunny, continued to scowl at me. "I just wanted to have fun," he said. "That was all. I just wanted to make a volcano erupt."

"Jackie, Jessi apologized to you," his father said gently.

"I know." Jackie finally managed a smile. But it quickly turned to a frown. "Oh, no," he muttered. "Here come John, Ian and Danny. They're going to laugh at me. I just know it."

But the three boys who approached us looked excited.

"Jackie," said one, "your volcano was totally rad. Make it explode again!"

"Yeah," said another. "That was so cool."

Jackie explained why he couldn't "explode" the volcano again.

"Oh, well," said the boys. "It was still awesome." They started to walk away. "See you at school on Monday!" one called over his shoulder.

Jackie grinned at me like the Cheshire Cat. "I don't believe it!" he cried.

Mr and Mrs Rodowsky were smiling, too. "You know," said Jackie's mum, "there'll be another science fair next year. Jessi, maybe you could try helping Jackie again."

"I don't think so," I said. "I'd better not."

"Good," replied Jackie. "Because if I'm going to lose, I want to do it all by myself!"

We laughed, even Shea and Archie. But while I was laughing, I was thinking about something. I needed to talk to my parents. And I needed to talk to them badly.

14th CHAPTER

I left the Rodowskys and searched for my parents in the crowded main hall. I finally found them at Charlotte's table, along with Becca, Charlotte's parents, Stacey, and of course, Charlotte.

I pulled my mother aside. "Mama? Can we go home now?"

"What's the matter, darling? Don't you feel well?" Mama's hand immediately went to my forehead. "No temperature," she murmured.

"I feel fine," I told her. "I'm not ill. But I need to talk to you and Daddy. It's about Jackie and – and Aunt Cecelia and some other things. Please can we leave?"

"Of course we can." Mama looked alarmed.

We couldn't leave straight away, though. Saying goodbye took a while. Becca had to congratulate Charlotte one more time and finger the prized yellow ribbon. Then I ran into Kristy.

"Sorry about Jackie," she said sincerely.

"Thanks," I replied. "Sorry about David Michael."

Kristy smiled. "Thank you. But it's funny – he doesn't seem upset at all."

At last my family had made our way out to our car. As we drove home, Mama said, "Becca, Jessi wants to have a talk about some things with Daddy and me, so when we get to our house, could you keep Squirt and Aunt Cecelia company for a while and let us have some privacy?"

"Okay." Becca sounded like she was on her way to the guillotine.

At home, Mama made tea, and she and Daddy and I sat at the kitchen table and sipped it.

"Now," said Mama, "tell us what's happened."

"Okay," I said, drawing in a breath. "It isn't something that's *just* happened; it's something that's been going on for a while. Only I didn't realize it – I mean, I didn't realize my part in it – until tonight, when Jackie didn't win a prize at the science fair."

My parents nodded, but they looked puzzled.

"See, this is what happened," I went on. "Jackie told me he thought it would be fun to build a volcano. He likes messy things. He also said the school science fair was coming up. So I pushed him into entering. . . .And then I did his whole project for him."

"You what?" said Daddy.

"I did almost everything. I researched volcanoes. I made him memorize that speech. I even lettered the sign for his project. It was as if I didn't trust him. I treated him like a baby. I didn't listen to him. I just forged ahead and did everything my way, thinking it was better."

"Well, you certainly seem to have recognized your faults," said Daddy.

"Did you apologize to the Rodowskys?" asked Mama.

I nodded. "But that isn't all. See, there's Aunt Cecelia, too. Becca and I," (I hadn't planned to say this) "we call her Aunt Dictator. She's running our lives. She moved in here and she tells us what to do and what not to do. Or she does things for us. And she never listens to us and she certainly doesn't trust us. Do you know that she once wouldn't let me go to a BSC meeting because I was ten minutes late getting home and hadn't phoned her? I'd have phoned if I was going to be later than that – but not for ten minutes."

"Darling, why didn't you tell us about that?" asked Mama.

"Well, I did try to call Daddy at work," I admitted, "but Ed couldn't reach him. He said you were out of the office, Daddy.

And then, well, Mama, I know your job is a big adjustment. I suppose I just didn't want to bother you with Aunt Cecelia problems. You neither, Daddy. She's your sister."

Mama and Daddy were silent for a moment. Then Daddy said, "I think it's time for a family conference."

(I knew he was going to say that.)

"Okay," I agreed. I guessed I could face Aunt Cecelia with Mama and Daddy and Becca around me.

Aunt Cecelia had just finished putting Squirt to bed, and she and Becca joined us in the kitchen. Mama poured tea for Aunt Cecelia and gave Becca a cup of orange juice.

Becca looked at me with eyes that were question marks.

"Cecelia," Daddy began, "it seems that Jessi hasn't been very happy lately. Nor has Becca. They feel . . . they feel that you don't trust them. They *are* big enough to do quite a few things on their own. We've been giving the girls a lot of responsibility. They're able to look after Squirt and to take care of themselves. But they think that you want to do things for them – things *they're* capable of doing."

Aunt Cecelia's face turned stiff. "Perhaps you don't need me, then?"

"Oh, yes, we do," Mama was quick to say. "The girls can't look after Squirt while they're at school, and – sorry, girls – but neither of them is much of a cook."

"I, um, I can understand how it happened," I spoke up. "I mean, why you took over, Aunt Cecelia. It's easy to do. I completely took over with Jackie and his volcano." (I had to tell the science-fair story again.) "But the thing was, I just wanted to show him that I care. I wanted him to feel good about himself."

"And *I* only wanted to show you that *I* care," Aunt Cecelia said. "I want you girls to grow up to be kind, responsible, neat, and polite. You know, it's an awful thing to have to say, but sometimes black people have to work twice as hard to prove themselves. It isn't fair, but that's the way it is – sometimes."

"That's sort of the way it is with Jackie, too," I said thoughtfully. "He's not stupid. He's clever. And he's kind and funny and a lot of other nice things. But he's a klutz, and that's how most people see him. So he has to work twice as hard to prove himself."

Silence. Then Aunt Cecelia, looking pained, said, "As long as we're baring our souls, I have to confess to something else. I was afraid I wouldn't be as good a sitter as you, Jessi."

"You *were*?" That was the last thing I'd expected to hear. "But you blamed *me* when Becca was stranded on the island."

"I know, but I shouldn't have. I needed

Something or someone to blame for that tragedy, and you were it. But I know you've been taking care of your brother and sister – not to mention all the kids you sit for – for quite a while now, and you're an expert. I wasn't sure I could live up to you.

"On the other hand," Aunt Cecelia continued, her voice changing, growing stronger, "there's a little matter I need to mention to your parents. I think I've kept quiet about it long enough now, don't you?"

Dum da-dum dum. The practical jokes.

Becca and I nodded, but we couldn't look at anyone, not even at each other. We stared into our cups.

"What is it?" asked Daddy warily.

"Ever since I got here," Aunt Cecelia replied, "from the very beginning, I've found spiders – fake ones – in my bed, shaving cream in my shoes, and more, plenty more."

"*Girls*," said Mama warningly.

"Well, we were angry. She was already taking over. She was our *babysitter*, ordering us about, making up rules. I don't need a sitter!" I cried. "I *am* a sitter. And a good one . . . like Aunt Cecelia said," I couldn't help pointing out. This time I looked directly at my aunt and held her gaze.

"Okay. Obviously we've got some problems to sort out," said Daddy. He turned to his sister. "Cecelia, I understand that you feel responsible for the girls, but they're used to certain things. For instance, Jessi never misses a meeting of the Babysitters Club. Not unless she has a special dance rehearsal or there's an emergency. We don't withhold that privilege as a punishment. I think that from now on, the girls should tell their mother or me about any plans they have. They can do this daily or weekly; we'll see what works best. We'll approve – or not approve – their plans, and then we'll tell you their schedules. Fair enough?"

"Fair enough," replied Aunt Cecelia. I could see her relax a little.

"Fair enough?" Daddy asked Becca and me.

"Yup," we agreed.

"Furthermore, the girls should be allowed to do the things we already trust them to do – do their own hair, choose their own clothes, that sort of thing," added Mama. "And perhaps," she went on, "it might be helpful if Cecelia is referred to simply as the children's *aunt*, not their sitter."

Aunt Cecelia smiled. "That sounds nice."

"Now," said Daddy, "there's a little matter of a punishment."

"A punishment?" squeaked Becca. "For who?"

"For *whom*," Aunt Cecelia corrected her gently.

"For you and your sister," Mama said sternly. "For spiders and shaving cream and I don't know what."

"Just a moment," interrupted my aunt. "Could I speak to you in private?" she asked my parents.

"Of course," they replied.

Becca and I escaped then. We didn't know what was going on, but we were glad to get out of there. That night, I slept like, well, like Squirt!

15th CHAPTER

Monday afternoon. Five-twenty-eight. Time for another BSC meeting.

We were all gathered. Kristy was sitting in the director's chair, visor on, pencil over her ear, watching Claud's digital clock, waiting for it to hit five-thirty on the dot.

Claudia was rummaging for junk food.

My friends and I were dressed in typical outfits. *Typical*, but not necessarily traditional. For instance, Stacey was wearing tight black trousers reaching just above her ankles, and sporting a column of four silvery buttons at the bottoms. (The buttons were just for decoration, I think.) Over the trousers she was wearing a *long* (past her knees) blue jacket made of soft material. Under that she was wearing a sleeveless blouse. Now that was unusual.

Claud was wearing a fake leopard-skin

vest, a fairly tame blouse, and blue leggings. She had made her jewellery herself – five papier-mâché bracelets that were painted in soft pastel colours.

Mary Anne and Dawn had swapped outfits, which they do pretty often. That's one nice thing about having a stepsister who's your best friend and also about your size. They were both dressed colourfully, and trendily, but not as wildly as Claud and Stace.

Then there was Kristy in her jeans and sweater. And finally Mal and me, also in jeans, but wearing (if I do say so myself) pretty *fresh* sweat shirts. And Mal had been allowed to buy high-top trainers with beaded designs on the sides!

Click. The clock turned to five-thirty.

"Order, please," said Kristy. "Treasurer, it's subs day."

Groan, groan, groan. We all produced our subs. Stacey counted the treasury money and looked pleased.

Before Kristy could even say, "Any club business?" the phone rang.

"Good sign!" she exclaimed, as Dawn answered it.

"Good afternoon, the Babysitters Club," said Dawn. Then, "Hi, Mrs Newton. . . Friday? I'll check and phone you straight back."

We arranged that job as well as two others before things calmed down.

Then Mal said, "Did everyone survive the science fair?"

"Just barely," I replied.

"David Michael is ecstatic," reported Kristy.

"Over an Honourable Mention?" asked Dawn. "Anyone who didn't win got an Honourable Mention."

Kristy smiled. "I know. That doesn't matter to David Michael, though. He's just thrilled with the idea of a prize – any prize. He wouldn't even leave the ribbon on his project at the fair. He brought it home on Friday night, slept with it, and carried it around with him on Saturday until Watson suggested having it mounted. Now it's hanging over his bed. You'd think it was the Pulitzer Prize."

"That's sweet," said Mary Anne. "I'm glad David Michael is so happy. You know, it's funny what these fairs do for different kids."

"Yeah," said Mal. "Margo's proud of her project, but not the Honourable Mention. It doesn't mean much to her. She just wants everyone to see Barbie on the moon."

"What about Charlotte?" I asked Stacey.

Stacey rolled her eyes. "Oh, wow. You should see her. She's in science heaven. She found out that the names of the three winners will appear in the *Stoneybrook News*. She's got a huge boost of self-confidence."

"Jackie's reaction is a little different from everyone else's," I spoke up. "He doesn't care about the Honourable Mention, either. But once he got over being humiliated when he couldn't answer the judges' questions, he returned to his usual self. He doesn't want me to help him with next year's project, though."

"I don't blame him," said Kristy.

"Neither do I," I answered.

Then I told the BSC members what had happened on Friday night when my family and I had got home from the fair.

"What did your aunt want to talk to your parents about in private?" asked Claud.

"I have no idea. That was three days ago and I haven't heard a word about it. I'm afraid to ask."

"You don't think she's leaving, do you?" asked Mal suddenly.

I paused. Then I said, "Gosh . . . I don't know. I thought we'd sorted everything out. We talked about how sometimes people take over when they just want to show they care. The way I did with Jackie and his project. And we laid down some rules. No. I don't think she's leaving."

You know what was weird? Just then, a little part of me *hoped* she wasn't leaving. If she did, what would we do about Squirt while Mama was at work? And who would be around to care *about* me (not for me) in the afternoons? The thought surprised me.

The phone rang then and we took a job call, and then another. When silence fell again, Dawn said, "Guess what? I'm going to California on our next school holiday. I'll get to see Dad and Jeff."

"That's *great*," said Kristy. "You know where Shannon Kilbourne is going?" (She paused dramatically.) "To Hawaii."

There was a huge chorus of "Oh, wows," and, "That is *so* fresh," and, "Boy, is she lucky."

Mal looked downcast. "I don't think I'll be going *any*where for a while. Dad's company is in trouble. He said he heard the chairman is going to lay off about half the people who work there. Dad says he thinks he'll be one of them."

"But he might not be," I pointed out.

"That's true. I suppose there's no point in worrying about it until it happens."

On that sombre note, the meeting broke up and I cycled home. I forgot about Mal and her father and his job, and began to feel cheerful. That was because this time I knew there would be no disapproving Aunt Cecelia waiting to pounce on me when I got home. There would be (I hoped) just an ordinary aunt who was probably making dinner and trying to entertain Squirt at the same time.

I was right on both counts.

When I entered our house I saw my aunt at the cooker, stirring things in pots. Sitting at her feet was Squirt, who was banging frying pans with a wooden spoon and looking pretty pleased with himself.

"Hi, Aunt Cecelia," I was saying, just as Becca appeared next to me and gestured wildly but silently for me to follow her. So I did. I followed her upstairs to her room, where at last she found her voice – sort of.

"Jes – Jes – Look at – I mean, see what—"

"Becca, what on earth is the matter?" I asked her.

"Go and look at my slippers," was her reply.

I opened Becca's wardrobe door, turned on the light, bent down, and saw that her slippers were filled with shaving cream.

"I almost put them *on*," she said, horrified. "Then, I needed my torch, so I pulled back my bedspread" (Becca keeps her torch under her pillow) "and I found *this* in my bed." My sister held up a huge, disgusting plastic fly. "You didn't do these things, did you?" she asked, narrowing her eyes a me.

"Of course not," I replied. "I bet it was. . ."

"Aunt Cecelia!" we said together.

Then we bolted for my room. I found shaving cream in my slippers and a furry mouse (fake) under my pillow, and discovered that my bed was an apple-pie bed.

Becca and I just looked at each other.

Then we heard gentle laughter. We turned round. Aunt Cecelia was standing in my doorway, holding Squirt on her hip.

"I think we're even now," said my aunt.

I couldn't help smiling. "I suppose so."

"Yeah," agreed Becca.

"Aunt Cecelia . . . I'm sorry," I told her. "We weren't very nice to you. We didn't give you much of a chance."

"I didn't given you two much of a chance, either," she replied. "I did move in and take over. But that's going to change now."

"Hey, Aunt Cecelia, want to hear a joke?" asked Becca, which I knew was her way of apologizing.

"Of course I do. Come downstairs and tell it to me while I finish dinner. . . Um, Jessi, you can watch Squirt for me."

"Thanks," I said.

So we returned to the kitchen and Becca told Aunt Cecelia a joke that I used to tell Becca.

"A long time ago, there was this Viking," Becca began. "And his name was Rudolph the Red. And one day he looked up at the sky and said to his wife, 'It's going to rain today.' And his wife said, 'No, it's not. The sky is blue and the sun is shining.' And Rudolph said, 'But it's still going to rain,' and his wife said, 'It's not,' and Ruldoph said, 'Is too.' So finally his wife said, 'How can you tell?' and her husband replied,

'Because Ruldoph the Red knows rain, dear.'"

Aunt Cecelia let out a burst of laughter like I'd never heard. Not from her, anyway. So we all began to laugh, even Squirt, although he hadn't understood the joke, of course.

And that was how Mama and Daddy found the four of us when they came home from work that night. All together in the kitchen, laughing.

"Well," said Daddy, "I think this household is finally settling down."

"Yup," I agreed. And I was pretty happy with the way things had turned out.

Later that night, I tore up the list of mean things to do to Aunt Cecelia.

The Babysitters Club

Need a babysitter? Then call the Babysitters Club. Kristy Thomas and her friends are all experienced sitters. They can tackle any job from rampaging toddlers to a pandemonium of pets. To find out all about them, read on!

1. Kristy's Great Idea
2. Claudia and the Phantom Phone Calls
3. The Truth About Stacey
4. Mary Anne Saves the Day
5. Dawn and the Impossible Three
6. Kristy's Big Day
7. Claudia and Mean Janine
8. Boy-Crazy Stacey
9. The Ghost at Dawn's House
10. Logan Likes Mary Anne!
11. Kristy and the Snobs
12. Claudia and the New Girl
13. Goodbye Stacey, Goodbye
14. Hello, Mallory
15. Little Miss Stoneybrook . . . and Dawn
16. Jessi's Secret Language
17. Mary Anne's Bad-Luck Mystery
18. Stacey's Mistake
19. Claudia and the Bad Joke
20. Kristy and the Walking Disaster
21. Mallory and the Trouble with Twins
22. Jessi Ramsey, Petsitter
23. Dawn On The Coast
24. Kristy and the Mother's Day Surprise
25. Mary Anne and the Search for Tigger
26. Claudia and the Sad Goodbye
27. Jessi and the Superbrat
28. Welcome Back, Stacey!
29. Mallory and the Mystery Diary
30. Mary Anne and the Great Romance
31. Dawn's Wicked Stepsister
32. Kristy and the Secret Of Susan
33. Claudia and the Great Search
34. Mary Anne and Too Many Boys
35. Stacey and the Mystery Of Stoneybrook
36. Jessi's Babysitter
37. Dawn and the Older Boy
38. Kristy's Mystery Admirer
39. Poor Mallory!

40	Claudia and the Middle School Mystery
41	Mary Anne Vs. Logan
42	Jessi and the Dance School Phantom
43	Stacey's Emergency
44	Dawn and the Big Sleepover
45	Kristy and the Baby Parade
46	Mary Anne Misses Logan
47	Mallory On Strike
48	Jessi's Wish
49	Claudia and the Genius of Elm Street
50	Dawn's Big Date
51	Stacey's Ex-Best Friend
52	Mary Anne and Too Many Babies
53	Kristy For President
54	Mallory and the Dream Horse
55	Jessi's Gold Medal
56	Keep Out, Claudia!
57	Dawn Saves the Planet
58	Stacey's Choice
59	Mallory Hates Boys (and Gym)
60	Mary Anne's Makeover
61	Jessi and the Awful Secret
62	Kristy and the Worst Kid Ever
63	Claudia's ~~Freind~~ Friend
64	Dawn's Family Feud
65	Stacey's Big Crush
66	Maid Mary Anne
67	Dawn's Big Move
68	Jessi and the Bad Babysitter
69	Get Well Soon, Mallory!
70	Stacey and the Cheerleaders
71	Claudia and the Perfect Boy
72	Dawn and the We Love Kids Club
73	Mary Anne and Miss Priss
74	Kristy and the Copycat
75	Jessi's Horrible Prank
76	Stacey's Lie
77	Dawn and Whitney, Friends For Ever
78	Claudia and Crazy Peaches
79	Mary Anne Breaks the Rules
80	Mallory Pike, No1 Fan
81	Kristy and Mr Mum
82	Jessi and the Troublemaker
83	Stacey Vs. the BSC
84	Dawn and the School Spirit War
85	Claudia Kishi, Live on Air
86	Mary Anne and Camp BSC
87	Stacey and the Bad Girls
88	Farewell Dawn

Goosebumps

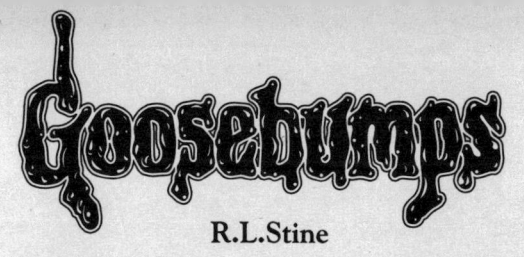

R.L. Stine

Reader beware – you're in for a scare!
These terrifying tales will send shivers up your spine:

1	Welcome to Dead House
2	Say Cheese and Die!
3	Stay Out of the Basement
4	The Curse of the Mummy's Tomb
5	Monster Blood
6	Let's Get Invisible!
7	Night of the Living Dummy
8	The Girl Who Cried Monster
9	Welcome to Camp Nightmare
10	The Ghost Next Door
11	The Haunted Mask
12	Piano Lessons Can Be Murder
13	Be Careful What You Wish For
14	The Werewolf of Fever Swamp
15	You Can't Scare Me!
16	One Day at HorrorLand
17	Why I'm Afraid of Bees
1o	Monster Blood II
19	Deep Trouble
20	Go Eat Worms
21	Return of the Mummy
22	The Scarecrow Walks at Midnight
23	Attack of the Mutant
24	My Hairiest Adventure
25	A Night in Terror Tower
26	The Cuckoo Clock of Doom
27	Monster Blood III
28	Ghost Beach
29	Phantom of the Auditorium

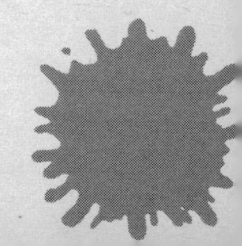

Goosebumps

30	It Came From Beneath the Sink!
31	Night of the Living Dummy II
32	The Barking Ghost
33	The Horror at Camp Jellyjam
34	Revenge of the Garden Gnomes
35	A Shocker on Shock Street
36	The Haunted Mask II
37	The Headless Ghost
38	The Abominable Snowman of Pasadena
39	How I Got My Shrunken Head
40	Night of the Living Dummy III
41	Bad Hare Day
42	Egg Monsters From Mars
43	The Beast From the East
44	Say Cheese and Die – Again!
45	Ghost Camp
46	How to Kill a Monster
47	Legend of the Lost Legend
48	Attack of the Jack-O'-Lanterns
49	Vampire Breath
50	Calling All Creeps!
51	Beware, the Snowman
52	How I Learned to Fly
53	Chicken Chicken
54	Don't Go To Sleep!
55	The Blob That Ate Everyone
56	The Curse of Camp Cold Lake
57	My Best Friend is Invisible
58	Deep Trouble II
59	The Haunted School
60	Werewolf Skin
61	I Live in Your Basement
62	Monster Blood IV

GOOSEBUMPS

Reader beware – here's THREE TIMES the scare!

Look out for these bumper GOOSEBUMPS editions. With three spine-tingling stories by R.L. Stine in each book, get ready for three times the thrill … three times the scare … three times the GOOSEBUMPS!

COLLECTION 1
Welcome to Dead House
Say Cheese and Die
Stay Out of the Basement

COLLECTION 2
The Curse of the Mummy's Tomb
Let's Get Invisible!
Night of the Living Dummy

COLLECTION 3
The Girl Who Cried Monster
Welcome to Camp Nightmare
The Ghost Next Door

COLLECTION 4
The Haunted Mask
Piano Lessons Can Be Murder
Be Careful What You Wish For

COLLECTION 5
The Werewolf of Fever Swamp
You Can't Scare Me!
One Day at HorrorLand

COLLECTION 6
Why I'm Afraid of Bees
Deep Trouble
Go Eat Worms

COLLECTION 7
Return of the Mummy
The Scarecrow Walks at Midnight
Attack of the Mutant

COLLECTION 8
My Hairiest Adventure
A Night in Terror Tower
The Cuckoo Clock of Doom

COLLECTION 9
Ghost Beach
Phantom of the Auditorium
It Came From Beneath the Sink!

Creatures

The Series With Bite!

Everyone loves animals. The birds in the trees. The dogs running in the park. That cute little kitten.

But don't get too close. Not until you're sure.
Are they ordinary animals – or are they creatures?

1. Once I Caught a Fish Alive
Paul's special new fish is causing problems.
He wants to get rid of it, but the fish has other ideas...

2. If You Go Down to the Woods
Alex is having serious problems with the school play costumes.
Did that fur coat just move?

3. See How They Run
Jon's next-door neighbour is very weird. In fact,
Jon isn't sure that Frankie is completely human...

4. Who's Been Sitting in My Chair?
Rhoda's cat Opal seems to be terrified ... of a chair!
But then this chair belongs to a very strange cat...

Look out for these new creatures...

5. Atishoo! Atishoo! All Fall Down!
Chocky the mynah bird is a great school pet.
But now he's turning nasty. And you'd better do what he says...

6. Give a Dog a Bone
A statue of a faithful dog sounds really cute. But this
dog is faithful unto death. And beyond...

Creatures – you have been warned!

HURRICANE HAMISH
Mark Jefferson

HURRICANE HAMISH
THE CALYPSO CRICKETER

Hurricane Hamish has always been a bit special – ever since he was found washed up on a Caribbean beach wrapped in an MCC towel. He's only twelve, but he can bowl fast. Really fast. So fast he might be about to play for the West Indies...

HURRICANE HAMISH
THE CRICKET WORLD CUP

Hurricane Hamish is back – and now he's in England, determined to help the West Indies win the Cricket World Cup. But England is so cold! The grounds are so wet and slippery that Hurricane can't even stay standing, let alone bowl fast...

"The ideal literary companion for this summer's Carnival of Cricket – the World Cup."
Lord MacLaurin, Chairman of the England and Wales Cricket Board

"Mark Jefferson has scored a real winner with Hurricane Hamish ... this pacey romp of a book."
Christina Hardyment, The Independent

"A novel which, like its hero, has pace and heart."
Nicolette Jones, The Sunday Times